England

Versus

Scotland

England
Versus
Scotland

Rupert Matthews

LEO COOPER

1409868
941

First published in Great Britain in 2003 by
Leo Cooper
an imprint of Pen & Sword Books
47 Church Street
Barnsley
South Yorkshire
S70 2AS

ISBN 0 85052 949 2

A catalogue record for this book is available from the British
Library

Contents

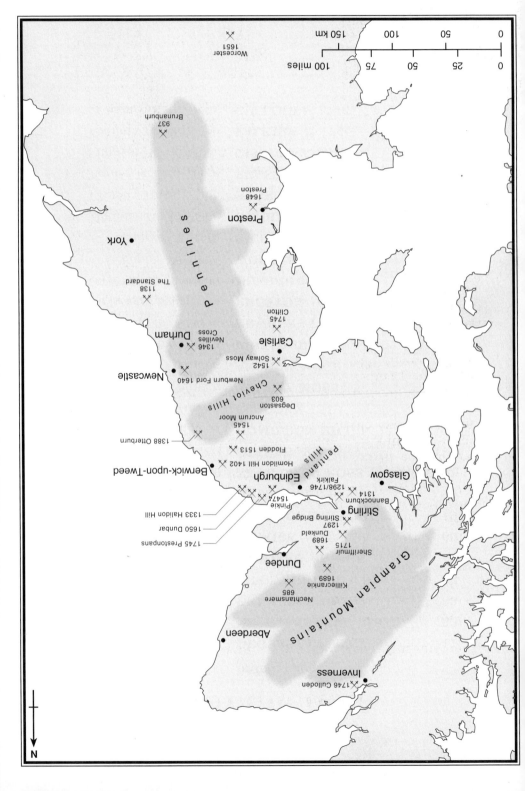

The locations of the battles described in this book. Detailed directions to find each battlefield and a guide to what there is to see on the site today are given at the end of each chapter.

Introduction

The island of Britain contains two kingdoms: England and Scotland.

Over the years the two kingdoms have been rivals, allies, friends and enemies. In the very earliest days, both the Scots and the English were foreigners to Britain. The Scots were an Irish tribe settled in the lands around Kintyre while the English were invaders from northern Germany.

As Roman control over the province of Britain collapsed in the fifth century the English and the Scots both expanded their power and their territories. It was inevitable that they would eventually clash and battle was joined at Degsaston in about the year 603. At the time neither the English nor the Scots were a unified people and some years later the northern English fought against the Picts at Nechtansmere. The climax of these early battles came at Brunanburh, possibly the most decisive battle ever fought in Britain.

The truth about these early battles can be difficult to trace in any detail. The chroniclers often blurred events and places, and were hopelessly inaccurate when dealing with figures. It is sometimes impossible to know exactly where the battle was fought and what happened. The author has walked the likely sites of the battles and closely studied the contemporary accounts. He is confident that he has been able to recreate what happened.

By the time of the Battle of the Standard, the Scots and English had left the Dark Ages behind them and had become unified states in name, if not always in fact. The Kings of England claimed a vague superiority over the Kings of the Scots, though it was never entirely clear what this meant. For the next four centuries the relationship between the two nations led to the battlefield as often as to the marriage altar or the negotiating table. Even when set piece battles were not taking place, relations were rarely peaceful. Numerous invasions led not to

The English/Scottish border marked by stone and flag beside the north bound carriageway of the A1 north of Berwick.

The monument to the battle at Nechtansmere. The battle was fought over 1,300 years ago, but the monument is only a few years old. The continuing relevance of the old battles between England and Scotland, as the two nations recover their identities, could not be more clearly demonstrated.

battle, but to ambush, siege and skirmish. And the borders were a place of continual raid, revenge and feud. The years were few indeed that did not see bloodshed of one kind or another.

Finally the death of childless Queen Elizabeth I of England gave the throne of England to King James VI of Scotland. The two nations, after centuries of conflict, were united under a single monarch. Even that could not bring peace. In 1640 Scotland invaded England once again and a fresh round of bloodshed began.

The final battles between the two peoples came after the English ousted King James II in 1688. James, a Stuart, was also King of Scotland and the old royal family of Scotland retained many supporters in the northern kingdom. These folk resented the removal of their Scottish king. The supporters of the exiled King James were known as Jacobites, from the latin version of the name James, and at first were found in England as well as in Scotland. The Jacobite uprising of 1715 saw fighting in England as well as in Scotland. By 1745, however, support for the Stuarts was found only in Scotland. The rising led by Bonnie Prince Charlie, which began in July, lasted many months and was the last time that armies of Scots faced the English in battle.

After 1745 the English and the Scots were united not just by a monarch and a Parliament but by a strong sense of mutual self interest. Working together, the Scots and English became British and set out to conquer the world. The British Empire was a joint creation of the two nations, as was the commercial wealth that flowed into Britain.

Even when the two nations were working together there was a rivalry between them. In the two World Wars regiments drawn from England and Scotland would engage in banter and the occasional fist fight. But woe betide any American, French or other outsider who took sides for they would soon find the Scots and English united against the foreigner.

After the collapse of Empire the rivalries and differences between Scots and English began to grow more pronounced. Some Scots began to wonder why they were ruled by a joint Parliament in London. In the 1970s a vote in Scotland failed to gain a clear majority for a Scottish Parliament, but such a vote was achieved in the 1990s. A Parliament was established in Edinburgh to look after domestic Scottish affairs. There was a growing feeling that Scotland could do without England.

The English, meanwhile, had been annoyed when the Scots 'Tartan Army' of football fans tore down the goalposts at Wembley

The site at Holyrood in Edinburgh where the main buildings of the new Scottish Parliament are being erected to mark Scottish nationhood – in the eyes of the Scots – and an enormous waste of English tax money – in the eyes of the English.

in 1977. But during the 2002 World Cup many English were seriously shocked by the vehemence with which Scots supported whichever football team was playing against England. The English noticed that Scots MPs in the Westminster Parliament could vote on English affairs, but English MPs could not vote on the same affairs which were dealt with in Edinburgh. And the English wondered why large sums of English taxpayers' money was spent in Scotland when the Scots seemed so anti-English.

With a growing sense of nationalism among both the English and the Scots it is perhaps time to look back to the days when the two kingdoms were, indeed, separate nations. It is possible to commemorate the heroism shown and great deeds performed on both sides and to trace the course of the campaigns and battles which contributed to the history of both nations.

Whatever the future may hold for the two peoples, it must surely be hoped that warfare is not included

Chapter One

DEGSASTAN 603

Introduction

The first clash between the English and the Scots came about because of the collapse of the post-Roman British power in the area around Hadrian's Wall. At the time both the English and the Scots were small in numbers and occupied only a fraction of the territories now covered by England and Scotland. The battle which took place at Degsastan looked at the time to be decisive, but was in fact just the opening round in what proved to be over a thousand years of warfare.

The Scots were, in AD 600, one of the less significant peoples in what was to become Scotland. They were recent arrivals from Ireland, to which they retained strong cultural links and important blood ties.

The Scots had begun arriving some time in the early fifth century. At first they came as isolated bands of settlers along the coasts and islands of Argyll and neighbouring areas. For a while,

The ruins of Hadrian's Wall at Banks. It was the collapse of Roman military power that enabled both the English and the Scots to expand their power and territory in Britain.

the Scots kingdom was ruled from the ancestral base near Coleraine. Then, in about 500, the Scots King Fergus left Ireland and established the centre of his kingdom on the Kintyre Peninsula. He brought with him a large stone on which the Kings of the Scots had for generations stood when being inaugurated as kings. Fergus and his grandson Gabran were famous soldiers and Scots power increased steadily. By 600 the Scots ruled the lands from Loch Linnhe south to Loch Long and probably exercised some form of overlordship over Mull, Skye and the Hebrides.

The remaining lands north of the Forth and Clyde were occupied by the Picts, a wild people who had never been tamed by Rome and who may have been descended from the pre-Celtic population of Britain.

South of the Forth and Clyde the land was divided between two Celtic kingdoms. The east was ruled by Mynydawc, King of Gododdin, whose power stretched from the Forth Valley to beyond the Tweed. The West was held by Riderch, King of Clyde. As the name suggests, Clyde was centred around the fertile lands of the Clyde Valley, but it reached south as far as Carlisle. Both these kingdoms had bordered Hadrian's Wall in the days of the Roman Empire. Their lands were criss-crossed by Roman-built roads and studded with Roman forts where legionnaries rested when on patrol. It is most likely that both Gododdin and Clyde had been client states of Rome – paying tribute and absorbing much Roman culture.

The English, meanwhile, had arrived in Britain in a series of waves of immigration from the 350s onwards. By AD 600 their power in northern Britain was based around two kingdoms: Deira and Bernicia. The Deirans were based around Driffield in Yorkshire and seem to have been the more numerous of the two English peoples. They were, however, more inclined to farming and trade than fighting. They seem to have lived on relatively good terms with their British neighbours. Bernicia was very different. Based on the fortress rock of Bamburgh, Bernicia was a warrior kingdom. Its kings were eager for power and they brought large numbers of land-hungry warriors over from Germany to help them secure it. King Athelferth came to the throne in 593 and began by raising a fresh army, before steadily increasing his lands and raiding deep into British territory.

In 598 the British of Gododdin marched south to fight the aggressive Bernicians. It is likely that Mynydawc was hoping for support from the British who still lived in large numbers around York, or even from the Deirans, for he led his army south on the

The overgrown mounds at Catterick which mark the Roman fortifications around which raged the Battle of Catraeth in 598. This English victory over the Britons paved the way for the first battle against the Scots five years later.

west coast before crossing the Pennines to enter Bernician territory down the valley of the Tees.

The two armies met at Catraeth, now Catterick, and the English achieved an overwhelming victory. Mynydawc and nearly all his men were killed – later tradition says that only one man returned home from this expedition. With its army wiped out, Gododdin was helpless. Bede, writing a century later, recorded of Athelferth 'He ravaged the Britons more cruelly than all other English leaders. He overran a greater area than any other king, exterminating or enslaving the inhabitants, making their lands either tributary to the English or ready for English settlement.'

Before long English warriors were stationed in the Forth Valley. It was this which brought the Scots into the picture. Their king, Aedan, could not ignore the growing might of the English, whose lands now bordered his around Callender.

Aedan realized that in Athelferth and the Bernician English he had a dangerous enemy. The Scots had traditionally recognized the Kings of Ulster as their overlords in some vague way. So Aedan asked the Ulstermen for help. Mael Uma, brother of the King of Ulster, promised to come to help in the expectation of acquiring rich loot.

It is most likely, though the chroniclers are unclear on this point, that Aedan also received help from King Riderch of Clyde.

The two kings knew each other well and both owed religious allegiance to the Abbots of Iona. It is more than likely that they would have united against the pagan Bernicians. It is possible that Riderch may, in turn, have appealed to the Britons of Rheged, the land between Hadrian's Wall and the Dee. However, Rheged was in the midst of a murderous civil war at the time and it is unlikely many men would have marched north to join the allies.

Athelferth, meanwhile, received news of the forces gathering against him. He sent out urgent orders to his scattered forces. They were to break off from pillaging or forcing tribute from the Britons of Gododdin and instead to gather for war.

The Opposing Armies

It is virtually impossible to know the sizes of the armies which met at Degsastan. The Dark Age chronicles tend to speak vaguely of 'a large army' or 'a small force'. On a few occasions, however, they are more precise and a good idea of numbers can be gained. It is not unreasonable to assume that a kingdom could raise a similar sized army on different occasions.

The army which Aedan led to attack the English was made up of contingents from his own Scots kingdom, from Ulster and from the British Kingdom of Clyde. A few generations later, the Scots were able to field a force of 3,000, perhaps they had a similar number in 603. It is reasonable to assume that Mael Uma brought less than half the fighting force of Ulster with him - perhaps another 1,500 men. The allied army may have numbered some 6,000 men all told.

The Ulstermen came from a land where cattle stealing and raiding were endemic. Lightly armed men, able to move swiftly, were ideally suited to such warfare. The Irish of the time would have fought on foot and been armed with two or three throwing javelins and a short sword about two feet long. They wore no armour and had only a small leather shield about twelve inches in diameter for defence. Richer men would have been armed with longer swords and are described as wearing richly coloured cloaks and gold jewellery into battle.

In Ireland the chieftains rode to war on chariots. These were light vehicles drawn by two swift ponies. However, it is unlikely these would have been brought over for the campaign of 603. The Irish crossed to Britain in boats known as curraghs. These were built by constructing a keel and ribs of supple saplings. Over this was woven a wicker skin, which was made waterproof with stretched cowhide. Even the largest curragh was no more than twenty feet long, too small to transport horses except in the calmest weather.

The Scots were, essentially, an Irish tribe. Archaeology reveals that in 603 they were still of a predominantly Irish culture, so it is most likely that their warriors would have been equipped in the Irish fashion. No records or archaeology have indicated that the Scots used chariots. Presumably the mountainous terrain of Argyll did not suit them.

The men of Clyde would have been quite different. Their military traditions and equipment were derived from late-Roman models. It was to rulers such as the Kings of Clyde that the Roman armourers and soldiers turned for employment when the money for their wages stopped coming from Rome.

The Clyde infantry would have worn a corselet of tough, boiled leather reinforced by metal strips and with leather flaps hanging down over the groin, backside and the upper arms. The conical helmet would also have been of boiled leather and metal. This boiled leather would not stop a determined sword thrust, but could turn aside spears or glancing blows. The men carried a large round or oval shield about three feet across. These were frequently painted with Christian symbols, such as a cross or image of Mary the Virgin. The weapons they carried were a stout, thrusting spear some seven feet long and a hand axe or large knife.

The Kingdom of Clyde also fielded a small number of cavalry. These men were armoured with short-sleeved tunics of mail and wore metal helmets. They carried throwing javelins and long swords for hand to hand fighting. In addition to this heavy cavalry there was lighter cavalry of unarmoured horsemen who would have been used for scouting and raiding.

Ensuring men of different backgrounds, different languages and different fighting styles would cooperate properly on campaign would have been a major challenge for Aedan. It is not clear that he succeeded.

The size of Athelferth's army is more problematic. He could draw on the manpower of his own kingdom, but his fame as a warrior attracted adventurous young men from elsewhere in England and from Germany. It is clear that he made a major effort on this occasion, so his army may have numbered anything from about 4,000 to 8,000 men.

Being made up entirely of Englishmen, Athelferth's army was more uniform in terms of equipment and appearance. The English of this period fought exclusively on foot, though some of the professional soldiers rode horses to reach the battlefield. The majority of men carried a large round shield for defence and a seven-feet spear and a one-sided knife for weapons. The professional men of the King's own troop would have had leather tunics and helmets. Only the king himself and the richest warriors would have carried mail tunics, metal helmets and long swords.

Tactics

The tactics of those who fought at Degsastan were simple and straight-forward. Most men were not professional soldiers and could afford only minimal time away from the farm for military training. That said, the styles of fighting of the various groups were quite different.

The Irish were accustomed to swift raid and retreat tactics and usually operated in small numbers. They preferred ambush or flight to fighting in open battle. When they did indulge in battle, however, the Irish would advance on the enemy and shower them with javelins. If the situation then looked favourable they would rush forwards to fight hand to hand with their short swords and knives. Otherwise they would retreat to fight another day.

The men of Clyde derived their tactics from those of the later Roman army. The armoured infantry formed up in a number of solid formations, bristling with spears. The heavy cavalry, of which there were rarely more than a couple of dozen present, lurked behind the infantry. If the enemy infantry became disorganized, the cavalry would charge forward to smash the formation apart. The enemy would then be vulnerable to an infantry attack or, if they ran, to pursuit by the light cavalry. If no such advantage could be obtained, the cavalry would remain inactive and the

When the Scots first appeared in Britain they dressed and fought much as did their ancestors in Ireland. This warrior has the distinctive Scot cloak, the brat, coming to a point at the rear, which was worn across northern Ireland at this time. All warriors would have carried the light throwing javelins or darts that this man has, and the stout thrusting spear. The short sword this man carries was known as the claideb and was more often used in ambush or skirmish than in a full-scale battle. The only protective armour this man has is the small wooden shield, showing that he is a relatively poor man who cannot afford even a helmet of boiled leather.

An English warrior carrying equipment typical of the seventh to ninth centuries. The shield is made of plywood covered in decorated leather with an iron rim and central boss. The heavy spear has a metal foot as well as a metal tip. The cross pieces behind the spear-head were usual at this date. They stopped the spear being driven so deeply into the enemy's body that it became caught and could not be extracted. The sword, carried on a belt slung around the shoulder, was usually found only on the more professional fighters, but anyone could pick one up at the end of a battle. Otherwise, this man has come to battle wearing his normal day-to-day clothes. A woollen cap is worn on his head and his body is covered by a leather jerkin over a woollen tunic. The legs are covered by gaiters over woollen hose and he wears leather shoes on his feet.

army would seek to disengage and fall back intact.

The English used more immobile tactics. They formed up in a single mass of infantry, often seeking to occupy a hill crest, gap between dense forests or some other tactically secure position. The better armed warriors formed the front rank. They would lock their shields together to create a solid obstacle known as the shieldwall. The spears would project forward from the shieldwall. When these were broken, the front ranks drew their swords or knives and stabbed forwards. The less well armed men, meanwhile, formed the rear ranks of the English formation. They showered javelins at the enemy and would step forward to take the place of any in the front ranks who fell dead or injured.

The Battle

The contemporary accounts of the Degsastan campaign are infuriatingly vague. Bede gives some detail of the course of the fighting, and says the battle was fought 'at a famous place known as Degsastan', but obviously thinks the place so well known that he does not need to say where it is. The Anglo-Saxon Chronicle is even more vague saying merely 'Aedan, King of Scots, fought Athelferth of Northumbria at Degsastan'.

There is no place in Britain today called Degsastan, though over the years such a name may well have become transformed into 'Dawston', 'Dayston' or something similar. There are several

The narrow defile where the Dawston Brook runs down from the Cheviots. It is here, the author believes, that the Battle of Degsastan took place.

of these in existence, and it is not immediately obvious which was the site of the battle. Given the political layout of northern Britain at the time, however, it is possible to recreate the likely course of the campaign and so to identify which place was then known as Degsastan.

Aedan was the aggressor, so the course of the campaign would have been dictated by his war aims. These were to drive the English out of Gododdin and to secure the safety of both the Scots and of Clyde. He also needed to meet up with his allies, the Ulstermen and men of Clyde.

These factors would have meant that Aedan had to gather his army at a point on the west coast where the Irish could land their curraghs and which offered easy marching routes into Bernician territory. There are two such places. The first is the Clyde. However, to muster an army here would have given only one possible line of attack – straight east to the Forth. Athelferth would have known from where the attack was to come and could have gathered his entire army to face it.

The second possible mustering place was the Solway Firth. This would have involved a longer march for Aedan's Scots, but allowed for men from Rheged to join the allied army. It also offered three routes into Bernicia, which would have kept Athelferth guessing and may have forced him to divide his army, which is what he did.

Assuming that Aedan chose the Solway Firth, he would most likely have gathered his army in the shelter of the stout Roman fortifications around Carlisle. From there the easiest route was the Roman road along Hadrian's Wall to Corbridge from where Aedan could have turned north along another Roman road to strike at the very heart of Athelferth's kingdom at Bamburgh. A second Roman road ran north up the valley of the Annan and over the Pentland Hills to reach the banks of the Firth of Forth.

The more daring option, however, would have been to abandon the Roman roads and advance up the valley of the Liddel. Some way up the river, the valley divides. The western spur offers a route over the Cheviots to the valley of the Teviot and thence to the Tweed. The eastern spur leads to the Tyne. The strategically vital fork in the Liddel Valley is occupied by the hamlet of Dawston – almost certainly the Degsastan where the battle was fought.

We can imagine Athelferth, knowing Aedan was mustering at Carlisle, being forced to divide his army. He sent one force under his brother Theobald to guard one route, perhaps the Roman road over the Pentland Hills, while he kept his main army under his own command, perhaps around Bamburgh. It is likely that Theobald's force consisted of an elite troop of infantry mounted on horses, which would have given him more mobility.

Hearing that Aedan was marching up the Liddel, Athelferth would have wanted to block his advance at Dawston, otherwise he himself might have missed the invaders completely and his lands would have lain open to pillage. It seems that Theobald reached Dawston first and drew up his men in a shieldwall in a strong defensive position. No doubt he hoped to block the valley until the main Bernician army came up.

Aedan may have sent forward his Irish and Scots to skirmish with the English shieldwall. Perhaps he hoped to lure Theobald off his position and disorder the shieldwall. The javelins and darts of the Irish and Scots would have inflicted casualties, but would have been unable to break the English defence. We do not know if Theobald stood his ground or attacked. But we do know that he and all his men were wiped out in the savage fighting.

It was at this point, with Aedan's army disordered after the victory over Theobald, that Athelferth and the main English army arrived. The disciplined English surged forward, cutting down the enemy and allowing them no time to reform. Both Mael Uma and Aedan escaped alive, perhaps they had horses, but the majority of the Scots and Irish were killed.

The fate of any men of Clyde involved is not mentioned. However, the Clyde army remained virtually intact and continued to hold off English attacks for years to come. Either it was not involved in the main fighting, or it had kept formation and not been caught in the disordered rout.

Aftermath

Writing a hundred years after the Battle of Degsastan, the English chronicler Bede boasted 'From that day until the present, no King of the Scots has dared to do battle with the English'.

Bede may have been exaggerating, but the victory for Bernicia was, indeed, dramatic. Within a couple of years, Athelferth had completed the occupation of the east coast south of the Firth of Forth. English farmers settled densely in Lothian and along the Tweed. The Britons who remained were subjected to English rule and became inferior citizens. The kings of Clyde and the disunited rulers of Rheged went on the defensive, leaving the English free to complete their conquests on the east side of the Pennines.

By the 650s the kingdoms of Bernicia and Deira had become united through dynastic marriage and all the English north of the Humber and south of the Forth were ruled by a single king. It would not be long before these Northumbrians would want to exert their power, leading to the next conflict with their northern neighbours.

Visiting the Battlefield Today

It is only fair to state that not all historians are agreed that Dawston in the valley of the Liddel is the correct site for the Battle of Degsastan. It is, however, the only site with a name that could be derived from Degsastan which makes any strategic sense given the political geography of northern Britain at the time. The fact that it is an ideal tactical position for an English army of the time would seem to clinch the matter.

To appreciate the Degsastan battlefield it is best to approach

The coastal fortress of Bamburgh. The buildings on the site today are medieval in date, but are built on the same rocky outcrop where King Athelferth had his stronghold.

from Carlisle. Leave the city on the A7 heading north, turning east on to the B6357 at Canonbie. Follow this B road as it twists and turns up Liddesdale, ignoring other B roads that branch off it. After the B6399 branches off left, the road passes through the scatter of houses that is Riccarton. Soon after this a side road goes right, signposted to Kielder Water. This is the route over the Cheviots towards Newcastle upon Tyne. The likely site of the battlefield is straight on where the valley suddenly becomes much narrower and steeper. This is Dawston Brook. Theobald and his advance guard would have found that the valley is easily defended with flanks that cannot be turned. The hillsides are open grasslands grazed by sheep, so take all the usual care needed in areas where livestock is kept.

The battlefield of Catraeth, now Catterick, is also worth a visit. From the A1, take the side turning to Catterick as far as the junction with the A6136 to Hipswell. Enter the large unsurfaced car park that is just west of this junction, beside Catterick Bridge. Large information boards by the car park entrance show the layout of the Roman fort of Catterick, its neighbouring civilian settlement and the bridge over the River Swale. It was around this river crossing and the fortifications that the battle was waged, though the exact location of the fighting is unknown.

Chapter Two

NECHTANSMERE 685

Introduction

The Battle of Nechtansmere took place some centuries before either England or Scotland were united kingdoms. It was, nevertheless, a defining moment in the warfare between the two peoples for it set a clear limit to the extent of English settlement in what is now southern Scotland.

By the 680s, the English kingdom of Northumbria stretched

The precise location of the armies when the Picts launched their ambush is unclear, but only the men at the rear of the English column were able to escape around the western shores of the lake.

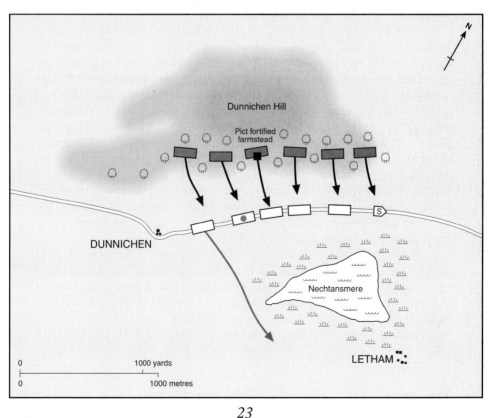

from the Humber to the Forth and from the North Sea to the Pennines. It also included stretches of countryside west of the Pennines north of Chester. The Kings of Northumbria were the most powerful in Britain, but they now sought to extend their control north into lands held by the Picts, Britons and Scots. At this time the Picts inhabited the lands north of the Forth and Clyde and the island of Skye. The British kingdom of Clyde occupied the lands bounded by the Solway Firth, the Clyde and the Cheviots. The Kingdom of the Scots occupied the islands and peninsulas of Argyll, Mull and the surrounding area.

In 655 King Oswy of Northumbria launched a major invasion into the territory of his northern neighbours. He defeated the Scots and Britons, and demanded regular tribute of gold and silver. The Picts were crushed and divided. The southern Picts were put under a puppet ruler and their lands opened up to extensive English settlement. The northern Picts remained free, but also had to pay tribute and they were restricted to the Highlands. When Oswy died in 670 the northern Picts took the opportunity to marry the heiress to their kingdom to Bridei mac Beli, from the royal family of the Clyde Britons, and so forge an alliance. The new King of Northumbria, Egferth, was too busy establishing his power to interfere.

In 681 Bridei, by now King of the Picts, took over the Orkneys. Feeling confident, he refused to pay tribute to Northumbria. Egferth could not ignore such a blatant challenge to his power. He gathered an army and marched north in the spring of 685. His enemies were waiting for him near the modern town of Forfar.

Although records of the campaign are scanty, it is relatively easy to reconstruct the routes that brought the rival armies to the place of battle. Bridei and the northern Picts were clearly determined to free the southern Picts from the puppet rulers who did English bidding, and to conquer the English villages and farms established after Oswy's conquests. As an opening move, Bridei marched south from his powerbase around Aberdeen. He ordered provocative raiding of Strathmore, where the native Picts outnumbered the immigrant English.

Egferth marched out of the English fortress of Edinburgh and along the southern shores of the Firth of Forth. This area had been part of English Northumbria for over a generation and Egferth was marching through friendly territory. Turning north, Egferth crossed the Forth near Stirling and marched into Strathallan. This area had seen the densest English settlements after the conquests of Oswy and the English probably outnumbered the Pictish population.

Egferth was following the old Roman road which had been built many years before to supply Roman forces on their patrols into hostile Pictish territory. Even after some generations of neglect, the road would have made for easier marching than dirt tracks. The Roman road would have taken him through Perth and then up the valley of the Isla to Inchtuthil. Here lay the Roman fortress of Pinnata Castra which, although ruined, would have provided a secure forward base for the English army.

It is unclear if the English king realized at this point that he was facing a full-scale invasion rather than a larger than usual raid. Certainly, Egferth behaved as if he did not realize the true strength of his enemies. Nor did he have any real idea of where the Picts were. The Picts, on the other hand, knew exactly where the English were and how many had marched north. They set a careful ambush for the English along the route they knew Egferth would choose on his march from the ruined Roman fortress towards the west coast.

The Opposing Armies

There are no contemporary records of the size of the armies which met at Nechtansmere. It is clear, however, that both kings had prepared for a major effort and would have brought powerful fighting forces with them.

It is easier to reconstruct the English army than the Pictish for more records survive from Northumbria than from Pictland. As with all English kings, Egferth had a personal bodyguard known as his Hearth-troop or 'Hird'. These were tough professional warriors drawn principally from Northumbria, but also hired in from elsewhere. They were equipped by the King and paid with regular gifts of gold and silver as well as by a share in any loot captured or tribute paid to the King.

The Hird were divided into two. The more experienced warriors, the dugud, were equipped as heavy infantry. They wore short-sleeved tunics of chain mail or lammelar armour together with a conical helmet. They also carried large, round wooden shields reinforced with metal edgings. Each man fought with a spear and sword, often richly decorated with gold and semi-precious jewels. They would have been given a horse or pony to ride on the march, but fought on foot.

The less experienced men of the Hird were the geogud. They were equipped with leather jerkins reinforced with metal plates for armour and had helmets and shields similar to the dugud. They were not given prestigious swords, however, but were equipped with javelins and thrusting spears.

The Hird not only formed a personal bodyguard to the king, but its members also served as royal messengers and could be put in command of towns or fortresses guarded by non-professional troops. At this time the Kings of Northumbria would have had a trained Hird of about 700 men and Egferth probably took most of them north with him.

The bulk of the Northumbrian army, as with those of all English kingdoms, was made up of the Fyrd, or militia. Like the Hird, the Fyrd was divided into two. If the kingdom was invaded, every able bodied man aged sixteen to sixty was expected to turn out with any weapons he could lay his hands on. This was the Great Fyrd and was called upon only in emergencies. In Northumbria a century later the men of the Great Fyrd were expected to serve for fifteen days free of charge, though the King had to pay them wages if he asked them to serve longer.

The more useful part of the Fyrd was the Little Fyrd. This was made up of one man from every five families. The families were responsible for providing the man with spear, shield, helmet and enough food to last for a campaign of sixty days each year. A few of these men would have brought hunting bows with them. Unlike the Great Fyrd, the men of the Little Fyrd were expected to undertake rudimentary military training and to be able to perform some simple manoeuvres.

Numbers are unclear before the ninth century but, at the time of Nechtansmere, Northumbria could probably have fielded some 7,000 men in the Little Fyrd. It is likely that Egferth would have left several units in Northumbria itself to deter other kings from taking advantage of his absence in the north to launch raids of their own. Perhaps some 4,000 Fyrd men marched north with their king.

The Picts left few written records at this time, but their enemies tell us much about their fighting men. Organization was much less sophisticated than among the English. It seems that a regional chieftain would answer the King's summons to war with whatever men he felt could be spared from working on the land. Sometimes the chieftain would not come at all if he thought the fighting was too remote from his territory or if he had better things to do.

The majority of Picts were largely unarmoured. Only chieftains wore helmets, and not all of them bothered. Every man did, however, carry a shield and these were almost universally of a distinctive square or oblong shape and richly decorated with painted swirls and spirals. Chieftains and men alike carried long stabbing spears, though most men had throwing javelins as well.

The men drawn from the rich, flat lands around Aberdeen rode horses and, unlike the English, fought from horseback. They rode bareback, without saddles or stirrups, which made them unstable in action and unable to wield swords or axes with any real success, nor could they have charged home with couched lances to produce a massive impact on enemy formations. It is likely they would have advanced at speed, throwing javelins at the enemy, then retreated to regroup.

How many men the Picts could field is unknown, but it is clear that at Nechtansmere they outnumbered the English. Perhaps Bridei had 6,000 men with him.

Tactics

In the seventh century tactics were simple and straightforward, largely because most men were part-time soldiers who rarely spent more than a few days each year in training.

The preferred English tactic was to form what was known as a shieldwall. In essence this was a dense phalanx at least five or six men deep. The name refers to the fact that the front rank of men linked their shields together to form a solid wall of wood and metal, a sort of temporary mobile fortification.

In practice the front rank or two was made up of the tough fighters of the Hird. It was their task to form the wall and to keep formation as the mass of men advanced or fell back. As men died or were injured, their bodies were pulled clear and men from the rear would step into their places. At all costs the front line of solid interlocking shields had to be kept intact. If the enemy managed to break the shield wall, the army was highly vulnerable and could break up with alarming speed.

Usually the king or commander would

A Pictish warrior from the later seventh century, based on carvings found on standing stones in the Pict lands. The pointed beard is typical of Picts of all periods up to the ninth century, as is the long woollen coat or tunic that this figure is wearing. The square shield with abstract designs was in common usage by the Picts, though some carried round shields. The heavy, thrusting spear with a large, leaf-shaped point was the usual Pictish weapon at this date, although cavalry usually carried lighter throwing javelins. Richer men would have been equipped with a sword and, possibly, a helmet.

station himself at the centre of the rear ranks, though sometimes he took up position on a flank if that gave him a better view of the battlefield. He would be surrounded by the very best men of the Hird. In victory, the king would use these men to occupy ground or to mount their horses and pursue the enemy. In defeat, these tough fighters would be relied upon to retreat in good order and prevent defeat becoming rout.

The tactics of the Picts were even more simple. Each body of men fought on their own with only casual attempts to cooperate with other units. They would gather in loosely formed groups and throw their javelins at the enemy. If there seemed a good chance of success, the Picts would then launch a wild charge of frenzied ferocity. Otherwise, they would melt away to fight another day.

The Battle

It is not known at what time of day, or even on which date, the battle took place. However, the Northumbrians were marching east from Forfar along the track which passed for a road.

East of Dunnichen the track ran between a steep hill and a wide lake with marshy shores – the Nechtansmere. A small fortified farm or house of some kind lay on the southern flank of the hill just 200 yards from the track. The Pictish army lay hidden in woods on the hill, out of sight of the advancing English.

The road east from Dunnichen. The English army was advancing along this road when it was ambushed by the Picts.

The slopes of Dunnichen Hill down which the Pictish army swarmed to attack the English army as it was vulnerable due to being strung out on the march. This photo was taken from the road along which the English were marching when attacked.

An English army on the march some generations later followed a traditional formation and there is no reason to suppose that Egferth's force was any different. In the front were men of the Little Fyrd, usually preceded by mounted men of the Hird who scouted out the route. Behind them came the bulk of the Hird and the King with his treasure chest, camping equipment and so on. Behind the King came the pack horses which carried the supplies and bringing up the rear the remainder of the Fyrd men.

Why the English scouts did not find the Picts before the ambush was sprung is unknown. Perhaps Egferth thought the enemy many miles away. Whatever the cause, the leading elements of the English army had almost passed the lake when the Picts leapt from cover and attacked.

It seems that the initial rush by Bridei's picked men – probably mounted men from Aberdeen – was launched on the Hird and King Egferth himself. The aim was to prevent the English from forming their formidable shield wall, and the Picts succeeded. As soon as the Hird was engaged, the mass of the Picts poured out of the woods and attacked the men of the Fyrd. Unable to form up behind the trained shield men of the Hird, the Fyrd turned and fled. Many of them became bogged down in the marshy shores of Nechtansmere and were butchered.

The Hird, meanwhile, had formed up around King Egferth and managed to construct a makeshift shieldwall. Lacking the support of the Fyrd, however, the Hird were isolated and outnumbered. They fought bravely but the end was inevitable. Almost to a man the Hird died with their King. The only surviving Englishmen were fugitives in wild country many miles from home. Only a tiny minority reached Northumbria with news of the disaster. The rest were killed or taken as slaves.

Aftermath

The most immediate result of the battle was that Bridei took over Strathmore and enslaved or expelled the English settlers. With these new lands, Bridei became the most powerful ruler in northern Britain. He later moved to take over the lands north of the Forth, but without expelling the large numbers of English. Instead, he and his successors forged a powerful multi-lingual kingdom which became known as Fortrenn. Over a century later a dynastic marriage saw Fortrenn pass under the rule of the King of the Scots and an alliance with the Britons of the Clyde then created the Kingdom of Scotland as we know it today.

The small pond that is all that remains of the mere at Nechtansmere. At the time of the battle the lake extended right across the fields now grazed by cattle and up the hillside beyond.

If Nechtansmere laid the conditions for the future Kingdom of Scotland, it proved disastrous for Northumbria. Egferth left no obvious heir and the nobles made the extraordinary choice of an elderly scholar named Aldfrith to succeed him. After Aldfrith's death in 705 Northumbria collapsed into anarchy as the nobles squabbled with each other for power and lands. When the Vikings arrived, they found the once powerful kingdom of Northumbria an easy target.

Visiting the Battlefield Today

Much has changed at Nechtansmere since 685, but it is easy to visit the site and to envisage what happened here.

Leave Forfar on the B9128 to Carnoustie. After about two miles the road enters the hamlet of Dunnichen and a road signposted to Letham turns left just as the B road makes a right hand bend. Take the side road and park beside the church which is on your right. Outside the church is a carved Pictish stone from the seventh century which probably pre-dates the battle. Return to the B road on foot and immediately on your left is a monument erected on the 1,300th anniversary of the Battle.

Return to the side turning and walk forwards to find the battlefield. As you emerge from the side of the churchyard, look down the slope to your right to see a small pond which is all that is now left of the Nechtansmere. The waters once came up to the side of the road and the mere was a substantial lake. Further on the road passes a farm before climbing to top a slight ridge almost a mile from where you have left your car. Above the left hand side of the road rears the steep slope of Dunnichen Hill. It was somewhere

The Pictish stone in Aberlemno Churchyard. Carved within a short time of the Battle of Nechtansmere, the stone is generally believed to show the warriors engaged in the battle.

along this stretch of road, from the Pictish stone to the slight ridge, that the Picts launched their ambush on the English marching along the road.

To see the battlefield from the hill, return to the B road, turning right, then turn right opposite the bus stop up a narrow lane. This climbs steeply up to the summit of Dunnichen Hill from which a panoramic view of the battlefield can be gained.

A short distance to the north is the village of Aberlemno where there are two large slabs of stone carved by the Picts in the late seventh or early eighth centuries. Both carry large crosses and enigmatic symbols, but the one in the churchyard also shows a battlescene with Pictish cavalry attacking infantry equipped with spears and round shields, perhaps Englishmen. It is generally thought that this scene is a contemporary depiction of the Battle of Nechtansmere.

Chapter Three

BRUNANBURH 937

Introduction

Of all the battles fought between the English and the Scots, the one fought at Brunanburh had arguably the most important long term results of all. It was at this battle that the English established themselves as the masters of what is now England – and that control has never been seriously in doubt since.

In the century before this climactic battle the map of Britain had been altered dramatically by the repeated hammer blows of the Viking invasions. The Battle of Brunanburh was to set the scene for further changes which led to the formation of the kingdoms of England and Scotland much as they exist today.

The Scots and the Picts had become united under the Scots royal family through dynastic marriage and by the 930s, King Constantine of Scotland ruled a kingdom which stretched from the Moray Firth south to the Forth and west to Mull and Kintyre. The Pictish lands north of the Great Glen had been lost to Viking Earls, who ruled a largely Pictish population. Allied to the Scots, more often than not, was the Kingdom of Strathclyde. This kingdom was based on the old Romano-British Kingdom of Clyde which had held off the barbarians in the collapse of the Roman Empire and now stretched from the Clyde south to include what is now Cumbria.

The English kingdoms of Northumbria and East Anglia had been overrun by the Vikings, as had much of Mercia. Most of northern and eastern England had thus been conquered and most areas heavily settled by the Scandinavian invaders. Even the Kingdom of Wessex had been threatened in the 890s, but southern England had been saved by King Alfred the Great and his successors.

Wales, too, had suffered Viking invasion and settlement. The Welsh princes had, however, managed to avoid being conquered and Wales was in the 930s divided among a number of local princes. Ireland had seen widespread Viking settlement, especially around Dublin, but most of that island remained in the hands of its native Celtic dynasties.

All these lands, kingdoms and dynasties were to be dragged into the destructive battle at Brunanburh, a conflict which all contemporaries recognized as being not only the greatest battle fought in Britain, but also one with truly historic consequences.

The series of events that led to the battle began in July 924. In that month King Athelstan of Wessex was accepted as King of Mercia. Athelstan had grown up in Mercia and was enthusiastically welcomed by the English lords and, grudgingly, by the Viking earls of eastern Mercia. Athelstan called the princes of Wales to a meeting at Hereford. At this meeting the various rulers promised peace to each other and fixed permanent boundaries between their realms. The Welsh princes promised Athelstan 25,000 cattle in yearly tribute and to come to his aid in time of war. Finally, in 926, Athelstan married his sister to Sihtric, the Viking King of York, to secure an alliance with the northern Viking earls. Athelstan seemed secure as the overlord of all southern Britain.

But in 927 Sihtric died and was succeeded by Olaf, a son by an earlier pagan wife. This Olaf Sihtricson had powerful connections, being cousin to Olaf Guthfrithson, King of Dublin, and son-in-law to Constantine, King of Scots.

Athelstan did not want such a powerful man as a northern neighbour. He gathered the armies of Wessex and Mercia, called on his Welsh allies, and marched north. In a lightning campaign, Athelstan captured York and expelled Olaf Sihtricson. He then made peace with the noblemen of Northumberland, most of whom were Viking, but some English. Athelstan allowed them to keep their lands in return for a pledge of loyalty. He left two noblemen, Gudrek and Alfgeir, in charge of the Northumbrians and returned home to Wessex.

In 934 Athelstan marched north again. Details of this campaign are sketchy and we do not know exactly why Athelstan chose to attack. The army included four Welsh princes and twelve earls from Northumberland. King Constantine fell back, refusing to fight a pitched battle. Having pillaged up the Scottish east coast, Athelstan retreated. It was this campaign which convinced the other rulers of Britain that Athelstan was determined to conquer the whole island. They began plotting his overthrow.

The prime mover in the alliance that sought to defeat Athelstan and pin the English into southern Britain was Constantine. He was giving refuge to Olaf Sihtricson, who wanted to regain his place as King of Northumbria. To this end, Olaf Sihtricson began recruiting an army of Vikings from Norway and Denmark and kept in touch with supporters in Northumbria itself. He also contacted his cousin, Olaf Guthfrithson, King of Dublin.

Constantine, meanwhile, was talking to King Owen of Strathclyde. Owen feared the power of Athelstan. He had acknowledged Athelstan as his overlord in 927, but he resented the relationship. It did not take much for Constantine to talk Owen into joining the war against Athelstan's English. In the spring of 937 the anti-English alliance began the great invasion.

Olaf Sihtricson loaded the Scots army and his Scandinavian allies into a fleet of longships and sailed to the estuary of the Humber, penetrating far upstream before landing. At this point Gudrek and Alfgeir called out the militia of Northumberland to attack the invaders. The turn out was patchy as many Northumbrians were supporters of Olaf. The Northumbrians were defeated and Gudrek killed. Alfgeir rode south to warn Athelstan of the invasion.

The army of Owen of Strathclyde, meanwhile, was marching down the old Roman road which runs west of the Pennines from Carlisle to Ribchester. At some point he met the Vikings and Irish brought over the Irish Sea by Olaf Guthfrithson. The combined army then crossed the Pennines to join the Scots and Vikings somewhere near the headwaters of the Humber. They may have met at Tadcaster, a small town which still retained sizeable Roman fortifications. Once the allies were gathered, they marched south, crossing into Athelstan's Mercia at Castleford and moving down the Roman road.

Athelstan by this time was gathering his forces. The Englishmen of Wessex and Mercia responded in large numbers, and Athelstan also called out the Norsemen of East Anglia and eastern Mercia. Athelstan also hired mercenaries, including an Icelandic Viking named Egil Skallagrimsson who brought about 300 men with him. The position of the Welsh is unclear. No chronicler mentions Welsh troops fighting on either side. Either Athelstan did not summon the Welsh princes to his aid, or they did not respond in time.

Athelstan seems to have mustered his forces in the Lichfield/Derby area towards the end of July. He then marched north to meet the Scots and their allies who were coming south from Castleford.

The Opposing Armies

It is notoriously difficult to establish the sizes of armies in this period. Chronicles were written by monks and clerics with little understanding of military matters. They tended to refer to 'great numbers' and left it at that. For the Battle of Brunanburh, however, it is possible to be rather more precise.

All the contemporary accounts agree that this was a major battle, the like of which had not been seen in living memory. The news of the battle spread far beyond Britain, being known about and commented upon in chronicles written on mainland Europe. Furthermore, when Egil Skallagrimsson returned home to Iceland he was treated as a famous and respected warrior, largely because he had fought at this battle. It can be assumed that all the kings involved made great efforts to get as many men as possible to the scene of conflict.

One eyewitness states that Olaf Sihtricson brought 615 ships full of fighting men to the Humber. Archeological evidence supports contemporary statements that each longship could carry about forty men, complete with weapons and supplies. This means that the combined numbers of the Scots army and the Scandinavian Vikings came to about 24,000 men. Some of these men would have been left to guard the ships and others to secure bridges, fords and the like. It is fair to assume that some 18,000 to 20,000 of these men were marching in the main army when battle was joined.

The majority of the Scots would have been fairly well armed infantry. The main weapon was a thrusting spear about seven feet long, though most would have carried a knife or axe as well. The majority of the men carried two or three small throwing javelins. For defence, they would have relied upon a round shield some three feet in diameter and on a jerkin of toughened hide. Usually a toughened leather cap or a metal helmet completed the outfit. Olaf Sihtricson would probably have been lent many men of King Constantine's personal guard. These men would also have relied on spear and shield, but probably had mail shirts and metal helmets.

A minority of the Scots army would have been equipped, as were their ancestors, with light throwing spears and hand axes or knives for close work.

The Viking contingent, likewise, had large round shields and spears. They were feared by their enemies for two distinct weapons. The first was the battleaxe. This was a terrifying implement that took years of training to use effectively. The five feet long wooden handle was topped by a curved axe head about a foot across. Wielded only by full time soldiers, the battleaxe

This Viking warrior carries equipment typical of that used by the wealthier and more important men present at Brunanburh. The Icelandic mercenary captain, Egil Skallagrimsson (see text) would have looked much like this. He is dressed in typical Nordic costume of a tunic reaching to the knees over baggy trousers and decorated boots. The hair was usually worn long and was washed and plaited for important occasions - such as battles! He carries the round wooden shield faced with leather and with a metal rim and central boss that was usual in northern European armies at this date. His conical helmet may be of boiled leather, but richer men tended to have metal helmets with a nasal guard, as shown here. He carries a pair of light throwing spears and a sword, as would all Vikings going to battle. His greater wealth and importance is shown by the mail jerkin he wears, a highly prized piece of equipment that would have cost much money. The axe he wields again shows him to be an important man. Its proper use in battle took a great deal of training, and such time was beyond the reach of an ordinary farmer. This man is clearly a professional fighter.

could slice a man in half and bring down a horse with a single blow.

The Vikings also had berserkers. These warriors worked themselves up into a frenzied battle rage in the grip of which they fought with the strength of madmen and ignored injuries or wounds which would have brought down most men. It is not clear if this frenzy was brought on by drugs, by religious devotion to the god Odin or to simple fury in the conditions of hand to hand combat. Although greatly feared, the berserkers were unpredictable.

King Owen of Strathclyde and Olaf Guthfrithson between them brought rather fewer men, perhaps 15,000. The combined anti-English army can be fairly confidently estimated at just over 30,000 men or thereabouts. The Irish were mainly of Viking extraction and would have been equipped as the Vikings arriving with Olaf Sihtricson. Owen's men would have been equipped much as the Scots.

The English army was smaller than that of the allies, though by how much is unknown. Aware that he faced a huge invasion force, Athelstan would have turned out as many men as possible.

Perhaps he had about 25,000 men with him as he marched north. The core of this army would have been made up of Athelstan's Hird, or hearthmen. These full time warriors lived with the King and kept warm at his hearth – hence their name. They would have been equipped with mail shirts and swords as well as the ubiquitous shield and spear.

Most of the army was made up of a semi-trained militia called the Fyrd. A group of families would join together to buy the equipment for one of their number to go to war. This equipment would have consisted of spear, shield, helmet and perhaps a tough leather jerkin. Given the emergency, Athelstan may have called out the Great Fyrd.

Tactics

By the time of the Battle of Brunanburh, most of the armies of mainland Britain had adopted the English style of fighting, though with variations. The core tactic was to form a shieldwall. Spears were thrust forward of the shieldwall to form a bristling hedge of metal points.

As the opposing shieldwalls moved towards each other, javelins would be thrown by the rear ranks and those men who had bows with them would shoot their arrows. Once the shieldwalls became locked together the men would thrust at the enemy with their spears and, when these broke, with swords, knives or axes.

Weight, numbers and sheer musclepower counted for much in these encounters. The object was to break into the enemy's shieldwall and push the formation apart, after which the enemy would usually flee. Sometimes the men in the shieldwall which was giving ground would not wait for the formation to break up, but would run first. It was considered an absolute disgrace for men of the Hird to abandon their lord. So long as he stood and fought, so did they. If he was injured or killed they were expected to guard or extricate his body. If the hearthmen could not remove their leader's body, they were expected to die on the field with him. Most did just this.

Although many of the hearthmen and richer warriors rode horses on campaign, they almost invariably fought on foot. In the opening stages of a battle, some horsemen would ride up to the enemy and throw javelins before retreating, but there was no attempt at a charge. Mounted men were used extensively in pursuit, when they used their extra speed to hunt down fugitives and secure loot or supplies.

The Vikings had some variations on the brutish tactic of the shieldwall. One often used tactic was the *svynfylking*, which involved pushing a wedge of especially well armoured men ahead of the main shieldwall. This was intended to punch a hole in the enemy shieldwall. Another favoured device was to advance a man armed with the terrible battleaxe in front of the front rank, backed by men whose task was to protect him. Again the aim was to disrupt the enemy formation.

The Battle

No contemporary accounts of the course of the fighting at the Battle of Brunanburh have survived in Britain. However, the Icelandic mercenary, Egil Skallagrimsson, became the subject of a saga after his death. This saga survives and includes Egil's detailed account of the battle. There can be little doubt that Egil exaggerated his own role in the fighting, but there is no reason to doubt the outline of events that he gives.

According to Egil, the armies were advancing towards each other along a road but halted when a day's horse ride apart. Athelstan sent forward messengers offering to pay a sizeable amount of silver and gold if the Scots and their allies would depart. Olaf Sihtricson, perhaps suspecting this was a ruse to

The view from the top of the ridge occupied by the English army along the modern B6067. Templeborough, where the Scots and their allies had their camp, is in the distance.

The densely wooded banks of the River Rother which formed the eastern edge of the battlefield.

make him disband his army, refused unless his men were paid even more money and he himself was given Northumbria. Athlestan refused and moved his army forward. Egil says the English halted on a ridge with a river on their right and a dense wood on the left. The land ahead sloped down towards a distant town. The next morning Olaf Guthfrithson launched a surprise dawn attack which Egil takes full credit for having beaten back.

The battle proper began with the Scots advancing along the river and their allies moving forward on their right, closer to the forest. As the Scots shieldwall approached that of the English a shower of javelins, darts and axes would have flown between the two sides, then the lines crashed together. The front lines hacked at each other, splitting open skulls and slicing off limbs. Egil records that one of his men killed an opposing Viking earl: 'He lunged his spear at the earl's breast, piercing his mail coat and body so that the point stuck out behind the shoulder blades. Then he raised the spear up and plunged the base of the shaft into the earth. So the earl died on the spear in front of everyone, before his own men.'

It was a brutal fight at close quarters with little room to move or manoeuvre. The *Anglo-Saxon Chronicle*, which usually restricts itself to bald statements of deaths, victories and treaties, reported, 'The field was slick with men's blood, many a man lay wrecked by spears'.

40

After some hours of fighting, the allies on the Scots' right began to give way. Then they collapsed and fled the field. The English left gave chase, then returned to the battle and fell on the open flank of the Scottish shieldwall. Within minutes the battle was effectively over and the Scots fled. The English pursued until dusk, cutting down and killing anyone they could reach.

Olaf Sihtricson was among the dead, as were seven earls and five men the *Anglo-Saxon Chronicle* describes as 'kings', perhaps from Ireland where there were many kings. By nightfall the English were far to the north and the only things moving on the battlefield were 'the black raven, with hard beak of horn, and hoary coated eagle eating the carrion,' at least according to the gleeful *Anglo-Saxon Chronicle*.

Aftermath

Once the initial rout was over, the northern armies seem to have retreated in reasonably good order. They did not stop to fight, however, and made no attempt to coordinate with each other. The Scots marched to the ships waiting on the Humber, and the Strathclyde army back up the Roman road west of the Pennines. The Irish moved swiftly to their ships, perhaps left near Ribchester, and sailed for Dublin.

After the defeat at Brunanburh the non-English peoples of Britain never again united to fight the English. It was the last chance they had had to ensure the English remained a small, divided people. Athelstan's victory gave him the prestige needed to weld the English and Vikings living in England, into a united country. It was to be some years before they merged to become a single people, but the foundations for that were laid in the bloody victory at Brunanburh.

Visiting the Battlefield Today

The precise location of the battlefield of Brunanburh has been disputed by historians for many years. The chronicles and Egil's saga taken together make it clear that the main Scottish army landed in the Humber and then marched south for some days before meeting Athelstan's army, coming north.

Assuming that the invaders were moving along the old Roman road, they would have been somewhere between Castleford and Derby. Egil's saga describes the topography of the battlefield clearly. The road south was climbing a slope to a long ridge, with a river just to the east. To the north was a town where the Scots and Vikings camped. There is only one spot along the road which matches that description; the hill south of Brinsworth beside the River Rother, which had the Roman town of Templeborough to the north. Interestingly the placename elements '-worth' and '-burh' are not too dissimilar in Old English so Brunanburh may also have been known as Brunanworth – or Brinsworth.

Assuming that the Battle of Brunanburh was fought on the ridge south of Brinsworth, outside Rotherham, there is not much left to see today. Nearly the entire battlefield has been built over and a main line railway runs across it.

However, it is easy to appreciate why Athelstan chose this place for his battle. The crest of the ridge is in full view of the 'distant town', Templeborough, where the Scots army was camped. The two Olafs could not have ignored the challenge of the English army drawn up in battle array. The approach to the ridge is a long climb and becomes noticeably steeper just before the crest. This fact is best appreciated on the B6067 off the A631. Although housing covers the surrounding land, the steepness of the hill is clear – especially if you walk up it.

Little remains of Templeborough as Rotherham has been built on top of it. However, there are some ruins in the grounds of Rotherham Museum, which also contains an interesting Roman Room and some impressive Roman tombs.

The ruins of the Roman city of Templeborough, now mostly covered by Rotherham, where the Scottish army was camped the night before the battle.

Chapter Four

THE STANDARD 1138

Introduction

The Battle of the Standard was an unusual battle in many ways. It was the first major clash between the English and the Scots for 200 years, but the reasons it was fought had more to do with internal English politics than with enmity between the two kingdoms. It was also fought at a time when weaponry and tactics were changing rapidly and both sides experimented with innovations in the art of war.

After the titanic clash at the Battle of Brunanburh in 937 both England and Scotland were kept busy with internal problems. The English were busy alternately fighting against, and then assimilating the Viking settlers who lived in northern and eastern England. Then, in 1066, England was conquered by the Normans under William I. Another generation was spent in pacification, assimilation and general reformation of the kingdom.

The Scots were also kept too busy to bother with major wars. In the 960s they added the Forth Valley to their domains and secured control of the old English border fortress city of Edinburgh while the English were distracted by a murderous feud within their royal family. In 973 the Scots King Kenneth received all the land from the Firth of Forth to the Tweed from the English King Edgar, in return for a personal pledge of loyalty. In theory the land remained part of England. Kenneth held it under terms similar to those by which English noblemen held their lands from the English King, but in practice the lands became permanently attached to the Scottish crown. The population of the area remained overwhelmingly English in language and ancestry.

In 1016 King Owen the Bald of Strathclyde was killed in battle against the English Earl Uhtred of Northumbria. With Owen, the Celtic dynasty of Clyde, which originated in Roman times and had held off the barbarians for centuries, became extinct. The Kingdom of Strathclyde was carved up. England got Cumbria and Westmorland while Scotland took the lands between the Clyde

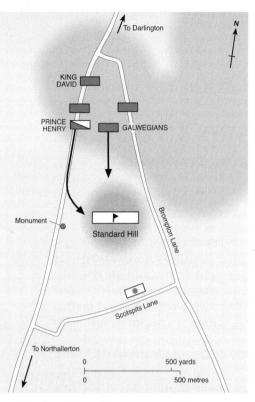

To Darlington

N

KING DAVID

PRINCE HENRY

GALWEGIANS

Monument

Standard Hill

Brompton Lane

Scotspits Lane

To Northallerton

0   500 yards

0   500 metres

The position of the armies at the opening of the battle. The English camp was guarded by only a token force and nearly all the fighting men were on top of Standard Hill.

and the Solway Firth. The fortified city of Carlisle thus became a border town.

The underlying cause of the conflict between Scotland and England which led to the Battle of the Standard occurred in 1135 when King Henry I of England died, leaving his crown to his daughter Matilda. The throne was, however, seized by King Henry's nephew the youthful Count Stephen of Blois. Although most of the English were content to accept the popular Stephen, Matilda had some powerful supporters among the nobility. She spent the next few years on the Continent rallying support and planning an invasion to enforce her claim to the throne.

One of Matilda's most powerful supporters was her maternal uncle, King David of Scotland. In 1137 and again in the spring of 1138, King David organized large scale border raids to coincide with localized rebellions by Matilda's supporters in southern England. In June 1138 David was planning another raid when the northern English Baron Eustace fitz John deserted Stephen and pledged allegiance to Matilda. He hurried north to join King David while his men held the key fortresses of Alnwick and Malton.

This altered the strategic situation and seems to have decided King David to change his planned raid into a full scale invasion. He ordered the entire fighting strength of Scotland to join him. In July King David crossed the border with about 25,000 men and headed south. The looting carried out by the army was organized, systematic and far more effective than the usual casual robbery of border raids. The bewildered English found it was not enough to bury their money in the fields and hide livestock in the woods. This time the Scots were stealing everything - including people who were driven off as slaves.

The sheer effectiveness of the Scots pillaging provoked the English response. King Stephen's royal army was busy in the south dealing with the rebellions there, so the northern English were on their own. The barons of the north gathered at York to discuss plans for resistance. Fortunately for them the King's Lieutenant in the north was Archbishop Thurstan of York. Aged about seventy, Thurstan was too bent with age to mount a horse, but he retained the formidable administrative skills that had won him his job in the first place. And he had the additional advantage of having travelled widely through Europe.

Thurstan ordered the barons to gather their men and return to York in the first week of August. Then he sent messages begging for help to the King and to anyone else he could think of. Finally he took the step that gave the coming battle its name; he ordered the construction of The Standard.

The Standard was a tactical innovation never before seen in Britain. It consisted of a large wagon pulled by oxen on which was mounted a ship's mast. Hanging from the yardarm of the mast were the sacred banners of the great northern saints, St Peter of York, St John of Beverley and St Wilfred of Ripon. These banners were regularly carried through the streets of their cities, but carrying them into battle was a new idea.

Thurstan had not, however, invented the concept himself. He had seen similar Standards in Italy during his journeys to Rome. Known as the *caroccio*, these massive, cumbersome wagons carrying sacred banners, relics and priests were commonplace in the armies of the Italian cities. They were used as rallying points for the citizen militia, and Thurstan was to use his Standard in the same way. He gave orders that all able bodied men were to follow their parish priests to Thirsk, where The Standard would await them.

As the northern barons marched their men into York they were joined by Bernard de Balliol who came with a small force of knights sent by King Stephen. Balliol had not only brought men, he also had terms for a truce. Stephen offered to recognize King David's son, Henry, as Earl of Huntingdon and Earl of Northumbria. These two titles carried with them substantial lands and wealth. It was a tempting offer with which Stephen hoped to buy peace in the north while he fought his civil war.

On about 14 August the baronial force left York to

The modern monument, which bears a stylized representation of the Standard mounted on its four-wheeled cart.

join the gathering militia at Thirsk. Thurstan was too ill to go with them, but he blessed the men before they left. Bernard de Balliol rode on north to meet King David and offer the truce. With him Balliol took Robert of Bruce, a nobleman who held lands in both England and Scotland and who knew King David well. The two men met David as the Scottish army crossed the Tees and made their offer. But David took the generous terms as evidence of English weakness. He laughed at Stephen's representatives and sent them packing.

When Balliol and Bruce rejoined the English army at Thirsk they found it much larger than when they had left. One of Thurstan's pleas for help had reached Sir Robert of Ferrars, the richest landowner in Derbyshire. Ferrars had not only turned out his own men, but had persuaded the entire landowning class of Derbyshire and Nottinghamshire to march with him. The importance of the arrival of Ferrars is often overlooked. At the time he was a relatively unknown youngster, though he had some experience of fighting the French. As a result the chroniclers merely record his arrival and give it no special importance. But Ferrars went on to become one of the toughest and most able soldiers of his generation and clawed his way up to achieve the position of the Earl of Derby. Although command of the army remained with Walter Espec, Sheriff of York, there are indications that young Ferrars had a hand in the tactical deployment on the day of battle. Certainly many of the knights looked to him for leadership once the fighting began.

On the afternoon of 21 August English scouts brought news that the Scottish army was some twenty miles to the north. The English army set out and by midnight was taking up position on top of a slight hill which dominated the road south and blocked the route of the Scottish enemy. Battle was about to be joined.

The Opposing Armies

At this time the Scottish monarchy lacked any real form of central administration. David relied upon his nobles to choose to support him. On this occasion the nobles scented the chance of easy booty in a disunited England and most of them came to join the royal army. The men of Galloway turned out in especially large numbers and even the Highlands sent contingents south. David also had the mercenaries he had hired for the summer to lead the raids. The main strength of the Scottish army was, however, made up of troops drawn from the Lowlands.

David had taken some 25,000 men with him when he crossed the border in July. Although he had left garrisons at captured castles and towns, and some troops were dispersed on the business of looting, it is likely David still had at least 16,000 men with him as the battle began.

It is difficult to be precise about numbers, but about 7,000 of the Scottish troops present at the battle were the Galwegians. These tough men from Galloway came from the lands of the Strathclyde British and reckoned themselves the best fighters in Scotland. They had no armour other than a simple helmet and a small, round shield of wood or leather. The vast majority were armed with a spear about twelve feet long, though a few had axes. Feudalism had not yet spread to Galloway so these men were free and semi-free farmers who had been raised by the old system of forinsec – a type of mass militia. The 2,000 or so Highlanders were also lightly armoured, but carried dirks, axes and swords in place of spears.

Another 6,000 infantry were made up of the Lowland soldiers. These men were raised through the feudal system which David and his father had introduced throughout the Lowlands, in the hope of producing a more disciplined and better equipped army. They were also intended to curb the activities of the more turbulent regional chiefs. The men had large shields and some would have had mail jackets. They were equipped with swords and axes as well as spears and a few men would have carried bows and arrows.

David had some 300 fully armoured mounted knights with him. These men were covered from head to foot in chain mail, topped by a conical or cylindrical helmet and they carried large, kite-shaped shields which protected their entire left sides. They were armed with lances eight feet long and with swords. Most of these knights were Norman or German mercenaries, though a few were Lowland landholders who had adopted the new style of fighting.

The English army seems to have been rather smaller but precise numbers are unclear. There were certainly very few mounted knights. So few, in fact, that they decided to dismount and join the main army on foot.

The armed retainers of the barons and nobles made up perhaps 6,000 men. They were heavily equipped and well trained. They had chain mail jackets together with helmets and long shields. The shape of these shields varied. but the men were trained to lock them together to form a solid barrier behind which to shelter.

The nobles also brought along several hundred, perhaps over a thousand, archers. These men did not carry the longbows with which the English would win spectacular victories in the fourteenth and fifteenth centuries, but short hunting bows with an effective range of about fifty yards.

Finally, the bulk of the English army was made up of the local militia raised by Thurstan's priests. It is entirely unclear how many of these men were actually present on the battlefield, but it may have been as few as 5,000 or as many as 10,000. They would have had only the most elementary training and came equipped with forester's axes, knives, scythes and a variety of other home-made weapons.

Tactics

In the later twelfth century most commanders tried to avoid battles. Battles were unpredictable and the outcomes often turned on unforeseen events. Much better, it was thought, to stick to the business of besieging castles and towns. However once battle was inevitable, well established tactics were used.

The infantry were formed into one or more solid bodies of men several ranks deep. These formations were usually deployed to guard, or capture, tactically important features such as fords, bridges or roads. At The Standard, the English deployed their infantry in one formation to hold the crest of the hill on which they had stationed themselves. This was a development of the old English and Viking shieldwall, but by the twelfth century new tactical innovations had been made.

The front rank or two were made up of heavily armoured and well trained men at arms. Suitably armoured and equipped with spears and axes or swords, these men at arms formed the main anchoring point of any army. With them the men at arms invariably had a smaller number of archers. The archers would deploy in front of the men at arms to shoot at an advancing enemy, but would dodge behind their comrades before hand to hand combat began. From this new position the archers would shoot at any target that offered itself.

When on the defensive this formation of men simply stood on the ground they had to guard. On the attack, the tactics were more subtle. The archers would usually advance to within maximum range and shower the opposing infantry with arrows. They themselves stood in loose groupings both to frustrate return arrow shots and to tempt the opposing men to charge and become disordered. When the archers had opened up a gap in the defending infantry the cavalry charge would take place.

It was this charge that was the battle-winning moment. The mounted knights were well armoured men riding big horses and could simply crush into the ground any but the most disciplined and skillfully placed infantry. An enemy caught spread out or disordered would be smashed by a charge of knights while even a force of rival knights could be pushed into headlong flight if not properly drawn up. Choosing the right moment to launch the charge of the mounted knights was the most crucial decision facing a commander at this period.

In those days all armies also had large numbers of poorly trained and poorly armed militia with them. The principal use of these men was to gather food and firewood, to make camp and to help with the unskilled labour of siegecraft. But even they had their uses in battle.

They were usually stationed immediately behind the trained men at arms and archers. From this position they could carry wounded to the rear, be sent to guard prisoners or simply add their noisy efforts to the flag-waving, chanting and singing that were as essential to raising morale on the medieval battlefield as they are at any modern football match. In most instances such untrained men were of little use in actual fighting, though they could be useful if the battle degenerated into confused mêlée – assuming they did not run away first.

The Battle

As the foggy dawn of 22 August broke, the English took up their positions. Whether it was Espec or Ferrars who decided on the disposition, it was done with skill. It was decided to hold the crest of the hill facing north and so force the Scots to attack up hill, which would put them at a disadvantage.

Thurstan's innovation, The Standard, was placed in the centre of the line and surrounded by a large body of men at arms. The rest of the men at arms were spread out like two wings on either side of The Standard. The knights and nobles were stationed at intervals along this front line as they were too few in number to act as a mounted battering ram, which conventional tactics would have dictated. The archers took up their usual position, slightly in advance of the solid wall of shields. Behind the two wings were stationed the militia raised by the priests.

Several hundred yards behind the hill was positioned a

makeshift camp. Here were the knights' horses and the pack mules which carried the food and drink brought up from Thirsk. Most of the baggage, tents, money and other equipment that normally encumbered a medieval army had been left behind the walls of Thirsk. This camp was guarded by a small number of men at arms.

King David drew his army up for battle more or less as it had arrived on the march. He stationed the bulk of his men in three formations. On his left David placed the Galwegians. In the centre was a force of Lowland infantry with a second identical force on the right. Hovering far out to the right was the compact body of mounted knights under his son, Prince Henry, waiting the chance to deliver their battle-winning charge. David positioned himself behind the centre, with a small guard made up of the Highlanders and a few hundred Lowland infantry.

Things went wrong for King David from the very start. The Galwegians, and their leader the Earl of Lothian, refused to be used for little more than a feint on the left wing. They were proud of their acknowledged role as the shock troops of the Scottish kings. Lothian demanded that his men be deployed as a front line and threatened to march off if he was refused. David gave in and allowed Lothian to redeploy his men in front of the two divisions of Lowland men at arms.

David has usually been blamed for this action which has long been seen as a crucial mistake, but in truth he had little choice. The independently minded Galwegians were quite capable of standing back from the fighting if they felt their honour had been slighted. In any case, Lothian was a particularly turbulent noble – even by the standards of twelfth century Scotland. David may not have been too upset to see him lose his best men.

As the Galwegians swarmed forward, David tried to alter his order of battle accordingly. Unfortunately the staff of a twelfth century army was virtually non-existent. The commander relied on mounted squires and knights to carry his messages to his subordinates. Such messages were rarely orders. The proud nobles and knights preferred to rely on their own judgement and scorned orders – even from a king. In the coming battle the confusion caused by the change in plan coupled with the poor communications system would prove fatal.

When the fog lifted soon after dawn, the English army was revealed to view. Lothian ordered his men forward in a determined charge. It must have been a terrifying sight. The rhythmic chanting of the men as they jogged forward brandishing their weapons was more than enough to unnerve the enemy. When this changed to high pitched shrieking as the Galwegians raced at top speed across the final few yards, more than one enemy had fled without striking a blow.

The Galwegians surged down the Scottish hill and began to climb the English hill. Only when the war shrieks of the Galwegians split the air did the Lowland infantry of the centre realize that this was no feint, as planned, but a real attack. They began to move forward to support the Galwegians, but it was already too late.

As the wild, painted Scots broke into a run they were met by a devastating volley of English arrows. Hundreds of Galwegians dropped, but the rest surged on. Another volley thinned their ranks still more and then they were on the English lines. But in those few crucial seconds the English arrows had disorganized the charge. Only at one point on the left did the Galwegian rush crash a hole in the English front line. The waiting dismounted knights soon plugged the gap.

The Galwegians drew back out of arrow range, then charged again. Neither the bravery nor the ferocity of these men could be in doubt, but Lothian had attacked without support from archers, necessary to keep the English archers on the defensive and upset their aim. Now he paid the price for he was killed by an arrow in this second attack. Having taken heavy casualties and with their

A view along the crest of the English hill. The front line of the English was positioned, approximately, along this line with The Standard in the centre. The wild Galwegian attack came from the right of the picture.

beloved Earl dead, the Galwegians fell back in disorder. Many drifted off to the left of the Scottish army and departed the field of battle.

It was at this point that the Scottish centre arrived. This attack was more ordered than that of the Galwegians with archers and men at arms playing their proper roles. There were too few Scots in this central division to defeat the English, but they did succeed in causing some disruption.

Prince Henry chose this moment to launch his mounted knights on their charge. He moved forward without orders from King David. More seriously he did not tell the right wing infantry, whose task it was to provide support, that he was charging. The mass of heavily armoured knights rode down from their position into the valley and then began to ride up the left flank of the English hill. Belatedly, the infantry of the Scots right wing set off to follow the knights towards the English lines. As they reached the base of the hill they met the retreating centre, which now turned back up the hill to renew the attack.

Meanwhile, Prince Henry was urging his knights into a full-blooded mounted charge. This was the moment for which knights trained their entire lives. With all the colourful panoply of chivalry the knights galloped forwards like a massive, armoured battering ram. Lances couched to extend the impact of the charge, the knights smashed into and through the English front line. Throwing away the broken lances, the knights drew their swords and powered on through the militia of the English rear line and on into clear country beyond.

They had torn a passage right through the English left. But the infantry whose task it was to move into the hole created by the knights were still struggling up the hill. By the time they arrived the English knights had managed to recreate a straggling, but continuous, line of shields and men. The Scots infantry made a half hearted assault, then drew back to see what would happen next.

The Scots and mercenary knights, who found themselves in the rear of the English army, were unsure what to do. Some rode off to pillage the baggage train, others trotted off to ride back around the English flanks in the hope of rejoining their own army. If any considered attacking the English rear, they did nothing about it. Their horses were blown and the English rear was rapidly turning about and bristling with spears. The Scottish knights and their mercenaries melted away. Some even threw aside their shields and favours so that they might be mistaken as English. Prince

Henry gathered a group of his companions and rode off to the west.

The Scots infantry, meanwhile, had been left stranded in front of the English army. Seeing themselves abandoned, they began to edge back down the hill in an attempt to disengage. But the retreat soon became a rout with men throwing away their weapons and equipment to be able to run quicker. The English followed with bloodthirsty vigour, cutting down any Scot they could reach.

Seeing his army disintegrate, King David realized his small reserve would be ineffective in attack. Instead he ordered the men to form a rear guard on which stragglers could rally and to march back to Carlisle. King David did not stop to help, but rode off at top speed. The day was still young, it was not yet 9 a.m.

It is generally accepted that 10,000 men were killed at the Battle of The Standard, most of them Scots. In fact the Chroniclers record only one English knight as being killed though several Scots knights were killed or captured.

Aftermath

As King David rode north, he sent out messengers to gather scattered units from their looting and from the garrisoning of castles that it would no longer be feasible to hold. He also sent Prince Henry to command the retreating main force as it straggled back from the battlefield. Within two weeks the Scots had an

The English hill seen from the area from which the Scottish knights, led by Prince Henry, began their charge.

army of 14,000 men concentrated around Carlisle. Morale was at rock bottom following the defeat and swift retreat, but David did have a united army to face any English counter-attack.

That counter-attack never came. The militia recruited by Archbishop Thurstan disbanded immediately after the battle and went back to their farms. The nobles, much though many wanted to launch a punitive raid into Scotland, were distracted by the troubles to the south. King Stephen had captured rebellious Shrewsbury, but new outbreaks of violence from the supporters of the dethroned Matilda were taking place. Fearing that full scale civil war might be imminent, the barons preferred to keep their private armies intact to protect their own lands.

Then, on 26 September the papal legate, Bishop Alberic of Ostia, arrived at Carlisle direct from Rome. He had come to summon the various British bishops to a General Council in Rome, but finding a war in progress saw it as his Christian duty to broker a peace. He began by asking the Scots to free all the peasants they had captured and were intending to keep as slaves. The Scots refused indignantly, but Alberic eventually persuaded them to release the women and children as a sign of goodwill.

Bishop Alberic then set off south to return the captives to their homes and to speak to the English. He found King Stephen eager to make peace before Matilda arrived with the army of mercenaries and adventurers she was recruiting in Europe. He therefore repeated his offer made to David before the battle. The young Prince Henry would be created Earl of Northumbria and Earl of Huntingdon and given the rich lands and revenues that went with the titles. Stephen, however, added some conditions. The mighty fortresses of Bamburgh and Newcastle upon Tyne would be garrisoned by royal troops and held by governors appointed by Stephen. And Prince Henry had to come to England – ostensibly to rule his new lands, but in reality as a hostage for his father's good behaviour.

David agreed readily and in April 1139 Prince Henry rode south over the border, but this time in peace. When visiting King Stephen at Nottingham Prince Henry met and fell hopelessly in love with Adeline, daughter of the Earl of Surrey. Love matches were not usual among royalty or nobility at this time, but King David allowed the marriage to go ahead. The mingling of English blood with the Scots royal family was to have profound dynastic consequences in future generations and was an unforeseen result of the Battle of the Standard.

Visiting the Battlefield Today

Not much has changed at the battlefield of the Standard in the nine centuries since the battle was fought. The main road, now the A167, follows much the same route it did in 1138 and the land remains largely undeveloped. Most of the battlefield is private farmland under crops, but good views of the scene of action can be had from the public roads.

Driving north from Northallerton on the A167, a fine monument is located on the right side of the road about a mile and a half beyond the outskirts of the town. There is a lay-by with parking for three cars beside the monument. From the monument you get a good view east, up the slight hill to the centre of the English position. The Standard itself stood more or less on the crest of the hill where a hedge from the north meets one running east to west.

If you walk 500 yards south along the main road you come to the overgrown entrance to Scotspit Lane. The lane is now fenced off, but a gate gives good views across the field to where the English baggage was located and where Prince Henry's knights came to grief. Returning to the monument, and walking 400 yards north you reach the crest of a low hill where Prince Henry was located when he began his charge. About 200 yards further on, just before the junction with Brompton Lane, is where King David took his stand. Looking back south you will notice that the crest of the English hill is out of sight, so David would have been unable to see what was going on. Brompton Lane offers views across the fields where the Galwegians charged and from which they retreated in disorder.

Chapter Five

STIRLING BRIDGE 1297

Introduction

The Battle of Stirling Bridge has a place in Scottish folklore. After years of growing English influence and interference in the affairs of Scotland, the ordinary people rose against the outsiders. At Stirling Bridge the men of Scotland proved they could defeat the English.

After the Battle of The Standard, Scotland underwent dramatic changes. The Western Isles were won back from the independent power of the Viking Lord of the Isles and the outer islands taken

The position of the armies in the opening phase of the battle when Sir Marmaduke Twenge led the English knights in a charge against the advancing Scots.

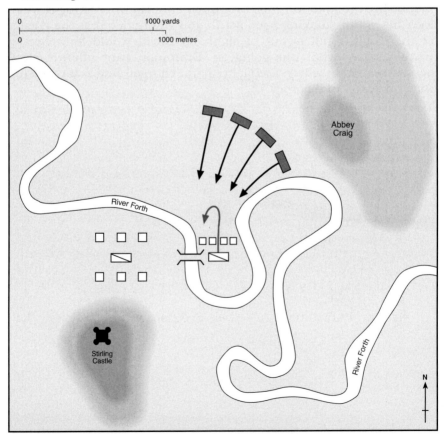

from the Norwegian kings. Loyalty to the Scottish king was enforced throughout the Highlands, though the semi-independent chieftains continued to make their own laws and to fight their own private wars.

Successive kings gave a number of Anglo-Norman knights lands in Scotland and made them powerful nobles. In return, the nobles taught the Lowland Scots the new tactics of mounted warfare from Europe. Among the most powerful of this new barony were the Bruce and Balliol families, both originally from Normandy but now based largely in England. These families held lands in both England and Scotland, which fact did not matter much while the two kingdoms were at peace with each other, but was to prove a cause of some trouble in the future. Opposed to what was seen as inroads of English culture and sympathy which these men represented, were the old nobility of the Picts, Scots and Britons led by the Comyn family.

In 1286 disaster struck Scotland. King Alexander III died when his horse stumbled over a cliff. The only legitimate heir was his infant granddaughter, Margaret, who was in Norway. A Regency Council was established to rule the kingdom until 'The Maid of Norway', as she was known, was adult.

It was at this point that King Edward I of England took a hand. The Kings of England were now far more powerful than they had been previously. They had inherited vast lands in France and had almost entirely subdued the Welsh. The English economy was booming and the population was increasing rapidly. Filled with self-confidence and a belief in the power of England, King Edward saw the Scots' misfortune as an opportunity. He suggested that his son, the future Edward II, should marry young Queen Margaret. The Scots nobles extracted a promise that Scots laws and customs would be respected, and then agreed.

But in 1290 the Maid of Norway died. There was no direct heir and no fewer than twelve Scottish nobles announced that they had a claim to the throne. Unable to resolve the conflicting claims by themselves, the Scots asked King Edward to choose the rightful king. In November, at Berwick Castle, Edward rejected the claims of all except John Balliol and Robert Bruce, both of them from the new Anglo-Norman nobility. Edward finally chose Balliol as the King of Scotland, having first extracted a promise from Balliol that he would recognize Edward as his overlord.

Neither Balliol nor the other Scottish nobles thought the

The narrow, deep valley of the Spott Burn near Dunbar. The English army forced their way across this barrier with ease in the face of a large Scottish army during their march north. It was this which gave the Earl of Surrey the confidence to try the same feat again at Stirling Bridge – but this time with fatal results.

promise anything more than a vague undertaking not to attack England. But Edward was taking it seriously and began issuing orders to Balliol. In 1296 the Scots repudiated the agreement, signed an alliance with France and began preparing for war. Edward, however, moved first. He captured and destroyed Berwick then led his army into Scotland before his enemies could gather enough men to face him. The few Scots who had mustered to defend Edinburgh were brushed aside in a fight on the banks of the Spotts Burn near Dunbar. Balliol was captured and sent to the Tower of London. To show his determination that Scottish independence was over, Edward removed from Scone Abbey the sacred stone on which all Kings of Scots had been crowned. He sent it to Westminster Abbey to be placed beneath his own throne.

In the autumn of 1296 Edward returned to England. He left behind John de Warenne, Earl of Surrey, who had won the fight at Dunbar, together with a tax official named Cressingham and a lawyer Ormsby. Unfortunately for all concerned, Surrey promptly fell ill and for months was unable to leave his room. This left Scotland in the hands of Cressingham whose greed for other people's money was legendary, and Ormsby who knew little about Scots law and cared less. By the time Surrey had recovered to realize how his subordinates were behaving, it was too late. Scotland was in revolt.

Most of the Anglo-Norman nobility of the Lowlands remained quiet, worried about their lucrative estates, but the Douglas and Stewart families expelled English garrisons from their lands and Robert Bruce, son of the Bruce who had lost the throne to Balliol, soon joined them. The heart of the rebellion, however, was in the wilder hill country around Selkirk and Moray. The rising in Moray was led by a knight named Sir William Murray and that around Selkirk by another member of the minor gentry – Sir William Wallace.

Wallace's background is rather obscure. He had received an education typical of the less wealthy knights of the time and had certainly travelled beyond his own country. His surname marks him out as a member of an old Strathclyde family which could trace its ancestry back to the days before Strathclyde was ruled by the King of Scots. He is said to have held lands in Renfrewshire, but is also linked to lands around Stirling.

Wherever he came from, Wallace got involved in a fight with some English soldiers near Dundee. It is said one of them insulted or struck Wallace's wife, for which the Scotsman killed him. Instantly outlawed, Wallace took to the hills and gathered a band of other Scots who had suffered at the hands of the English. He led a successful raid on English barracks at Ayr, then captured and burnt Lanark where he executed the English sheriff Hazelrigg. By August 1297 Wallace had joined forces with Murray and had captured or expelled all the English north of the Forth except those at Dundee, which he had under siege.

Faced by a popular revolt, Surrey gathered the English soldiers in Scotland together and marched to Irvine, where he forced the submission of most Scottish nobles, before moving on to relieve Dundee. At Stirling, Surrey found his path blocked by the army of Wallace.

The Opposing Armies

The size of the English army at Stirling Bridge has been the subject of much speculation. Estimates have ranged as high a 40,000 men, though on the most slender of evidence. Official correspondence from the tax collector, Cressingham, shows that he was willing to pay for supplies for 300 mounted knights and 10,000 infantry. Even allowing for squires, serjeants and various other support soldiers, it is unlikely that the English army numbered more than 15,000 men.

By this time the English were moving away from a purely feudal military structure. Although most of the men in any English army were raised on the basis of a feudal levy, they would serve much longer than the standard forty days in return for cash payments. There was also a growing tendency to hire mercenaries, usually specialists such as archers or siege engineers.

The army which marched to Stirling Bridge was spearheaded by about 300 mounted knights. These men were the social and military elite of England. They held extensive estates from the king or from the great nobles and in return promised to serve as mounted knights in time of war. There were about 7,000 such men in England and many served as government officials or royal servants as well as under arms.

In battle, the armoured knights were formidable. They were trained from childhood to fight from horseback, charging with the lance or fighting hand to hand with sword, axe or mace. By this date, a knight would have worn trousers

This English knight is equipped in top quality armour of the period. By this date a rich knight would have worn an all enveloping suit of mail armour. The body was covered by a tunic of mail which reached to the wrists and down to the knees. The hands were protected by mail mittens. The legs had mail leggings, rather similar to modern stockings in shape, which were tied to a belt under the mail tunic. The head was covered first by a soft leather cap for comfort, then by a mail coif which looked rather like a modern balaclava helmet, though it reached down to the shoulders and chest. Over this was worn a helmet of solid steel, carefully shaped so that swords or lances would tend to glance off it. For weapons, this knight has a lance with which to skewer opponents when charging forwards and a sword for use at close quarters. As the armour became more effective, the shield grew less important and smaller. This knight carries his shield strapped to his upper arm. His identity is proclaimed by his coat of arms, repeated on his shield, the lance pennon, his linen surcoat and the linen coverings of his horse.

of mail, often overlain with plate armour on the foot and lower legs. The mail coat extended to the wrists and he wore mail gloves to protect the hands. The head was protected not only by a mail cap, but also by a helmet of solid steel plates which completely enclosed the head, except for narrow eyeslits and small breathing holes.

When they rode to war the knights would have been accompanied by two squires whose task was to look after the war horses and armour. When battle was joined, the squires were used either as fast-moving unarmoured cavalry or put to guard the baggage train.

Probably half the English infantry was made up of freemen serving for pay. The fortunate minority had mail coats reaching to the knees and elbows, but most wore suits of quilted cloth. This style of armour had been copied from the Saracens in the Crusades. It consisted of up to eighteen layers of linen or wool which were sewn together and then treated with a mixture of salt and wine. Although not as tough as mail, quilting could turn aside glancing sword blows and offered some protection from lances and arrows. Most men had a metal helmet.

These infantry were equipped with a triangular shaped shield, usually painted with the heraldic device of the knight they served or, if they were mercenaries, of the man paying their wages. The prime weapon of such men was a spear about eight feet long, though most would have had a sword or axe for close fighting.

The remainder of the infantry at Stirling Bridge were Welsh mercenaries, most of them archers. These men served unarmoured, except for a metal skull cap and wore the sort of woollen tunic common among farmers. The formidable longbow with which they were armed was typically over five feet long and enormously powerful. The arrows could puncture most types of armour, particularly at ranges under 100 yards. The trained archers could shoot three or four arrows a minute, each aimed at a target. They typically carried thirty-six arrows with them on campaign.

The Scottish army was very different from the largely professional English force. It was, for a start, considerably smaller, perhaps about 7,000 strong. The feudal levy which had been scattered at Dunbar and overawed at Irvine was similar to the English as regards equipment, but only a few hundred such men were at Stirling Bridge. The men who came to join Wallace were more typical of what was called the Common Army.

The Common Army was the Scots nation in arms, made up of

one man from every ploughteam, or carucate. Effectively this meant that each group of five or six families, which joined together to afford a plough and the oxen to pull it, was also expected to produce one man for the army. These men were armed with heavy thrusting spears about twelve feet long and small shields about eighteen inches in diameter. Most had metal helmets, but body armour was virtually unknown. The Common Army did not generally field trained archers, though some men would have brought along hunting bows. Wallace had only small numbers of cavalry, and no heavily armoured knights.

Tactics

The professional English army had, by this time, developed some fairly sophisticated tactics. To be successful these depended not only on the training of the men, but also on having a commander who knew his business and subordinate commanders willing to take orders.

English infantry was, in theory, organized in groups of 100 men led by an officer known as a constable. In practice most units had fewer men due to casualties and sickness, while a few units might have more where different constabularies, as they were known, were merged. Each constabulary would form up in a dense formation about five men deep and with interlocked shields facing the enemy. Unlike the earlier shieldwall from which this tactic evolved, the constabulary was mobile and flexible. Different constabularies could join together to form a solid wall of men, separate to allow cavalry to charge through, form into columns to give maximum impact in a charge or fall back alternately to provide cover to each other in retreat.

At this period, the archers were dispersed among the armoured infantry. The infantry would provide defence to the archers, who shot over their heads at the enemy as they advanced.

The key battle-winning tactic, however, remained the massive impact of the charging armoured knights. The crushing blow of big men on heavy horses advancing at the canter was usually decisive on the battlefield. An army struck by such a charge could be turned into a rabble in flight in seconds. But it took skill and timing by the army commander to make full use of this weapon. If the knights charged too soon, they might dissipate their strength on a well formed enemy. If they charged too late the enemy might already be withdrawing in good order. As a rule, the charge of the mounted knights could only be used once. Once launched forward, a body of knights would crush everything in its path, but generally the knights were unable to turn or regroup for another charge.

To face such a formidable army, Wallace had been teaching his men a new tactic. It became known as the shiltron, from the name of the small shields carried by the men. Drawing on the experience of the infantry militias of European cities, Wallace was seeking a way to defeat the charge of the knights, of which he had none himself. The shiltron consisted of several hundred, sometimes a thousand, men formed into a circle or oval. Each man in the front rank knelt down and placed the butt of his spear in the ground, point facing outward. This made an impenetrable line of spear points. Any horseman charging forward would be impaled on the spears. Meanwhile the rear ranks of the shiltron thrust forward with their spears, hoping to unseat any knight who tried to push between the spears of the front rank. The few archers Wallace had, stood in the centre of the shiltrons while the cavalry were close, and shot from outside when the knights fell back.

At Stirling Bridge, Wallace's shiltrons were put to the test for the first time.

The Battle

The key feature on the battlefield was the River Forth, which is deep and flows swiftly at this spot. There was only one bridge across the river at Stirling, a wooden structure about nine feet wide mounted on stone piers. The north side of the bridge gave on to a wide meadow in a bend of the river. Wallace drew his men up on a steep hillside about 1,000 yards north of the bridge.

From the English side of the river, the full strength and location of the Scots army could not be seen. The Earl of Surrey knew that Wallace and his men were there, but could see only a few scouts and isolated men. Surrey's only personal experience of fighting the Scots had been at Dunbar the previous year. On that occasion he had sent a small force over a river to secure the crossing, then marched across in force before mounting a charge. The Scots, outnumbered and demoralized, had fled. Surrey decided to try the same plan again.

About mid morning, Surrey sent forward a force of infantry to cross the bridge and hold the meadow beyond against an expected Scottish attack. This would give time for the main body of the English army to cross and form up for the advance.

At this point a Scottish knight serving in the English army, Sir

The battlefield seen from the ramparts of Stirling Castle. The English army gathered on fields in the foreground, now covered by housing. The bridge is in the bottom left of the picture. In the middle distance is more housing and some open fields, which is where the main action took place.

Richard Lunday, pushed past the men around Surrey and demanded to be heard. He told Surrey that there was a ford about two miles downstream where sixty men could cross at a time, whereas the bridge would take only two men abreast. The English army, said Lunday, should cross at the ford. But Cressingham objected that the march downstream would take too long. In any case the English commanders did not think the Scots would stand up to a charge any more than they had at Dunbar. Surrey gave the order to cross the bridge, sending Cressingham over to supervise the deployment on the far bank.

Wallace, from his hill, watched the English crossing. He planned to wait until enough of the English were across that their defeat would be a serious blow, but not until so many were across that they could beat the Scots. It would take careful timing.

At noon, Wallace gave the order to advance. The Scots formed up into their newly invented oval formations and marched forward. Seeing the Scots advance, Cressingham ordered the senior knight, Sir Marmaduke Twenge, to lead the hundred or so heavily mounted knights who had crossed the bridge in a charge to smash the Scots.

Twenge and his men surged forward, but the Scots did not flee. Instead the shiltrons came to a halt and bristled with spears. A few knights were killed as they charged home, others were speared by the rear ranks or shot down by the archers. The English knights milled around in confusion for they were unaccustomed to being held off, then trotted back towards the bridge.

The Scots came after the retreating knights and plunged into the English infantry. The fighting turned to hand to hand combat and the English, now outnumbered, were faring badly. Twenge did not have enough space to organize his knights for another charge.

Surrey, seeing the course the battle was taking, decided that the Scots could be beaten if a new charge of cavalry could be delivered. He did not believe Wallace would be able to reform the knight-proof shiltrons in time now that his men were engaged in an infantry battle. Surrey therefore ordered his infantry to fall back from the bridge and sent his remaining knights forward at the canter to cross the bridge and charge on without giving the Scots time to respond.

But as the heavily armoured men pounded across the bridge, there was a sudden groaning crash. The timbers, unused to such a thundering burden, gave way and collapsed. Those knights who had not already crossed, pulled their horses to a halt.

The English on the north bank, perhaps a third of the army, were now isolated and outnumbered. The Welsh archers turned and ran for the river. Unencumbered by armour most of them managed to swim across to safety. Marmaduke Twenge gathered his knights and launched a desperate charge. He and a few men managed to cut a path through the Scots, then spurred away to find another way across the river. But for the armoured English infantry there was to be no escape. Nor was there any mercy.

With so many of his men dead, and with Wallace's jubilant Scots surging across the ford which Lunday had pointed out, Surrey had no choice but to retreat. He headed first for Torwood, where he halted for stragglers to come in, then fell back again to Berwick. His army was harried the whole way, losing more men to ambush and raid. Among the dead Surrey left behind at Stirling was Cressingham. The Scots skinned the body and tanned the hide for use in souvenir purses and pouches.

Aftermath

When Surrey reached Berwick the only English soldiers left in Scotland were the garrisons of a few isolated castles and towns. Most surrendered as soon as they heard the news of Stirling Bridge. The Scottish nobles also reacted to the news of the battle. They declared their allegiance to 'the Community of the Kingdom of Scotland', by which was meant all the free men of the country.

The nobles were not sure what to do next. John Balliol was still alive, but imprisoned in England and had abdicated. The abdication, however, had been forced by the English at swordpoint and may not have been legal. As a temporary measure, Wallace was appointed as Protector of the Kingdom. All power passed into Wallace's hands while the nobility decided what form the new government should take.

England's King Edward, meanwhile, had been in France when he received the news of Stirling Bridge. He returned to England and promised bloody revenge on the Scots.

Visiting the Battlefield Today

The battlefield of Stirling Bridge lies, appropriately enough, where Stirling Bridge carries the A9 over the River Forth, just north of Stirling town centre. The A9 is now carried by a modern bridge, but the old medieval bridge, built to replace that destroyed in the battle, lies some fifty yards upstream. There is a convenient lay-by just south of the river beside a newsagents and cafe. It was in this area that the English army gathered

Stirling Bridge as it stands today. This all-stone bridge was built to replace the part-timber construction which was destroyed during the battle.

The commanding heights of Abbey Craig where Wallace stood on the morning of the battle to watch the English army take up its positions. The Gothic-style tower is the Wallace Monument, erected in the nineteenth century.

before crossing the bridge to the fatal field beyond.

On the far bank of the river the battlefield is divided between an area of modern housing and open fields which are under crops and not generally accessible. However, the Wallace Monument has been built on the crest of Abbey Craig, where Wallace stood on the morning of the battle before descending to lead his men into action. A car park serves the monument, from which panoramic views over the battlefield can be obtained and the course of the battle easily visualized.

If you feel in need of refreshment, the city of Stirling has plenty to offer, as well as numerous historic places to visit including, of course, the castle.

Chapter Six

FALKIRK 1298

Introduction

The battle fought at Falkirk in 1298 was not what it seemed to those who fought there. It appeared to be an overwhelming English victory, but in fact laid the seeds for eventual English defeat. At a tactical level, the battle appeared to confirm the superiority of the heavily armoured knight, but in fact heralded their demise as a major feature on the field of battle.

Such results were far away in the spring of 1298. The Scots victory at Stirling Bridge had driven the English from Scotland. Indeed, the Scottish leader Sir William Wallace had led an army into Northumberland to loot and pillage on a grand scale. However the Scots had not yet solved their underlying weakness:

The routes taken by the charging knights of Hereford and Beck against the Scots on the slopes leading up to Callendar Wood.

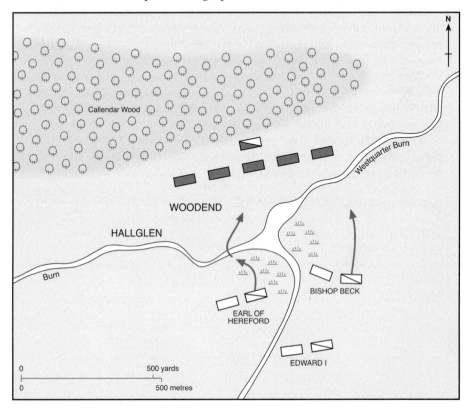

a lack of a clear heir to the throne recently left vacant.

Wallace had been appointed Guardian of Scotland with almost regal powers. His authority rested on his military success and this was not enough to ensure the cooperation of the proud noblemen who looked on him as a mere rustic upstart. Many of them thought that his invasion of Northumberland had been a dangerous provocation of the formidable King Edward I of England and that it would have been better to negotiate. Now it seemed they were being proved right for Edward was gathering a large army. Even worse, it was the rich lands of these same nobles which were the first to feel the vengeance of Edward.

Wallace, however, had been following a clear plan. Knowing he could not rely on the nobles, he preferred to put his trust in the ordinary commoners. They had won him his battle at Stirling Bridge the previous year and had followed him through the grim winter. Wallace calculated that loot and revenge were the best ways to keep the common folk of Scotland loyal, so he had given them both in large quantity during his raid south.

In June Wallace learned that Edward was in Yorkshire mustering a large army. Rather than face the English army as it crossed the border, Wallace decided to fall back. Northumberland had been pillaged so thoroughly that the English army would get few supplies there. Now Wallace stripped the lands between Berwick and the Forth of cattle, food and supplies. He hoped to starve the English into retreat. If that did not work, it would at least seriously weaken their army. Then Wallace would meet it somewhere in the Forth Valley with the full might of his supporters.

Like Wallace, Edward had some problems of loyalty with his own men. He was suffering financial difficulty and many of the lesser nobility were refusing to pay new taxes until Edward reformed the judiciary. Of more immediate concern was the fact that many of the northern nobles did not support an invasion of Scotland. They had suffered badly at Stirling Bridge and in Wallace's raid. They blamed Edward for having taken the main army off to France and left them to their fate. They preferred to negotiate peace with Wallace rather than risk having the King leave them with the job half done once again.

Edward solved both problems in the winter of 1297. First he issued a revised and updated version of Magna Carta, which took care of the problems of the lower nobility. Second he went on solemn pilgrimage to the shrine of St John in Beverley Minster in Yorkshire. This was one of the leading holy sites in

Beverley Minster, possibly the most beautiful early Gothic church in Britain. It was only after King Edward came to this church, then newly built, to take a vow on the sacred relics of St John of Beverley that the northern barons agreed to follow him on the invasion of Scotland.

northern England and the relics of seventh century St John were considered among the most sacred in Europe. Here King Edward took a solemn vow to protect his people against the Scots. It convinced the northerners. Edward could now plan his campaign.

Edward ordered his army to muster at Roxburgh. He knew that northern England would offer him little in the way of supplies, and guessed that Wallace would strip southern Scotland of food. Edward therefore ordered his fleet north. These ships had ferried his army to France the year before. Now he loaded the vessels with food, drink and military supplies and ordered them to sail slowly up the east coast, keeping in close contact with the army. When he needed supplies, Edward only had to call his ships into shore. There was little danger that they would be attacked, for the Scots had no navy.

In mid June Edward crossed the border and marched his army north. By mid July Edward and his men were in Edinburgh, but he had found no sign at all of the Scots army. The situation got suddenly worse when a storm scattered the supply fleet. Only one ship got safely into harbour at Leith and that was loaded not with food, but with wine. The men got hold of the wine and before long a violent drunken brawl had broken out between the English infantry and the Welsh archers. Only a fit of towering rage and promises of vicious punishments from the King himself restored order.

Disgusted, Edward moved his army a few miles west to Kirkliston to get them away from any other ships that came to harbour. Unknown to Edward, Wallace and his entire army were just five hours march away at Falkirk. Wallace decided to lead his men on a daring night march and assault the English camp at dawn.

That evening, 10 July, Wallace realized that two of the most powerful Scottish nobles had left the army, taking their men with them. The Earl of Angus and the Earl of Dunbar had, in fact, gone to join King Edward. Not only did these noblemen dislike Wallace, but they feared for their lands and wealth which were both being destroyed in the fighting. They betrayed both Wallace's position and his plans to the English.

Edward promptly gathered his army and left camp, marching west towards Falkirk. Next day, the English advanced again and came across the Scots army drawn up on a hill in front of Callendar Wood.

The Opposing Armies

As usual in this period, precise numbers are not available for the armies which fought at Falkirk. It is thought that Edward had about 25,000 men with him when he left Roxburgh in June. Some of these men would have been left to guard river crossings and captured castles, and some would have fallen sick. It is likely that Edward had about 18,000 men with him as he approached Falkirk. All contemporary chroniclers agree that the Scots army was rather smaller than the English, perhaps about 14,000 strong.

The two armies were very different in the types of troops they fielded and the tactics they intended to use. The Scots army was, in general, not very different from that which had fought at Stirling Bridge. Wallace made an attempt to introduce a mass call up of all able-bodied men, but with little success. The vast majority of his troops were derived from the Common Army, a militia recruited from the farming families of southern Scotland. These men were armed with a small shield and a twelve-feet spear and many had a helmet, but they were otherwise unarmoured.

Wallace also had some archers with him at Falkirk. These men came from the area of Selkirk Forest. They were unarmoured and came equipped with short hunting bows which had an effective range of about fifty yards. It is thought that about a 1,000 archers were present under Sir John Stewart.

At Falkirk, Wallace had small numbers of cavalry provided by the nobles and under the command of John Comyn. This nobleman was a possible heir to the throne and was known as the Red Comyn because of his vivid hair colour – his father was for similar reasons known as the Black Comyn.

Most of the Red Comyn's men were armoured knights. These were big men on big horses. The men were armoured from head to toe in chain mail and wore large helmets which totally enclosed the head in sheet steel. The main weapon of these knights was the lance, used to devastating effect in the mounted charge. Once hand to hand combat was joined, they would use swords, axes or maces as each preferred. There were about 180 such armoured knights with Wallace. The remaining forty or so cavalry were unarmoured and rode bareback. They would have been little use except for skirmishing or scouting.

Most of these men came from the Lowlands where they held estates of land in return for equipping and supplying themselves in time of war. Crucially, they owed loyalty to their feudal lord from whom they held their lands. Their loyalty to the king was always tenuous and in 1298 Scotland was without a king.

The English army was more professional and more mixed than that of the Scots. Many of the men were mercenaries or, at least, part-time soldiers who were paid a wage when on campaign. In theory the King of England could call on able-bodied men to form a national army, like the Common Army of the Scots. In practice most English farmers preferred to pay a tax called scutage, or shield-money, instead. Those young men who did go to war could therefore be assured of good wages and would campaign for much longer than the forty days expected of the militia.

It was these part-time semi-professional infantry who had formed the bulk of previous English armies. They were equipped with varying degrees of armour, a large triangular shield and an eight-feet spear as well as sword or dagger. As they spent many weeks together, these men could usually be relied upon to know basic formations and drills and to carry them out even in the heat of battle. In 1298, however, this armoured infantry was very much in a minority in Edward's army. It is thought there were only about 3,000 of them.

Far more numerous were the Welsh and Irish mercenaries whom Edward had hired for the summer. These men had fought well for several seasons in France and served for hard cash only.

The Welsh were hired for their skills in archery. They came to battle effectively unarmoured, though most had helmets and many had light armour of various kinds. They were equipped with the longbow. This formidable weapon was up to six feet long and made of yew. It could shoot an arrow with startling accuracy and enormous power. A man needed years to learn to use a long bow effectively, but its arrows could pierce armour at ranges up to 100 yards and the aim was extremely accurate at such distances. Edward had about 8,000 Welsh archers with him at Falkirk.

The Irish lacked any such speciality. They fought unarmoured and were equipped with spear and knife. Their key weapon was the double-handed axe which they had borrowed from the Vikings. This formidable weapon could slice a man in half and bludgeon its way through any sort of armour, but it took great skill and long hours of practice to wield it effectively. The main use of these men on campaign was to guard camps and to raid the countryside through which the army passed, but they could be handy in a defensive battle. The numbers of Irish in Edward's army is unknown.

Edward also had a large force of knights, perhaps as many as 2,000. Again these were, in theory, raised on the basis of a feudal levy but in practice many who held lands paid scutage instead. Most knights with Edward were paid fighters, but they were distinctly less professional than the infantry. Knights were more inclined to ignore orders and to make their own minds up about what needed doing. As proud aristocrats in a military society they were keen to win glory and honour in battle – especially younger sons who had little hope of inheriting family wealth.

Tactics

At Falkirk, Wallace again deployed his main body in shiltrons, formed up on the slopes in front of Callendar Wood. The few cavalry he had were placed behind the shiltrons and the archers interspersed in pockets among and between the shiltrons. His plan was to lure the English cavalry into charging against the shiltrons where they would be halted by the spears, shot down by the archers and then tumbled into defeat by a counter charge from his own knights. With the English knights defeated, Wallace hoped, the rest of the English would retreat as they had done at Stirling Bridge. To further ensure the charge of the English knights was disrupted, Wallace placed his men behind a small burn which had marshy banks.

The tactics of the various elements of the English army would be much the same at Falkirk as at Stirling Bridge, but with one crucial difference. Up until this time it was usual to spread the archers evenly through the army and rely on their skill at aiming to shoot down enemy troops. But Edward had been listening to his commanders who had been defeated at Stirling Bridge and he knew the key to victory was to defeat the apparently impervious shiltrons.

Edward reasoned that the shiltrons were invulnerable to a traditional charge of armoured knights, but only so long as the infantry formation held firm. Once the formation was disrupted, a cavalry charge would succeed. He knew that the archers at Stirling Bridge had tried to pick holes in the Scots ranks, but had failed. Edward decided to try a new archery tactic.

He ordered his Welsh archers not to bother aiming at individual enemy soldiers at all. He reasoned the shiltrons were so closely packed with men that an arrow hitting roughly the right area was bound to find a target. Edward told his men to concentrate on the speed with which they could shoot, not on accuracy. Then he bunched his archers into large formations of over 2,000 men each. So many men shooting rapidly in the same direction would create an 'arrow storm' which would lash an area of ground like a sudden storm of rain.

The Battle

At dawn the English broke camp and marched towards Falkirk, coming within sight of the Scots about mid-morning. As the English army came into view, Wallace stood in front of his army and gestured defiantly at the advancing enemy. 'I have brought you to the ring', he shouted at the Scottish army. 'Now dance if you can.'

Edward had given orders that the army was to draw up in its proper formations before attacking. But the Earl of Hereford, who commanded the vanguard, had other ideas. Sending the Welsh archers under his command to one side, Hereford led his armoured knights forward. He intended to launch a devastating charge against the Scots centre, smash a hole in their formation and scatter them in the traditionally approved fashion.

Unfortunately for Hereford, his heavy knights quickly got bogged down on the marshy banks of the Westquarter Burn. As his men tried to extricate themselves and move to firmer ground to their left, they were peppered with Scots arrows. The light hunting bows were unable to penetrate the knights' armour, but

The view Wallace and his men had across the valley towards the line of hills over which the English army appeared in mid-morning.

injured many of the horses.

Meanwhile, the English centre had arrived. Commanded by Bishop Beck of Durham it was composed largely of the northern English knights and infantry. Bishop Beck ordered his men to deploy as ordered by the King, but his second in command, Lord Basset of Drayton, disagreed. Seeing the vanguard bogged down, Basset decided to lead the knights of the centre in a charge to the right of the boggy ground and, he hoped, gain the glory for himself. He contemptuously pushed Beck aside saying loud enough for all to hear 'Go to your Mass, Bishop. Leave us men to fight.'

As Basset led his knights around to the right, Hereford got his

The view from the Westquarter Burn up the hill to the crest where Wallace drew up his shiltrons at the start of the battle.

men formed up again and launched a charge on the left. The Scots army were struck simultaneously by two massed columns of charging heavy knights. The shiltrons held steady in the face of this assault, and the knights were left to mill helplessly around the formations of infantry. Scottish archers managed to bring down a few knights by killing the horses, and the men were speared by the infantry as they tumbled to the ground. Those English who attempted to charge home were killed by the spears. Within a quarter of an hour the pride of English chivalry was reduced to an aimless mob.

This was the moment for the Scots cavalry to charge. Although few in numbers, they were in tight formation and could have driven the disorganized enemy back to the burn. But when Wallace turned to them, his cavalry were gone. It is usual to blame this on a deliberate act of treachery by the Red Comyn, as was so graphically illustrated in Mel Gibson's movie *Braveheart*. It is alleged that the Red Comyn left the upstart Wallace to his fate so that the nobles could reassert their rule over Scotland. This may have been the case, but it is also possible that Comyn thought the battle lost when he saw the thousands of English knights charge and that he preferred to keep his own forces intact to fight another day.

Whatever the reason for Comyn's disappearance, it was fatal to the Scottish army. Realizing they were getting nowhere, Basset and Hereford led their cavalry back down the slope to the valley of the Westquarterburn. By this time, King Edward had arrived on the field and, after raging at the stupidity of his knights for disobeying orders, drew his thousands of archers up into massed formations. As soon as the knights were clear of the shiltrons, Edward gave the order to start shooting.

Following orders to ignore individual targets, but to concentrate on letting fly as many arrows as quickly as possible, the Welsh went to work. About 30,000 arrows a minute rained down on the closely packed and unarmoured men in the shiltrons. The powerful longbow arrows tore through flesh and bone, even cutting through the small shields of the Scots to transfix arms and bodies. To the watching English knights, the shiltrons seemed to shiver as the merciless arrows injured and killed the Scots.

First one, then another shiltron lost its formation under the deadly hail. And then the English knights charged again. This time the Scots formations were badly disrupted and collapsed almost at once. The knights pounded into the Scots infantry, lancing and slicing with their swords almost at will. Wallace and the Earl of Fife tried to rally their army on the steep slopes of Callendar Wood, but Fife was cut down and Wallace was pushed on to a horse by his men.

The pursuit went on for miles as the English knights, followed by lighter cavalry and infantry, chased after their fleeing enemies. About a third of the Scots army was killed by nightfall. The English had lost about 200 knights in the initial attack, but few other men were killed.

Aftermath

The Scottish army effectively ceased to exist as a single unified command after Falkirk. More seriously for the Scots was the fact that Wallace had lost his reputation for never having lost a fight. Those nobles and knights who had remained loyal to him now deserted his leadership. Some paid homage to Edward, others continued to resist the English. Some families made sure that they had members on both sides so that, whoever won, the family would keep its estates. Wallace himself fled back to the hills where he had begun his rising. He raised a new force of guerrilla fighters and began all over again.

The English army, meanwhile, was desperately short of supplies. Leaving a few garrisons at strategic strongholds, Edward marched back to England. He returned in 1300, but again a lack of supplies prevented him from keeping a large army in the field for more than a few weeks. The war became a long succession of raids, ambushes, sieges and counter-attacks which looked set to drag on indefinitely.

In 1305 Wallace was betrayed and captured by Edward. Taken to London, Wallace was sent to the hideous fate of being hung, drawn and quartered as a traitor. He was no traitor, for he had never sworn allegiance to Edward, but the English King was not prepared to accept what he saw as a legal quibble.

Wallace was dead and, it seemed, Scotland was set to become a mere province in the realms of Edward I.

Visiting the Battlefield Today

The field where Wallace was defeated is difficult to find. It has no monument, is not signposted and there is nowhere to park your car when you get there. This is a shame as the battle saw brave feats on both sides and, once you get there, the site is such that you can trace events fairly clearly. But Falkirk does not appear to encourage visitors to its battlefields, for the site of the 1745 conflict is equally as difficult to access.

To find the battlefield, it would be best to have a streetmap of Falkirk. Find the modern housing estates of Hallglen and the modern road that runs from them to the older suburb of Westquarter. The battlefield lies along this road where a footpath signposted to Shieldhill turns off it to the south. This footpath is the old medieval road along which King Edward was advancing on Falkirk and it remained a cobbled road up until the nineteenth century. Further to the east an unmade road turns off north towards Woodend Farm and Callendar Park. This is the area you need to explore on foot, the residential roads of Hallglen being the nearest place to leave your car.

Begin at the lane to Woodend Farm which takes you up the hill to the position taken by the left wing of Wallace's army. Where the lane divides into the bridlepath to Callendar Park and the farmyard you can look south across the valley to the ridge over which the English army appeared. Return to the main road and walk west to the start of the footpath. Walk down the footpath to the valley floor. The meadows on either side are where the English knights became bogged down in the mud during their initial charge – and the ground is still muddy after rain. Further on the path crosses the two streams which flow down this valley, then climbs the hill beyond. About fifty yards beyond the streams is an open field on the right which is approximately where Edward massed his archers to open the second English attack.

A nineteenth century statue of William Wallace in Stirling which presents a romanticized image of the Scottish hero.

Chapter Seven

BANNOCKBURN 1314

Introduction

Bannockburn established Scotland as a free, independent and united kingdom after decades of English occupation and civil strife. Though English armies were to invade Scotland in the future, it was never with any real chance of annexing the kingdom and ending the independence won at Bannockburn.

The road to Bannockburn began after the capture and execution of William Wallace by the English in 1305. This left the leadership of the resistance against the occupying English in the hands of two great noblemen, Robert Bruce, Earl of Carrick, and John Comyn, Earl of Buchan. Both men had a claim to the throne and both were experienced military commanders. It was

The dawn attack of the Scottish army on the second day of the battle, which led to the utter defeat of the English.

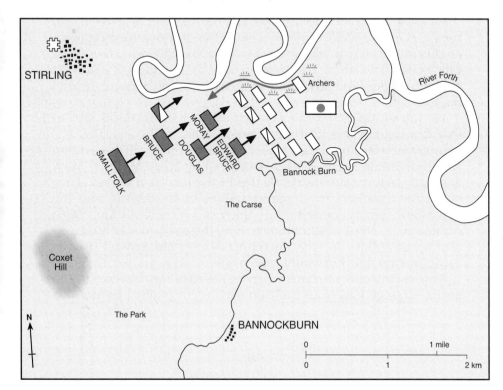

clear that the resistance to the English needed a unified command if it were to succeed, so the two factions agreed to meet to discuss a way forward.

Because of mutual distrust, the two noblemen arranged to meet alone and unarmed in the sacred church of the Greyfriars at Dumfries. It is unclear what happened in the church, but there was a fight in which Comyn was killed. Robert Bruce claimed he had been attacked and acted in self defence. Others thought he had deliberately murdered Comyn.

Whatever the truth of the events at Dumfries, Robert Bruce was left as the undisputed leader of the Scots in their war against the English. In March 1306 Robert Bruce was crowned King of Scotland in Scone Abbey. The ceremony lacked the traditional coronation stone of the Scots as King Edward I of England had taken it south to Westminster. However, the traditional circlet of gold was used and the ceremony was regarded as valid by those Scots nobles and churchmen who attended.

The English, of course, did not regard it as a valid coronation and the war went on. At first Bruce came off worst and in June 1306 his army was scattered by the English at Perth. It was in the following months, when Bruce lived as a fugitive in the mountains, that the famous story of the spider belongs. Bruce was said to have watched a spider trying repeatedly to complete a web across a great gap in a cave and was inspired to try one more time to drive the English out of Scotland.

In 1308 Bruce took to the field again with a small army of 700 men and at Old Meldrum won a skirmish. It was a turning point as this minor victory was enough to lend his leadership credence. The Scots flocked to his banner and by a series of guerrilla actions, sieges and lightning strikes the English were beaten back.

By Christmas 1313 the only stronghold in Scotland still in English hands was Stirling Castle. Edward Bruce, Robert's younger brother, made an agreement with the English garrison that they would surrender if not relieved by 25 June 1314. Such agreements were standard practice in the medieval period. They saved the attackers the huge casualties of an assault, and the defenders were spared the horrors of starvation. Both commanders would estimate how long the castle could hold out, and agree a date for the surrender if no help arrived. In the meantime no fighting would take place.

Robert Bruce was furious when he heard of the agreement. His entire strategy had been built on avoiding a pitched battle with the English, but instead relying on the raiding tactics at which the Scots excelled. He now feared that the English would march north in large numbers and, if he were to save face, he would have to fight a battle to stop them reaching Stirling.

The English King was also angered by the agreement. Edward I had died in 1307, leaving the crown to his impulsive, but weak-willed son Edward II. The new King had promptly alienated the leading nobles by heaping honours and wealth on his homosexual lover, Piers Gaveston. In 1312 Gaveston was murdered by the Earl of Warwick and civil war was averted only by the fact that neither Edward nor the nobles were certain of victory.

When news of the Stirling agreement reached Edward, he was still planning revenge on Warwick. However, he knew he had to try to relieve Stirling to save his honour as a King and prepared to march north. He ordered the royal army to muster at Wark in the first week of June and sent messages to all the leading nobles to bring their armies to the muster. Warwick and his closest allies stayed away, and Edward knew he could not trust all those nobles who did arrive. More promisingly, two great soldiers – the Earl of Hereford and the Earl of Gloucester – had answered the summons. This was the same Earl of Hereford who had disobeyed orders at the Battle of Falkirk, but he had learnt his lesson over the intervening sixteen years and was now a wiser and more experienced man. Edward knew the advice of these men would make up for his own inexperience in warfare.

Edward also had the services of some 2,000 Scotsmen loyal to the memory of Sir John Comyn who were eager to avenge his murder. They knew the territory well and were to prove invaluable with their advice and local contacts.

The Opposing Armies

The army which Edward II led north from Wark on 17 June 1314 was outwardly formidable. It was certainly one of the largest English armies to cross the Scottish border in the medieval period and had a high proportion of knights and nobles, perhaps because Edward was reluctant to leave these men behind him in England.

The size of the English army which left Wark was about 25,000 men, of whom some 5,000 men were mounted. Not all of these men would have been knights as they would also have included lightly armoured troops used for scouting and raiding. There may have been some 2,000 armoured knights, plus about another 1,500 armoured horsemen who were squires or hired assistants to the knights. All these men would have worn armour and equipment broadly similar to that of the knights who fought at Stirling Bridge and Falkirk.

In order to understand the actions of the English knights at Bannockburn, it is important to understand that by this time few of them were raised by feudal levy. In theory the King could call on about 7,000 knights to serve him for forty days free of charge and thereafter for pay. The men were granted lands in return for their service and had to pay for their own equipment. In fact relatively few of these tenants actually served as knights by this period. Instead they either paid a cash sum, known as scutage, to hire a mercenary or they sent a younger brother or son instead. These younger sons would not inherit the family lands and their only chance of earning a fortune was to catch the eye of the King or a leading nobleman by their bravery and skills in combat. They were, therefore, prone to be brave and daring even when the situation demanded caution and care.

The 8,000 archers in the English army were largely Welsh and would have been equipped and organized as those who fought at Falkirk. They all had the deadly longbow and were well trained in its use. Some Englishmen, particularly from Cheshire and the North, were beginning to train with this weapon and joined Edward's army.

The 12,000 infantry, as at Falkirk, were a mixed force. About 8,000 of the Englishmen in the ranks were equipped with helmet, shield and spear, while some had mail shirts and swords as well. There was an increasing tendency for the knightly commanders of infantry units to fight on foot alongside their men, rather than on horseback with the other knights. Such men would have been fully armoured and were supported by equally well-equipped squires, companions and a standard bearer.

The remaining 3,000 infantry were unarmoured men armed with a spear and long knife. Such men were of only limited use in a full-scale battle and instead were set to guard the baggage train, help with pitching camp and work in the trenches during sieges.

Robert Bruce had a far more rudimentary system for raising soldiers. He had no regular supply system and relied on his men bringing enough food with them from their home farms. It was largely for this reason that he had relied on a guerrilla war. He would call out the men of a local area for just long enough to capture a castle or ambush an English patrol, then send them

Throughout much of the Middle Ages, the bulk of the Scottish armies were composed of spearmen like this, recruited from the Lowlands. These men rode ponies or cheap horses on campaign, but dismounted to fight. Like most of his fellow fighting men, this warrior has brought the minimum equipment laid down by the government. He has a conical helmet of metal and a small shield of wood, covered with leather and featuring a metal boss. His main weapon is the spear, the great length of which was commented on by many of the Englishmen who faced the Scots in battle. The spear ends in a simple metal point. Many men would have carried a long hunting knife or a small axe as well, but this was down to personal taste. Otherwise he is dressed as he would have been on his home farm. The short tunic is of wool, but most warmth would have been provided by the very heavy cloak he wears over his shoulders. Many Lowland Scots at this period went bare-legged and often barefoot as well.

back to their farms. Faced with the need to muster a full army, Bruce gave orders that as many men as possible should gather south of Stirling by 20 June. Bruce calculated that the English would be forced to arrive before the 25th, and that his own men would have brought enough food to last them at least that long.

In the event about 10,000 men turned up to join Robert Bruce. Of these some 6,000 men were from the semi-feudal Common Army. They came equipped with twelve-feet spears, shields and helmets, as had their counterparts at Falkirk. Another 500 or so were archers equipped with small hunting bows. Bruce had some 600 mounted men, of whom less than half were armoured knights. The remainder of the army was made up of lightly equipped Highlanders and Borderers. At the last moment some 3,000 town militia and almost unarmed farmers turned up, to be termed the 'Small Folk'.

Tactics

The armies converging in 1314 had similar equipment to those that had fought at Stirling Bridge and at Falkirk. Likewise, their commanders were expecting to use similar tactics.

The English were hoping to implement Edward I's original plan for Falkirk. They would begin by using the power of the longbowmen to unleash a storm of arrows on the Scottish army from a safe distance. Once the Scottish formation had been disrupted by casualties, the armoured cavalry would charge

The level ground of the Carse over which the English army marched to their campsite on the first day of the battle. The hill of Abbey Craig, where Wallace had defeated another English army seventeen years earlier looms ominously on the skyline.

forward to sweep all before them. The infantry would be used to protect the archers from any Scottish attack and to mop up any particularly stubborn pockets of resistance.

Robert Bruce was relying on the shiltron formation developed by William Wallace. This oval formation of infantry bristled with spears pointing outward and, if it held steady, was invulnerable to the charge of the armoured knights. Knowing that the shiltron was vulnerable to the arrow storm, Bruce planned either to goad the English into attacking too early or to surge forward and close with the enemy before the archers could inflict too much damage.

It was with this in mind that Bruce drew his army up across the road leading to Stirling Castle in an area known as the Park. This was a patch of raised land, covered with woods, in front of which flowed the Bannock Burn. To the left of Bruce's position the burn ran across a marshy plain called the Carse to join the River Forth. Bruce knew the Forth was impassable and believed the English knights were too heavy for the Carse. He therefore intended to use the trees of the Park as defence against the deadly arrow storm and to use the shiltrons in a defensive role to break up a charge of the knights before advancing to engage the infantry. To make doubly certain, Bruce dug a series of concealed pits in front of the trees, each one just large enough to trap and break a horse's leg. Bruce then prudently placed a single shiltron under the Earl of Moray in his rear in case any English troops crossed the Carse.

On 23 June the English army came in sight. They were marching straight up the road to Stirling towards the waiting Scots in the Park.

The Battle

As the English army advanced, King Edward took advice from Hereford and Gloucester. It was decided to advance on the Park with archers and the bulk of the armoured cavalry while the infantry were held back. Meanwhile, a force of 500 knights under Lord Clifford was sent to cross the Carse in an attempt to get behind the Scottish army.

The Bannock Burn, which lends its name to the battle. The stream with its marshy banks hemmed in the left flank of the English army and made it impossible for them to deploy properly to meet the Scottish attack.

It was while the English were deploying to advance that young Sir Henry de Bohun, nephew of the Earl of Hereford, saw his chance to win great glory for himself. He spotted Robert Bruce mounted on a small pony and without full armour a short distance in front of the main Scottish army. Bohun spurred forwards with lance couched to ride down the enemy King and win the battle with a single blow.

Bruce watched the fully armoured knight approaching. The moment before Bohun reached him, Bruce turned his pony nimbly aside and stood in his stirrups to swing his battleaxe. Bruce's aim was true and the axe smashed through Bohun's helmet and sliced his skull in half. Bohun's horse continued on at full speed and the axe was so firmly lodged in the dead man's skull that Bruce was jerked off his horse. He

85

The view from the English camp towards the Park. It was across this field that the Scots advanced as dawn broke on 24 June.

hurriedly remounted, however, and rode back to his cheering men.

The main English force now came on. As Bruce had planned, the arrow storm was ineffective because of the trees and the Scots took few casualties. The advancing English horsemen soon found the pits made a fast charge impossible and held back. The desultory fighting continued, but the English were reluctant to attack an enemy still in perfect order, while the Scots did not wish to leave the protection of the trees. Trying to urge his men forward, Gloucester was thrown from his horse and had to walk back to get another under the jeering of the Scots.

Meanwhile, Lord Clifford's force had crossed the Carse and was swinging left to enter the Park a mile to the north, close to the Forth. As the knights rode up out of the marshy valley, they found their path blocked by Moray's shiltron. Eager for glory, the English charged, but without archers the horsemen could make no impression on the shiltron. The first clash was bloody, but indecisive. Soon the fighting was reduced to the English circling, looking for a weakness that was not there. Insults and battle chants were shouted, but not much bloodshed took place.

About 3 p.m., Edward again consulted Hereford and Gloucester. It was realized that the well defended direct approach was impossible to force. Instead, it was decided to launch a co-ordinated attack with archers, infantry and cavalry across the open ground where Lord Clifford had been halted by Moray. Getting the entire army and its baggage across the Carse would, however, take many hours. The attack was called off and arranged for the next morning.

Seeing the English pull back, Robert Bruce was satisfied. He had held the entire English army to a draw, which was the best he had hoped for. He intended now to disperse his army and return to his tried and tested guerrilla tactics confident that within a year or two he would have complete control of Scotland.

It was at this point that Sir Alexander Seton, one of Comyn's men, abandoned the English and rode over to join the Scots. He eagerly reported the tensions between Edward and his men and explained that morale was low after the failure to defeat the Scots at the first charge. At the urging of Moray and Sir John Douglas, Bruce now changed his mind and ordered an attack on the English camp the next morning.

'Now's the time,' Bruce declared.

Meanwhile, the Earl of Atholl was convinced Bruce was about to retreat. He took this opportunity to attack and plunder the Scottish baggage in the grounds of Cambuskenneth Abbey, north of the Forth.

Dawn came just after 3 a.m. As soon as it was half light the Scottish shiltrons marched down from the Park on to the marshy Carse. Bruce held back the lightly armoured Highlanders and Borderers, together with the Small Folk on the higher ground to act as a final reserve. His few horsemen kept close behind the advancing shiltrons to be on hand if needed for a sudden charge.

The English were taken by surprise. They had been intending to deploy on the Carse before advancing, but were now hemmed in between the Forth and the Bannock Burn. The knights were ready first and charged forward led by Gloucester. The charge was broken by the firm ranks of the shiltrons. Gloucester was unhorsed and killed while the rest of the mounted knights fell back.

Not waiting for the dreaded archers to come into action, the Scots surged on and soon were in hand to hand combat with the English infantry. Crammed between the river and the burn, the English could not deploy to make their numbers count. When one body of archers did get out on the right flank to open up on the Scots, they were swiftly ridden down by the Scottish cavalry. The battle was becoming a slogging match between the two masses of infantry, with the Scots pushing steadily forwards.

Then two things happened. First the Small Folk came surging down the hill to join their comrades. The English could not see these were unarmoured and undisciplined men but took them to be a fresh shiltron advancing. Almost at the same time, King Edward decided to flee the field and head for the safety of Stirling Castle.

Seeing the enemy strengthened and their own King fleeing, the English army began to break up. Before long the English had disintegrated as a fighting force. The more lightly equipped men managed to swim the Forth and most of the surviving cavalry galloped out of reach of the pursuing Scots. The armoured infantry, however, could neither swim nor run and were butchered. It was said that next day it was possible to cross the Bannock Burn dry shod by using the dead English as stepping stones. In all about a third of Edward's army was killed at Bannockburn. Scots losses barely numbered a thousand, probably much less.

As he rode towards Stirling, King Edward was protected by a small band of knights led by the Hospitallar, Giles d'Argentine. After winning through Scottish scouts, the King put his spurs to

The route taken by the fleeing English as their formations broke up in confusion. The invitingly open ground is misleading, for just 100 yards distant are the deep waters of the River Forth – a death trap for men weighed down by heavy armour.

his horse and galloped off. D'Argentine, however, shouted at the retreating King 'I am not accustomed to running away, nor shall I do it now'. He returned to the fight and was killed. At Stirling, Edward was told bluntly that the castle had not been relieved and would surrender as promised. He had to ride on to Linlithgow where he took ship for England.

Aftermath

Bannockburn won Scotland her independence and Bruce his crown, but it was not the end of the war. Raiding and skirmishing continued for some years. In 1322 Edward II led another army north and reached Edinburgh before lack of supplies forced him to retreat. But such forays were useless and merely took place to try to wipe out Edward's sense of shame for his defeat at Bannockburn. Edward never formally acknowledged Robert Bruce as King of Scotland.

Robert Bruce was rapidly reorganizing his kingdom. He swept away the old administration and power structures, which had in any case been largely destroyed by the English occupation, and instituted a thoroughly modern system of government.

A key step was the Declaration of Arbroath of 1320. This document retold the semi-mythical history of the Scots nation and its 113 Kings before stating 'so long as a hundred of us remain alive we will never be subject to the English'. The resounding rhetoric of the Declaration made it a key document in Scottish nationalism, but its constitutional impact was just as great. The Declaration speaks of the 'whole community of the realm' – there is no longer a division between Scots, Britons, English or Pict. More revolutionary still is the concept of the kingdom distinct from the King for the Declaration states that Bruce would be set aside if he capitulated to the English, effectively giving the citizens the power to choose their King.

Bruce also reorganized the armed forces of Scotland. In 1318 he issued his famous Statute of Arms which laid down exactly who was liable for military service and what they should bring with them in the way of equipment and supplies. The crucial feature turned out to be the stipulation that all men should present themselves for service mounted on horses, even if they fought on foot. This gave the Scottish army a degree of mobility unusual at the time.

Edward's reputation suffered dreadfully as a result of Bannockburn and for some months he was too ashamed to

A statue of Robert Bruce erected on the ramparts of Stirling Castle which gazes out over the site of his greatest victory.

appear in public. Hereford was so disgusted by his King's behaviour in fleeing the field that he went over to the side of the rebellious nobles. For years England was torn apart by feuding and quarrels between the King and the various factions of nobles. Finally, in 1327, Edward was murdered.

Visiting the Battlefield Today

As befits the crucible in which Scotland was born, the battlefield of Bannockburn is the centre of a sizeable tourist industry. The spot where Bruce raised his banner and mustered his army in the Park is now marked by a Heritage Centre which boasts a magnificent statue of the Bruce, a gift shop and a better than average cafe. Pretty well everything you could want to buy concerning the Battle or the Bruce is on offer here. It is, however, out of sight of the main scene of the fighting.

To find the main battlefield, turn right out of the Heritage Centre and then south along the A872. At the junction with the A91 turn left and drive north to the junction with the A905. You are now in the middle of the Carse, the marshy area which the English army crossed after it had been repulsed at the Park. At the next roundabout to the north a narrow lane signposted to Taylorton and Balfornough turns right. This lane twists and turns across the battlefield, making a sharp left hand bend at the approximate centre of the English line and then bending right to dip down behind the low ridge on which the archers tried to form up. The lane eventually peters out in the area across which the English army fled before being brought to a halt by the Burn and the Forth. The battlefield is now private farmland, so stick to the lane.

The ruins of Cumbeskenneth Abbey lie down a side road off the A907 and are signposted. They are open to the public free of charge.

Chapter Eight

HALIDON HILL 1333

Introduction

Few victories have been more overwhelming than that gained by England's King Edward III on the slopes of Halidon Hill in 1333, nor have many turned out to have had so little long term impact.

England's Edward II had been murdered in 1327 by a gang of nobles who were more interested in keeping power in England than in looking after England's interests abroad. They signed a treaty recognizing Scotland's full independence and acknowledging Robert Bruce as King Robert I of Scots. Soon

The intended Scottish attack plan was disrupted when the heavy cavalry became bogged down on marshy ground, forcing the infantry to veer to the left.

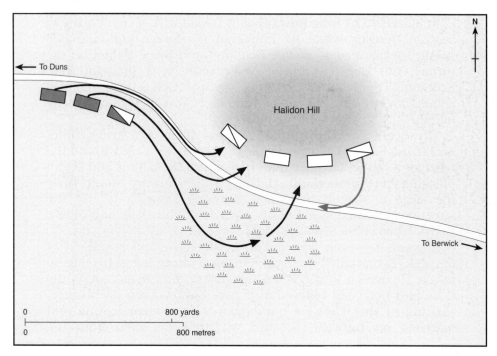

afterwards the barons were ousted in a palace coup by the youthful Edward III.

Meanwhile Scotland also lost its king when Robert Bruce died in 1329. He left a son, David, aged just five years old. Seeing a chance to grab the throne for himself, Edward Balliol declared that he was the rightful King. Edward Balliol was the son and heir of John Balliol who had ruled Scotland for a few years in the 1290s before being sent off to exile by England's Edward I. Balliol's claim to be the heir of the ancient royal house was as good as that of young David Bruce and he had the great advantage of being a grown man able to take up the reins of power in a troubled time.

After much discussion, and some bloodshed, the majority of Scottish nobles opted for young David Bruce with a council to advise him. Balliol was packed off to exile once again. Thus the boy David was crowned in 1331 at Scone and nobody could legally contest his right to be King of Scots.

But Edward Balliol was determined to try and asked England's Edward III for help. Edward was only too happy. Not only would civil war in Scotland make it unlikely that northern England would suffer raids, but he wanted to regain control of the Tweed Valley. Balliol agreed to hand over these lands if he became King and the war began.

In March 1333 King Edward sent Balliol with a small army to besiege Berwick while he mustered his forces and marched north. He planned to invade Scotland and place Balliol on the throne, but Berwick proved to be more of a problem than expected. The Scots governor, Sir Andrew Seton, was a skilled commander and by the end of June there was no sign of the city falling.

The Scots had meanwhile gathered their own army under Archibald, Earl of Douglas. Hoping to break the siege without the need for a battle, Douglas marched across the border and began pillaging Northumberland. He hoped that Edward would raise the siege to defend his lands, allowing Douglas to use the superior marching speed of his army to double back and relieve Berwick before the English could respond.

Edward, however, was not to be deterred and remained at Berwick. Eventually hunger and disease forced Seton to come to terms. He agreed to surrender Berwick to the English on 4 July if he had not been relieved and gave his own son as hostage. Hearing of this Douglas gathered his men from looting and marched on Berwick. Edward withdrew his men from the

The Market Square at Duns, where the Earl of Douglas mustered the Scottish army before marching east to face the English on Halidon Hill.

siegeworks and drew up for battle, but Douglas suddenly turned aside and made a dash on Bamburgh where Edward's Queen Philippa was staying. Bamburgh shut its gates in time, but in the confusion half a dozen Scots riders broke through the thinly manned English siege works and entered Berwick.

Seton declared that these few men constituted a relief and so refused to surrender. Edward was furious and hanged young Thomas in full view of the Berwick garrison. In response, Seton again promised to surrender, this time by 19 July. Edward was not to be fooled a second time and forced Seton to sign a written agreement. This stated that a relief force had to be at least 200 men strong and had to enter Berwick Castle. Edward also offered to forego the surrender if the Earl of Douglas defeated him in open battle. When Douglas heard of the new agreement he realized he would have to fight a battle to save Berwick. He abandoned his siege of Bamburgh and marched quickly to Duns.

On 19 July, Douglas led his men down the main road from Duns towards Berwick. As he drew close to the city he saw the English army drawn up on the slopes of Halidon Hill. It was almost noon.

The Opposing Armies

The long wars of independence had shown the Scots the need to update their military organization, and King Robert Bruce had introduced many reforms during his fifteen years in power. The army which approached Halidon Hill in 1333 was largely the product of his reforms.

The new Scots Army was ranked in feudal fashion with every man aged between sixteen and sixty expected to turn out to serve in the army for forty days each year, bringing with him arms and equipment suitable to his wealth. Noblemen were to serve in person and to bring with them private armies, made up as was the Royal Army. Knights were to serve in full armour and to bring with them a similarly armoured squire and a servant. Non-knightly men who owned £20 or more of goods were to wear a mail jacket and steel helmet and to carry a sword, shield and small bow. Those owning less than £20 were to bring a shield, helmet, spear and long knife. All these men were expected to ride a horse or pony, giving the army much-needed speed of travel. Those men who owned one cow or less were asked only to turn up on foot with a spear and were termed 'Small Folk'. In practice there were usually enough ponies for most or all of these men to be mounted. Each Easter the men of the kingdom had to parade in front of royal officers to prove they had their weapons ready for service.

Because of the need to garrison castles and city walls with rotas of men serving forty days each and the supply difficulties caused by gathering the entire army in one place, Douglas did not have the full strength of the Scottish army with him. His force consisted of 1,200 knights and armoured cavalry supported by 13,500 spearmen, though it is unclear how many of these were the lightly armoured men worth £20 or less and how many were 'Small Folk'.

Exactly how many men Edward had with him at Halidon Hill is unclear. He had left a sizeable force in the siege works on this occasion and had sent other parties of men to guard his Queen and to safeguard the supply routes. Contemporary sources are agreed that he had substantially fewer men than Douglas on the day and it would seem that about 9,000 men were with King Edward on the slopes of Halidon Hill. Of these about 800 were knights and another 4,000 heavy infantry equipped with spear, sword and varying degrees of armour. The remaining men were archers carrying longbows.

Edward had one innovative weapon with him at Berwick. For

The ruins of Berwick Castle rear up above the River Tweed. It was to relieve the Scottish defenders of this vital border stronghold that Douglas risked an open battle with England's King Edward I.

the first time an English army was using cannon in a siege. The guns were big, cumbersome and embarrassingly inaccurate. They were of little more use in the siege than more traditional catapults, though the morale effect of their noise and smoke was enormous. Too difficult to move easily, the guns were left in the siege trenches and played no part in the battle.

Tactics

Scottish tactics in 1333 were, in theory at least, still those developed by William Wallace and perfected by Robert Bruce. The equipment specified to the men serving in the army was designed to meet these tactical needs.

The spearmen would form up in a shiltron. The few archers that Scottish armies fielded were placed within the shiltrons or nearby so that they could take shelter quickly. They were equipped with short range hunting bows which were used to pick off the enemy as targets presented themselves. The armoured cavalry, of which Scottish armies were usually short, would be stationed behind the shiltrons ready to charge at any enemy formation which looked vulnerable.

At Halidon Hill there was no cover for the shiltrons, so Douglas knew he had to close the gap with the English line as quickly as possible. Douglas could also make use of a larger force of armoured horsemen than was usual in Scottish armies. His plan at Halidon Hill was to send his knights forward in a swift charge to get to grips with the English at first sight. The horsemen would hopefully disrupt the English front line, but in any case would mask the advancing shiltrons from the deadly arrow storm. Once the shiltrons were engaged in hand to hand combat, Douglas relied on weight of numbers to overwhelm the English.

King Edward was a much younger man and less experienced at warfare. But he had with him his uncle, Thomas, Earl of Norfolk, a battle toughened soldier able to give advice to his nephew and master. The two men decided on a novel deployment. It had been usual for English armies to have a centre formed of the armoured infantry to serve as a strong anchor able to resist enemy attacks. On the flanks were placed the longbowmen in solid masses which were pushed slightly forwards. The armoured knights sat their horses in the rear or on the flanks awaiting a chance to launch their battering-ram charge and win the day.

The key to victory was the arrow storm produced by the longbowmen. By the 1330s this tactic was nearing perfection. At Falkirk the archers had abandoned aiming at individual men and instead concentrated on massed volleys of arrows all aimed at an area of ground, hitting whatever targets were to be had. To achieve success a high rate of shooting was needed, and a plentiful supply of arrows. At Falkirk the archers are thought to have been able to shoot three or four arrows a minute and to have had a sheaf of twenty-four arrows each. At Halidon Hill the archers were trained to let loose six or eight arrows a minute and were issued with four sheafs, ninety-six arrows, each.

Edward chose to vary the usual layout of the troops while retaining the same basic battle plan. He divided his force into three self contained divisions, or 'battles'. Each battle had a centre of armoured infantry and flanks of archers. The battles were lined up alongside each other so that there was a continuous line of infantry with wedge-shaped formations of archers pushed forward where they met. This formation ensured that the archers were in the masses needed to create an arrow storm, but were spread along the length of the battlefront. Because each commander was free to choose his own targets, there was a flexibility about the formation unusual at the time. The right wing battle was under the command of the Earl of Norfolk, the left wing under Edward Balliol and the centre under King Edward himself.

Edward allowed only 200 of his knights to remain on their horses, and placed them on the flanks. Their task was not to launch a battle-winning charge but oppose any charge by the mounted Scots knights. The rest of the knights were ordered to dismount and stand with the armoured infantrymen. Edward believed he would need all his fighting strength to halt the Scottish attack. If the Scots were defeated, he thought, there would be time for the knights to remount and charge the retreating foe.

Edward had had the entire previous day to decide where to station his troops to block the Scots advance from Duns. The key consideration was to give his archers unlimited space over which to shoot and to try to slow down the Scottish advance so that the archers could drench them with the deadly arrow storm for as long as possible. He chose the ground with skill.

Edward drew his men up on the slopes of Halidon Hill where they dominated the road to Berwick and could not be bypassed. There were no trees or other cover for the Scots to shelter behind. The slope up to his position would slow down the Scots and give the archers extra time to inflict casualties. Finally, the lower reaches of the slope were boggy and marshy, and the mud could again be counted on to slow down the Scots.

Berwick from the battlefield. This was as close as Douglas got to his objective for his army was cut down wholesale before they could reach the Scottish defenders of the city.

The Battle

The day of battle began badly for the English. They saw the Scots army advancing and realized it greatly outnumbered them. One chronicler records that the advancing spearmen looked like a moving forest. The men were downcast and morale fell badly. King Edward mounted his horse and rode out in front of his army. He was tall, muscular, good looking and aged just twenty-one.

With a great show of nonchalance he turned his back on the advancing Scots and faced his own men. He called out to the knights and nobles, addressing them by name and praising them or their men. He swapped coarse jokes with the common soldiers and got the translators to render his wit into Welsh for the archers to appreciate. We do not know exactly what Edward said, but it was vulgar and common and it cheered his men. Then Edward ordered his minstrels to play a lively tune to keep the spirits up. By the time Douglas began deploying for battle, English morale was restored. Edward dismounted, sent his horse to the rear and took his place in the battle line.

The Earl of Douglas had been inspecting the English position as he advanced. It might have been possible to slip 200 men around a flank towards Berwick, but it was clear large numbers of the English army were absent from the hill and must be in the siege trenches, so that trick was unlikely to work.

Instead, Douglas decided to move swiftly and get to grips with the enemy as quickly as possible. He ordered his armoured knights and cavalry to trot down the road until they were opposite the English, then swing left and charge home as quickly as possible. Douglas could not see the English mounted knights, for the simple reason that they were dismounted and with the infantry, and he may have worried where they were. He put his infantry into shiltrons to resist any cavalry charge which might be made and ordered them to follow the cavalry as quickly as they could.

As the Scottish knights reached the foot of the slope, their horses found themselves in the marshy bog. The ground was unexpectedly soft and the hooves soon turned it into a quagmire. All formation was lost and many of the knights had to dismount and lead their horses out of the mud. The following infantry were forced to veer to the left to avoid the milling mass of knights, and so lost their own formation and momentum of advance. That was when Edward ordered the arrow storm to begin. The archers bent to their bows and let fly. With 4,000 men each shooting six

The battlefield seen from the road along which Douglas and the Scots were advancing. Edward and the English army were gathered on the hilltop to the left, from where they could have launched a devastating flank attack if Douglas had not attacked first.

arrows a minute, the Scots were lashed by over 20,000 arrows a minute. The arrows tore through flesh and splintered bone. They punched holes through armour and penetrated skulls. The Scots began to fall in their hundreds.

Douglas urged the men on, knowing that they had to cross the killing ground and close with the English infantry if the arrow storm was to stop. The Scots pushed on up the hill, crouching down and bending their heads as if walking into heavy rain. Still the arrow storm continued, the air humming as it was filled with a dense cloud of arrows. More and more Scotsmen were falling dead and injured in to the slippery, blood soaked grass of Halidon Hill. A few men reached the right flank of the English army but at this critical moment Douglas was killed.

The Scottish army broke and fled, pursued down the hill by the merciless arrows of the English archers. As the fleeing Scots got out of range of the archers, Edward unleashed his 200 mounted knights, ordering the dismounted knights to get in the saddle and join the chase. Only when the surviving Scots got to their waiting horses and rode off did the killing stop.

The slaughter had been frightful. Not only was Douglas dead, but so were the Earl of Ross, the Earl of Sutherland and the Earl of Carrick together with 500 other knights and noblemen and some 4,000 infantry. The English had lost one knight, four 'men of worth' and a handful of infantry.

Aftermath

The most immediate result of the battle was that Berwick surrendered. Edward quickly refortified the city and castle, making it an impregnable stronghold on the Scottish border. A few months later young King David was sent to France for safekeeping as Balliol and his English supporters ranged widely across Scotland. But Balliol was never accepted as King of Scots and by 1341 David was back on his throne. The slaughter on Halidon Hill had achieved little, except the transfer of Berwick from Scotland to England.

Visiting the Battlefield Today

To reach this battlefield, leave Berwick on the A6105. About half a mile beyond the A1 bypass road, a narrow lane to the right is signposted to the battlefield. Follow this lane until nearly at the crest of the hill where a car park opens on the left.

In the car park is an informative display mounted on a curved stone wall. This display indicates views across the battlefield, and much of the area around Berwick. It is located on what was the extreme left of the English line in the battle. The English army extended to the right, around the shoulder of the hill. Looking downhill, the road along which the Scots were advancing is at the far end of the field hidden behind a hedge. The main road visible a mile away is the modern A1 bypass, which did not exist at the date of the battle. It was up this hill that the Scots had to advance.

You can return back down the lane to the A6105 and turn right towards a lay-by. This is a busy road, so take care if you walk. From the lay-by it is possible to get an idea of the daunting task the Scots had in attacking the English army. The field in which the Scots tried to deploy, but got bogged down, is close behind the lay-by. It is private farmland and so should be treated as such. In any case, it remains very muddy after even light rain.

It is possible to follow the route of the Scottish advance along the A6105 from the Market Square in Duns. Halidon Hill is a major landmark and first comes into sight when it is still three miles away, so Douglas would have seen the English host an hour or so before he reached the scene of battle. However, he would not have been able to see the precise layout of the land and Edward's army until he came over the shoulder of high ground at the aptly named Brow of Hill some 600 yards before being forced to fight.

Since the battlefield is little more than an open hillside, the visitor would be wise to seek refreshments before leaving Berwick, or Duns depending on which way he comes to the field.

Chapter Nine

NEVILLE'S CROSS 1346

Introduction

The causes of the Battle of Neville's Cross had little to do with Scotland, but they still brought the Scots army south to disaster. And an even greater disaster was to follow.

In 1328 King Charles the Fair of France died without leaving an heir. The throne was taken by his cousin, who thus became King Philip VI. King Edward III of England disputed the claim on the grounds that he himself was a nephew of Charles and therefore closer to the throne. The French, however, did not recognize Edward's claim as it was through his mother and women were barred from the French throne. For some years Edward pursued legal manoeuvres and recruited allies among

While Douglas and his men negotiated the ravine, the rest of the Scottish army advanced up the slope towards the waiting English.

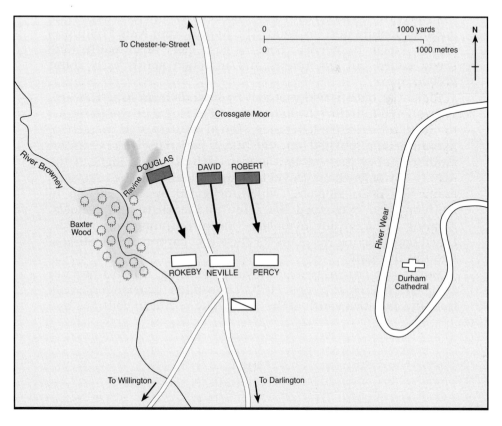

France's enemies. Then, in 1346, he gathered a mighty royal army and invaded France.

After capturing the cities of Caen and Lisieux, Edward swept across northern France. On 26 August he was cornered by a vastly superior French army at Crecy. The French had about 40,000 men and Edward only some 13,000. The French, however, had never before encountered the arrow storm tactic. Edward drew up his men in exactly the same manner as he had at Halidon Hill and proceeded to slaughter the French. Eleven princes, twelve Counts, 1,540 knights and 18,000 others fell victim to the longbow, while Edward's army suffered fewer than a hundred deaths. Even King Philip was injured in the slaughter.

King Philip of France was desperate. He ordered his cities to prepare for siege, asked the surviving nobles and knights to raise new troops and appealed to the Pope for peace. He also sent money, armour and some troops to King David II of Scotland begging him to invade England and cause a diversion to distract Edward.

As it happened David needed little prompting. He was twenty-two years old and had only recently taken over the reins of power from the Regents appointed when he inherited the throne as a child. Sir William Douglas had already been on a cross-border raid and had burnt Penrith without encountering serious opposition. David knew Edward had stripped much of England of troops for the invasion of France and believed the land to be wide open for looting and invasion. The appeal from King Philip was all the reason he needed. Sensing easy glory and wealth, King David called out his troops and marched south with about 25,000 men.

Almost at once David was met by heralds from King Edward. They offered him the city and castle of Berwick if he would return to Scotland and pledge peace. David saw this as a sign of weakness and pushed on. He burnt Lanercost Priory, looted Hexham Abbey and on 16 October, arrived within sight of the mighty city of Durham. David took up residence in the luxurious manor of Beau Repaire, which belonged to the Bishop of Durham, and encamped his army in the surrounding fields. Sending his men out to pillage the surrounding countryside, David began laying his plans for the siege, capture and looting of wealthy Durham.

But in one crucial respect David was wrong. Edward had not stripped England of troops. He had raised his invasion force only from the counties south of the Trent. The northern counties had not been raised. Now the Archbishop of York, acting in the King's name, sent out a Commission of Array to the northern armies and asked the famous fighting noblemen Lord Lucy, Ralph Neville and Henry Percy to take command. The army was mustered at Bishop Auckland and, by 17 October, it was about 15,000 strong. Lord Lucy had not arrived, but Percy ceded overall command to Neville and the English army set off.

The English army had marched just three miles when it met the first party of looting Scots at the village of Merrington. As it happened this raiding party was led by the same Sir William Douglas who had earlier burnt Penrith. Douglas took one look at the size of the host advancing on him and fled. He did not move fast enough and his force was overtaken by a force of English 'hobilars' who harassed the Scots all the way to Sunderland Bridge.

Galloping on, Douglas burst in on King David at Beau Repaire with news of the advancing English. None of the Scots had expected to face an army, never mind one almost as strong as their own. Douglas and others recommended immediate retreat, but David would have none of it. He sent out orders to recall his men from their looting and from the building of siege works. As David waited for his men to come in, English scouts appeared on a ridge to the southeast.

These scouts included Ralph Neville. Laid out before him he saw the pavilions and tents of the Scots together with the rapidly gathering Scottish army. Neville decided to draw up his army on the ridge with his left protected by the River Browney and his right by a steep bluff. Moreover the centre of the ridge was marked by a stone cross erected by his own family and called Neville's Cross. Perhaps he thought it was a good omen.

The Opposing Armies

King David had made great efforts to call out as much of Scotland's army as possible before marching south. In theory at least the main body of the army was expected to assemble within eight days of the King calling a muster, but in practice the units from more distant areas would take longer to arrive. Nevertheless, David probably marched with the majority of his Lowland troops. The Lord of the Isles, still semi-independent at this time, did not call out his troops so there were no Highlanders nor Islanders in the Scottish army.

The troops the English met at Neville's Cross would have been familiar to them from earlier encounters at Halidon Hill and

This English foot soldier carries equipment typical of the later thirteenth and early fourteenth century. On his head he wears a hat-like helmet known as the kettle which was popular with the English, but rarely seen in other armies. His body and upper arms are heavily protected by a scale tunic worn over mail. The scales were better at deflecting glancing blows than was mail, but mail was needed to stop the impact of heavy direct thrusts. He carries a large shield over his shoulder. In action this would have been strapped to his left arm and brought forward to form a solid wall with those of his companions. It would have been painted with the heraldic device of the knight or lord in whose service the man was serving at the time. His principal weapon is the thrusting spear, though he also carries a sword for use in a mêlée or if his spear snaps.

Falkirk. The bulk of the army were infantry armed with spears, shields and helmets and a fair number would have had mail or scale armour jackets. It is unlikely that David would have brought many of the 'Small Folk' with him. Such men were unmounted and David was on a looting raid, which demands speed of movement.

David did, however, have about 2,000 knights and armoured horsemen in his army. By this date the chain mail suits and large, round helmets of previous battles were going out of favour. The head of a knight was now more likely to be protected by a sphere-like helmet called a bascinet with a moveable visor over the face. The body was still protected largely by chain mail and the shield, but the legs and arms were now being covered in plates of steel.

The Scottish army also had the French troops sent by King Philip. It is not clear exactly how many such men were at Neville's Cross, but there were certainly fewer than 500. These men would have been equipped with spears, swords and shields much like the Scots infantry, though the spears would have been shorter at around ten feet compared with fourteen for the Scots. The key difference was in armour. The French would have worn full suits of chain mail and heavy, enclosed helmets. Over the armour was worn leg and arm guards of tough leather, often with metal plates attached.

We know rather less about the English army than about most forces at this period as all the senior heralds and clerks were with the King in France. We do know, however, that this army was different from earlier forces in a number of key ways.

First, there were considerably fewer archers than would have been the case if the king had been present. The expert bowmen from Wales and the Marches were in France. Lancashire sent 1,200 archers to join the army, but the other northern shires may have been able to raise only as many again between them. Lord Neville would be unable to let loose an arrow storm as devastating as he would have liked.

Second, the armoured infantry were beginning to use a new weapon: the bill. The bill was first used a century before Neville's Cross, but was becoming widespread about this time. It consisted of a heavy blade mounted on the end of a six feet haft and was replacing the spear as the pole weapon of choice among the infantry. Bills came in a wide variety of shapes, but most had a point at the end and an eighteen inch cutting blade down one side. Later examples had a hook or spike on the back. They could be used to thrust like a spear, chop like an axe and the hook could pull a man from a horse. In the hands of an expert they were deadly.

The final innovation in the English army was the type of troop known as a hobilar. It was these men who attacked and pursued Douglas's raiding party in the morning. The English had borrowed the idea from Ireland and, indeed, many hobilars in English armies were actually Irish mercenaries. Mounted on ponies, the hobilars were equipped with sword, knife and spear and armoured with a quilted or leather knee-length coat and iron helmet. These men were used for scouting, foraging and raiding, but were also useful in battle against less well-equipped troops and could, in an emergency, fight on foot as infantry.

Tactics

The tactics that King David and Lord Neville intended to follow at Neville's Cross were not much different from those planned by Douglas and Edward III at Halidon Hill. David intended to draw his men up in shiltrons. He would minimize the English superiority in archers by closing to hand to hand combat as quickly as possible and then rely on the greater number of Scots to secure victory. Neville intended to take a position from which his archers could shoot at the advancing Scots and where he could place his armoured infantry in a secure defensive position.

Matters were, however, complicated by the fact that Neville did not have as many archers as he really needed. He knew that he would be unable to stop the Scottish attack by archery alone and so he abandoned the by now traditional tactic of putting archers on the flanks. Instead, he placed his archers in advance of the armoured infantry. They had orders to shoot at the Scots, then duck behind the infantry at the last moment.

Neville did, however, follow the plan of Halidon Hill as regards his armoured knights. Most dismounted and joined their infantry contingents in the main battle line. Only a few hundred knights remained mounted. Along with the hobilars they were stationed in the rear to be used as a reserve as and when they were needed. They stood ready for action under the command of Edward Balliol, pretender to the Scottish throne.

The Battle

The battle itself began in a most unusual fashion. The monks of Durham Cathedral held a procession across the field of battle. Led by Prior Fossor, a group of a dozen monks processed out of

Durham Cathedral. It was on top of the Cathedral Tower that the monks of Durham held a prayer meeting during the battle to call on God for divine assistance for the English army.

the city gates and up to the hills where the two armies were deploying. With them they carried the sacred burial shroud of St Cuthbert, patron saint of Durham, mounted on a spear. The monks erected their strange banner on a small hillock located off to the Scottish left and knelt around it in prayer. Meanwhile the remaining monks gathered on top of the great tower of Durham Cathedral and chanted psalms and prayers. All this was in response to a vision one of the monks had received in which St Cuthbert appeared and instructed his monks to throw back the Scots by this strange ceremony. Quite what the fighting men made of all this is unknown, but King David gave orders the monks were not to be attacked.

David drew his large army up in three divisions, each of which was divided into three or four shiltrons. The right wing was commanded by Sir William Douglas, the centre by King David and the left wing by Lord Robert Stewart. Robert's actions in the battle were to be the subject of

The view from the ridge occupied by the English left wing under Rokeby towards the north-west from which direction Douglas advanced. Hidden in the valley is a deep ravine which broke up the Scottish advance.

much controversy. He was the son of David's sister Marjory and the great nobleman Walter Stewart. He was thus a rich man in his own right and the heir to the King. If David were to have a son, however, Robert would lose his claim to the throne. Such considerations may have affected his decisions as the battle unfolded.

Once the Scots were properly drawn up in their shiltrons, David ordered the advance. The Scottish formations marched forward toward the ridge on which Neville's men waited and almost at once Douglas's men on the right got into difficulties. A line of trees to their front hid a small, but very steep ravine. Douglas's shiltrons were forced to swerve to their left, file around the ravine and then reform before continuing the advance. As they reformed, the English archers let fly. Although there were not enough archers to create a truly effective arrow storm, Douglas took many casualties and his advance was seriously delayed.

King David's men, meanwhile, had faced no such obstacle and marched up the gentle slope to their front without much difficulty or delay. The Scottish infantry crashed into the centre of the English line and began pushing it back. On the Scottish left, the lead shiltron of Robert Stewart had even more success. The English right under Lord Percy suffered badly, the united front being broken up into its component units. As these fell back, the advancing Scots themselves became disordered.

This was the moment for which Edward Balliol had been waiting. He gave the order to charge and the English armoured cavalry swept forwards. The disorganized Scots stood no chance. Caught outside their firm shiltron formation, they were cut down mercilessly. Robert Stewart's remaining two shiltrons were intact and advancing up the slope, but Robert ordered them to halt. If he had continued his advance it is probable he could have brushed aside Balliol's disorganized cavalry and swept on through Percy's infantry before they could reform. But Robert did nothing. His men stayed put and watched while Percy reformed his line.

On the Scottish right Douglas had by now reached the English. In this part of the field the slope up to the English position was steep and Douglas was unable to gain any momentum to his advance. The hand to hand fighting was savage, but short lived. Douglas at first gave ground, then tried to disengage and eventually fled back down the slope.

Seeing his left wing advancing and with his centre holding its own, Neville gave Percy orders to advance. As soon as Percy's men started forward, Robert Stewart led his men off the field. Whether he did this to further his own ambitions to replace David or as a wise precaution in the face of an attack is unknown.

David's central division now had both flanks exposed and before long was being attacked by the advancing English wings. The Scottish centre fell back, but in good order and continued to fight stubbornly.

After an hour's hard fighting, the Scots saw a fresh force of English troops surge over the ridge crest beside Neville's Cross. These were the men of Lord Lucy who had been late arriving at the mustering point and had spent the entire day marching to catch up with the main army. Their arrival was enough to dishearten the Scottish centre which collapsed and fled.

A band of knights and nobles formed around King David and set themselves to fight their way out of the English forces to get the King back to Scotland. They managed to get as far as the River Browney before they were overwhelmed by the pursuing English cavalry. King David himself was wounded twice in the confused struggle at the river before being grappled to the ground by a Northumbrian squire named John Copeland. Copeland refused to let go of his prize even when the Scottish King knocked out his front teeth with a mailed fist.

Aftermath

The remaining Scottish troops were gathered together by Robert Stewart, who led them in a rapid retreat over the border, pursued and harried by the English cavalry. With David a prisoner in England, Scotland fell into the hands of Robert Stewart, though he was compelled to confer with a Parliament drawn from the leading families of the realm. King David, meanwhile, was taken to the Tower of London by the jubilant John Copeland. King Edward knighted Copeland and endowed him with lands paying over £500 a year in rents. The young man was made for life.

The English raided over the border the following summer and Edward Balliol again began to think about regaining his lost throne. Ralph Neville celebrated the battle by taking down the old Neville's Cross and replacing it with a magnificent creation adorned with stone statues and carvings. He did not live to see the work completed as he died in 1347. In thanks for his great victory he was buried in Durham Cathedral, the first layman to receive the honour.

The wooded banks of the River Browney. It was here that the Scottish King David was wrestled to the ground and captured by a youthful English squire who thus became rich for life.

But a more deadly enemy than archers or knights was about to arrive. In 1348 the Black Death arrived in Britain. Within months the entire population was overwhelmed by a catastrophe which carried off a third of them. The economy was severely disrupted, land was left unploughed, government posts were unfilled and society teetered on the edge of collapse.

The plague returned year on year, though in less virulent form and both the English and the Scots had more important things to do than fight each other. A treaty was patched up and King David went home to nurse his ailing country. It would be more than a generation before warfare flared again.

Visiting the Battlefield Today

Most of the battlefield is now covered by modern housing estates; however, enough can be seen to make a visit worthwhile.

109

The broken stump of Neville's Cross – it was smashed in the Reformation – stands protected by iron railings beside the A690 a hundred yards east of the junction of that road and the A167. A large pub called the Neville's Cross stands beside the crossroads.

North of the crossroads the A167 crosses a railway bridge and then enters the battlefield. Immediately south of the railway bridge, there is a narrow road running west called Quarry House Lane. This runs between houses before emerging into open countryside. This is where the English left wing stood and the lane, now unmade, offers good views across the land covered by the advancing Scottish right wing. Further north on the A167 another turning, Toll House Road, leads you to the position where the Scots drew up just before they began their advance. A bridlepath to the south, just beyond the last house, leads to the ravine that caused so much trouble to the Scots under Douglas. Further down the lane is the River Browney.

If you follow Toll House Road for a mile or more and turn right by a sign pointing to 'Bearpark Colliery' you will find yourself in a maze of disused industrial land and semi-derelict Victorian buildings. Perseverance will lead you to a turning on the right, which appears to be a dead end, but is in fact merely a blind corner. The road then becomes unmade and dips sharply down to the valley floor. Where this road crosses the river a footpath leads off to the right to the ruins of Beau Repaire Manor, now known as Bearpark Manor. These are worth a visit in good weather and if you are wearing stout shoes. They are well cared for and the main rooms can be made out, but mud makes them difficult to visit in wet weather.

The broken stump of Neville's Cross. This monument was erected by the English commander to celebrate his victory, but largely smashed during the Reformation by Protestant zealots.

Durham City offers much to the visitor, including the cathedral and its tower where the monks prayed for victory. Neville's tomb lies in the nave, but three centuries after the battle Scots soldiers captured at the Battle of Dunbar were imprisoned in here. They found Neville's splendid tomb and smashed it, so only sad remnants are to be seen.

Chapter Ten

OTTERBURN 1388

Introduction

'Of all the battles that I have described in this book, this was the best fought and the most severe, for there was not a man, knight or squire who did not fight gallantly hand to hand with his enemy.' So wrote the chronicler Jean Froissart before launching into enormous detail about the Battle of Otterburn. He was not alone in his opinions. Three Scottish ballads appeared within months of the Battle, as did two English versions and within a few years the Battle had taken on legendary and mythical status among Europe's minstrels and troubadours.

An enduring mystery of medieval warfare is how the Scottish force of Douglas and the English troops of Umfraville managed to miss each other when marching in opposite directions through the same wood. The solution proposed here is that Umfraville advanced along the crest of the wooded hill, while Douglas moved along the lower slopes

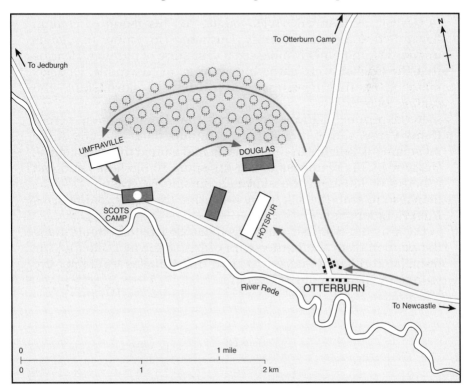

This was a battle which excited the imaginations of noblemen and chroniclers throughout Christendom. It was a not a particularly large battle nor were its results far reaching nor even permanent. It was the pure chivalry and romance of the Battle that made it so famous.

The campaign began with a great feast of the Scottish nobles held in Aberdeen. King Robert II was not invited. This was the same Robert Stewart who had retreated so quickly from the field of battle at Neville's Cross and it appears that the nobles did not want him present because they did not trust his judgement when it came to war with England. In any case, he was over seventy years old and sick.

Led by James, Earl of Douglas, and William, Earl of Fife, the nobles decided to take advantage of civil unrest in England by launching a massive border raid. They knew that the English were not only weakened by the anarchy under Richard II but by the fact that the two greatest noble families of the north – the Nevilles and the Percies – were engaged in a bitter quarrel over titles and honours.

The nobles decided to order the Scottish army to muster at Jedburgh early in August. The bulk of the army would march under the Earl of Fife to lay siege to, and hopefully capture, Carlisle. A smaller, mobile force under the Earl of Douglas would meanwhile conduct a plundering raid on north-east England to divert the English forces.

At first the Scottish plan went well. The Earl of Fife laid siege to Carlisle as planned while Douglas led his mounted column down Redesdale into County Durham. He found the lands unguarded and quickly amassed a vast store of plunder. Hearing that the English were gathering an army at Newcastle, Douglas marched on that town and several days of skirmishing and raiding followed.

It was in one of these skirmishes that Douglas came across Henry Percy, son of the Earl of Northumberland and one of the most famous knights in England. He had gained the nickname of Hotspur by his readiness to put his spurs to his horse and join a battle or joust. In the skirmish outside Newcastle, Douglas managed to grab the silk pennon bearing the Percy coat of arms from Hotspur's lance.

Back at the Scottish camp, Douglas boasted he would hang the pennon from the battlements of his castle at Dalkeith. The humiliated Hotspur angrily declared that Douglas would not live to take the pennon out of England.

Alnwick Castle, ancestral home of the Percy family. It was from here that Harry 'Hotspur' Percy set out to do battle at Otterburn, and here that his descendant, the Duke of Northumberland, still lives.

With fresh English reinforcements arriving at Newcastle almost every hour, Douglas decided to march back to Scotland with his plunder intact. The morning after the skirmish the Scottish army began its retreat. Seeing his pennon heading for Scotland, Hotspur gave orders for an immediate attack, but he was overruled by the other northern barons who insisted that they wait until they outnumbered the Scots.

While Harry Percy kicked his heels at Newcastle waiting for more men, Douglas marched back up Redesdale. On 18 August he reached Otterburn, where a border castle was held by a tiny English garrison. Douglas decided to try to capture the castle and let it be known he was waiting just south of the border to allow Hotspur to come and get his pennon back. To make the point, Douglas tied the Percy pennon to a pole in front of his tent.

The next day a Scottish attack on the castle failed. It was fairly late in the afternoon by the time Douglas had accepted defeat. He ordered his men to return to camp, cook their supper and get to sleep. Scouts were posted on a ridge between the castle and Douglas's camp in case the English garrison tried a sortie. Dusk fell and satisfied with his arrangements, Douglas retired to his tent and a hot meal.

It was at that moment that a scout galloped into camp from the ridge. An English army marching under the banner of the Percies had come up the road from Newcastle, marched past Otterburn Castle and was deploying for battle.

The Opposing Armies

The contemporary chronicles differ slightly about the size of the force which Douglas had with him at Otterburn. However, it is clear that when he crossed the border at the start of his raid, Douglas had about 6,500 men with him, of which 300 were heavily armoured knights and an unknown number were servants and grooms. Given that he had gathered his various plundering detachments before retreating from Newcastle, it is likely that Douglas had pretty much his entire army with him.

The armoured knights would, by this date, have been entirely encased in plate armour. Even squires could expect to have at least some plate armour, though not of the best quality. Chain mail was still a vital part of any knight's armour for it was used to cover the elbows, knees, groin and other areas where a knight needed flexibility. Shields were becoming smaller and less important as the quality of the body armour increased, but most knights still carried them.

By this date many knights provided their horses with armour. This usually came in the form of quilted cloth a dozen layers thick with a metal plate over the front of the animal's head and, sometimes, the chest as well. Particularly wealthy noblemen are known to have had horse armour of chain mail which covered the animal's head, neck and body but it is unclear if this was for tournaments or would have been used on campaign.

The bulk of Douglas's army, however, would have been nothing like this well equipped. They were infantry equipped with shield, spear and helmet, and often with a sword or long knife. Axes seem to have been gaining favour in Scottish armies by the later fourteenth century. They had curved blades about ten inches across and were wielded one handed. Most of the

By the time of the Battle of Otterburn, plate armour was reaching its most sophisticated forms. Only the very richest knights and noblemen could afford custom-made suits such as that shown here. Each piece was made by the armourer to match the body of the wearer. This made the armour extremely flexible as well as surprisingly lightweight. Less wealthy knights bought less well-fitting standardized pieces while men at arms relied on mail reinforced with any odd bits of plate they could pick up. The helmet is of the type known as a bascinet, a strong conical design with a full face visor that could be lifted up when not in action. Underneath is a mail coif, a balaclava helmet shaped cap which reached down to cover the shoulders and chest. The breast and back plates are covered by a linen jupon on which is embroidered the man's coat of arms, repeated on the shield. The notch on the top edge of the shield was used as a lance rest when charging on horseback. The long, heavy blade of the sword was needed to make an impact on an enemy similarly encased in armour and was balanced by a heavy metal knob at the base of the hand grip.

infantry had jackets of mail, scale or quilted armour. All would have ridden horses or ponies on campaign, but fought on foot.

Unlike the Scottish army, raised by royal decree on a feudal basis, the English army of the period was more professional and better equipped. The English had abandoned the feudal levy, by which men were granted land and in return were expected to march to war with arms and supplies provided by themselves. Instead, English kings had turned to levying cash taxes on their subjects and using the money to hire troops.

A feudal element remained in English armies, however, as the king would raise relatively few troops himself – usually foreign mercenaries. Instead he relied upon his chief nobles to provide him with troops raised from their estates. In turn the greater nobles relied on their tenants and followers to raise smaller contingents to make up the total. Each leader had a written contract with his superior which set down how many men he was to raise and how they were to be equipped, together with rates of pay and conditions of service. Once agreed, the contract was torn down the middle and each kept half. At the end of the campaign, the two halves were brought together and the outstanding payments made. The indented torn edges gave this contract its name – an indenture.

In 1388 it was usual for indentured knights to be paid four shillings a day for themselves plus two shillings for each armoured squire or man at arms they brought with them. Hobilars, a form of armoured infantryman who rode a horse for transport, could expect sixpence a day and an archer threepence a day. Pay was often at half-rates for garrison duty, but might be doubled for hazardous overseas campaigns. Indentures were for a minimum of a month and a maximum of a year, though most were for three months.

The indentured men that Harry Hotspur summoned to Newcastle would have been well-equipped professional soldiers. They would have been equipped in a similar manner to those who fought at Neville's Cross, although now there was a tendency for the infantry to have more in the way of armour. A new weapon was appearing at this time. In addition to their usual weapons, most English infantry carried a maul. This was a long handled hammer with a heavy lead head which was used to crush or crack open plate armour.

It is certain that Hotspur had just over 8,000 men with him as he approached Otterburn. Of these about 600 were heavily armoured knights and some 3,000 archers. The remainder were armoured infantrymen equipped with shields, helmets and chain jackets. They would have had spears and swords, but many were equipped with bills, stout pole weapons with cutting edges as well as spear points.

Tactics

At the time of the Battle of Otterburn, military tactics had changed little for nearly a century. Most fighting was done by the infantry who formed up in solid blocks of 50 to 150 men with overlapping shields. Each body of infantry could move independently or cooperate with neighbouring units to form a solid phalanx thousands strong, or more flexible formations. It was these formations which held or captured terrain, and battles were increasingly decided by the success or failure of the foot soldiers.

The armoured knights could launch mounted charges on favourable terrain, which could have a devastating impact on any infantry formations they met. Among both sides, however, there was an increasing tendency for the knights to fight on foot alongside the men they had brought to the battle. The English cavalry was usually made up of men at arms and knights with special indentures for this purpose.

Archers were a decisive factor on many battlefields. Scottish archers were few in number and used shorter, hunting bows, the techniques of which were easy to learn and to use. They tended to be spread among the infantry and picked off targets as they saw them. Archers in the English armies, many of whom were Welsh, used the long bow which took years to learn to use properly. They could unleash an arrow storm, drenching an enemy formation with thousands of arrows a minute. Such tactics were devastating, but needed open land to provide a good field of fire and the archers had to be protected from enemy attack by sensible use of the other infantry.

The Battle

When Hotspur passed Otterburn Castle the garrison told him the Scots were encamped just beyond the ridge to the west. Knowing that his army outnumbered the Scots and confident of victory, Hotspur detached a small force under Sir Thomas Umfraville. Umfraville was ordered to march up the hill to Percy's right and swing wide through the woods that topped the hill so as to come down behind the Scottish camp. There he was to block the

Scottish retreat and so trap Douglas and his men. While Umfraville marched off, Hotspur rearranged the bulk of his army. This gave Umfraville time to get into position, and also gave the English army a more disciplined formation.

Douglas, meanwhile, had not been idle. He had already drawn up his plan for what to do if an English army appeared and now he put it into action. He sent a force of armoured infantry up to the crest of the ridge with orders to hold the English attack for as long as possible. He then formed up the rest of his men and led them in a column into the woods through which Umfraville was marching in the opposite direction. A small guard was left in the Scottish camp to look after the horses and plunder.

By the time Percy had marched his men up to the ridge held by the Scots, night had fallen. But this was the night of a full moon and the sky was cloudless and clear. By the pale silver light the battle opened. Percy and his men surged up the hill at the Scots, crashing into the armoured front line and pushing them back a few yards. The English began their battle chants, but the Scots fought in grim silence.

At some point in this initial phase of fighting, Sir Ralph Percy, Hotspur's younger brother was wounded by a Scots knight by the name of Maxwell. Sir Ralph fell to his knees and surrendered with the somewhat unglamorous words 'I yield. I am so wounded my drawers are full of blood'.

It was at about this time that Umfraville arrived in the Scottish camp. The guards fled and Umfraville took up position to block the Scots retreat. Some of his men slipped away to see what they could plunder from the camp.

Meanwhile Douglas had got his own column of men into position at the edge of the woods. From there he was on the

The open field just north-west of the village of Otterburn where the fiercest fighting took place. Douglas led his flanking attack down the slope from the left to strike the English army in the right flank. At the time of the battle most of the ridge was covered by dense woodland.

exposed right flank of the English army as it battled with his men on the ridge. Raising his banner, the Earl let rip the battle cry 'Douglas, Douglas' and led his men in a ferocious charge. The impact of Douglas's men hitting the right flank of the English army was immense. The right wing collapsed almost at once and the men fled. Some two miles from the battlefield, the fugitives met Walter Skirlaw, Bishop of Durham, who was advancing with 5,000 reinforcements. Thinking the battle already lost, Skirlaw halted his men then turned back towards Durham.

Meanwhile, the battle hung in the balance. Hotspur managed to rally his centre but soon afterwards was knocked unconscious and taken prisoner. Shortly afterwards the English began to fall back, a retreat that soon became a rout. The English were spared heavy casualties when the moon set and blackness engulfed the land. Realizing the battle was lost, Umfraville led his men away from the Scottish camp and into the wooded hills.

At dawn next day, the Scots found they were in possession of the battlefield. The only English within sight were the 1,800 dead and 700 prisoners, which included both Percy brothers and forty knights and nobles. The Earl of Douglas, however, was nowhere to be seen. At first it was thought he was leading a force in pursuit of the English, but then his body was found. He had been wounded in the thigh by a lance, but killed by an axe blow to the head. The Scots hurriedly erected a boulder on the spot where they found the body of their leader, then carried him to Melrose Abbey for burial.

Aftermath

The Battle of Otterburn had little lasting impact. On hearing the news of the victory, the Earl of Fife called off the siege of Carlisle and returned to Scotland. He claimed that he feared an English army could cut him off now that Douglas's army had fallen back, but it may have been that Carlisle was proving more difficult to take than had been expected. Within a few weeks the two Percy brothers had been released on payment of a large ransom by their father, the Earl of Northumberland and most of the other prisoners were likewise released.

The only long lasting effect of the battle was on the reputations of those who had fought there. Douglas was hailed as a national hero, as were most of his men. The Percy brothers had been humiliated and wanted revenge on the Scots. All were celebrated by the minstrels and balladeers, often being credited with actions and words that had never taken place.

Visiting the Battlefield Today

Otterburn stands on the A696 just south of the border. Some 300 yards north-west of the village there is a clump of trees on the right of the road with a driveway entering it. This is the car park which serves the monument and is a convenient starting point for visiting the battlefield. Walking past the monument to the stone wall beyond brings you to a large information board. To the north can be seen the ridge along which Umfraville moved and to the west a large clump of trees marks the position of the old Roman earthworks which are known as Greenchesters. Umfraville probably descended the slope to attack the Scottish camp from this position.

The village pub at Otterburn, which carries an appropriate name and sign. This being England, the pub commemorates the losing English commander rather than the victorious Scots.

To find the Scottish camp, walk north-west along the main road to the junior school. Cross the road where an overgrown public footpath runs across fields to the river. The Scottish camp was probably positioned in the meadows north-west of this path. A better view of the area can be gained further along the main road where a second footpath is less overgrown and more welcoming. Returning to the car park and walking south-east along the main road brings you to the main scene of the fighting. A ridge descending from the hill to your left is the position taken by the Scottish army at the start of the battle.

The monument at Otterburn. It is said that the upright stone is a chimney lintel removed from the ruined Otterburn Castle.

You can now walk on to the village, or get your car and drive there. The Tower Hotel was built on the site of, and using stones from, the medieval Otterburn Castle. Otterburn Hall, signposted up a lane from the village, is open to the public. For such a small village, Otterburn is well provided with a pub, a hotel and a coffee shop as well as a good village store. Whatever you feel like snacking on after walking the battlefield, you should find it in the village.

South of the village, the B6341 leads after a few miles to Eldon, where there are the finely preserved remains of a motte and bailey castle as well as, perhaps more important, some well maintained public toilets.

119

Chapter Eleven

HOMILDON HILL 1402

Introduction

The last of the medieval confrontations between England and
Scotland was not so much a battle as a slaughter. It was a battle
in which leadership and tactical skill won out against muddle
and indecision. Which is not to say that there was a lack of
courage, as the events of the battle clearly show.

After his defeat at Otterburn, Harry 'Hotspur' Percy, heir to the
Earl of Northumberland, craved revenge on the Scots. First,
however, he took a hand in sorting out the internal unrest in
England. King Richard II had ruled well for many years, but after

*Goaded beyond endurance by English archery, the Scots abandoned
their position on the hill and charged down into a carefully prepared
killing ground from which few escaped alive.*

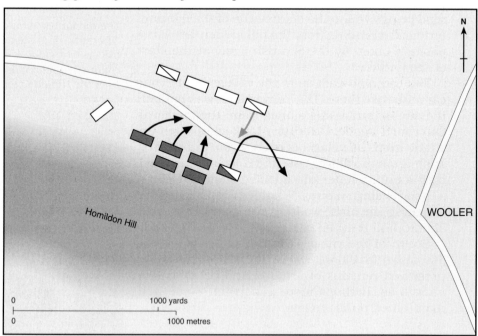

The River Till at Milfield. The English laid an ambush for the Scottish army at this ford, but Douglas heard of the ploy and withdrew to Homildon Hill to decide his next move.

the death of his beloved Queen Anne something snapped in his brain. He indulged in every luxury known at the time and gave himself over to gluttony and drink. He hired a large private army, not to fight the kingdom's enemies, but to crush resistance to his heavy taxes and arbitrary whims. He ordered the murder of the Duke of Gloucester and personally beat the Earl of Arundel senseless. Other nobles and bishops were executed, thrown into prison or exiled. The economy was in a mess and the common people suffered terribly.

When Henry Duke of Lancaster raised a rebellion in the summer of 1399, the powerful Percy family joined immediately. Richard sent out the summons to raise the royal army, but nobody came. Abandoned and alone, Richard was captured and deposed. A few months later Lancaster announced that Richard was dead and took the throne as King Henry IV.

Almost immediately a man with a strong resemblance to Richard appeared at the court of King Robert III of Scotland. The Scots hailed him as the real King Richard and refused to deal with King Henry on the grounds that he was a usurper. The Scots stepped up the number and scale of their border raids. In July 1402, Henry led a large army into southern Scotland, but failed to capture any major cities or to bring the Scottish army to battle.

As soon as King Henry was gone, Archibald, Earl of Douglas mustered a force and marched south over the border. Like his grandfather in 1388, Archibald plundered Northumberland and

Durham before turning back at the gates of Newcastle. He led his army, now laden down with a vast amount of plunder, north along the coast road. He turned inland to avoid the great fortress of Alnwick intending to pass through Wooler and cross back into Scotland at Coldstream.

The English had not been idle. The Earl of Northumberland had gathered an army and laid an ambush beside the ford at Milfield where Douglas would have to cross the River Till. Scottish scouts discovered the trap and Douglas halted just north of Wooler to decide his next move. The next morning, 14 September, the English army led by the Earl and his son Harry Hotspur advanced on the Scottish position. Battle was inevitable.

The Opposing Armies

Archibald, Earl of Douglas, had about 9,000 men with him when he camped on the slopes of Homildon Hill. The approaching English army under the Earl of Northumberland was smaller, probably about 7,000 strong. But the English were so confident of victory that Northumberland's son, Harry 'Hotspur' suggested an immediate attack. His confidence was based on the different equipment and tactics of the two armies.

The Scottish troops were overwhelmingly infantry, who rode horses on campaign but fought on foot. These men were armed much as Scottish armies had been for the previous century. In addition to his infantry, Douglas had several hundred heavily armoured knights – though it is not known exactly how many. In theory these men were raised by traditional feudal levy, being expected to serve forty days at their own expense. In practice, however, the full levy was raised only when the king went to war on the grand scale. Noblemen, such as Douglas, could call out the levy of their estates for cross border raids, but they also hired men for cash payments called Bonds of Retinue, or for the promise of a share of any loot captured. It is thought that the Scottish army on this occasion was hired by Douglas and his fellow nobles on the basis of Bonds.

The English army at this battle was, essentially, the private army of the Percy family and other northern noblemen. The great wealth of these families gave them the money to hire and equip soldiers, while their spreading estates gave them a large reservoir of men who felt a direct loyalty to the noble family. The English had long ago abandoned the feudal levy and instead relied upon a minority of the men in the population who effectively worked as full time, professional soldiers. As a result the English armies of this time were consistently better trained and equipped than their Scottish rivals.

At Homildon Hill, the Percies brought an army accustomed to fighting on foot. About half the army was made up of archers, many of them Welshmen hired by the northern families to stiffen the bowmen of their own estates. At this date the longbow was at the peak of development. The best archers were those who began training as boys, for the years of practice as the body grew produced massively broad shoulders and overdeveloped arm muscles which together gave greater power in the shot arrow. The remainder of the troops in the English army were infantry equipped with more or less effective armour. Most men wore mail jackets and steel helmets and carried wooden shields bound with iron.

The English also had their heavily armoured knights encased in full plate armour. These men usually fought on foot alongside the men they had raised, using their extra weight to stiffen the battle line and their authority to give orders in the heat of battle. Some English knights chose to fight on horse at this time, but not at Homildon Hill.

Tactics

The early fifteenth century saw large battles fought with similar tactics to those of the fourteenth century. Battles tended to be won or lost by the formations of armoured infantry. Not until the enemy's divisions were broken and in flight was the battle won.

To achieve this aim, the Scots and English employed quite different tactics. The English used the longbowmen to produce an arrow storm. The armoured infantry were held back while the archers did their work and were brought into play only if the enemy threatened to overrun the lightly armoured and vulnerable archers. At this point in the battle the archers could not shoot for fear of hitting their own men and the battle would become a mass of men engaged in bloody hand to hand combat. If the English were getting the worst of the encounter, they would seek to disengage again covered by archery or by mounted knights whose presence would deter too rash a pursuit. If it were the enemy who fell back, the English would use archery to inflict casualties until their targets were out of range, after which mounted men would take up the pursuit.

To counter these tactics, the Scots came up with a number of ploys designed to neutralize the arrow storm and get to close quarter fighting. The Scots might attack at dawn, as at

Bannockburn, or launch a surprise attack from a forest, as at Otterburn. Alternatively they could launch a swift cavalry charge to ride down the archers, or at least mask their aim and enable the infantry to get to grips. If none of these tactics looked possible, the Scots usually preferred to avoid a pitched battle and rely on ambush, raid and sieges to grind down the English campaign.

The Battle

As the English army advanced and deployed for battle, the Scots realized they had a problem. Encumbered by a large train of wagons and pack animals, loaded down with plunder, they could not march as quickly as the English and so avoid a battle. Nor could they scramble up the steep slopes of the hills at their back where their height would render the longbowmen far below almost useless. Nor would the Scots abandon their plunder and flee. Uncertain what to do, Douglas did nothing.

The Earl of Northumberland agreed with his son that an immediate attack was needed, but the wily old man ignored Hotspur's calls for a frontal assault. Instead Northumberland drew up his armoured infantry on level ground directly in front of the Scots and halted. The front rank of this battle line was filled with archers. A strong body of archers, perhaps 2,000 strong, was then sent out to the right wing. If the Scots tried to attack, the archers could scamper back to the cover of their armoured support.

As the archers moved forward, Douglas did nothing.

The hidden gully halfway up the slopes of Homildon Hill where the Scots secreted their baggage train which was loaded down with loot from their lengthy raid into England.

Once in position, the archers let fly a deadly arrow storm. Some 12,000 arrows a minute plunged into the Scottish army. Wounded horses screamed in agony and fell to the ground lashing out with their hooves. Men raised their shields, but were hit nonetheless, the arrows tearing into flesh and shattering bones. Hundreds of Scots fell wounded or dead.

Still, Douglas did nothing. Perhaps he panicked, perhaps he was frightened. Whatever the reason, the inactivity of the Scottish commander was condemning his men to death.

Suddenly a lone knight rode out in front of the Scottish army. It was Sir John Swinton, a champion jouster at Scottish tournaments. He turned to face the army and shouted angrily 'What has bewitched you today? Why do you not attack these men who hurry to destroy you with their arrows as if you were deer? Those who are willing should come with me and we shall strike our enemies to save our lives, or at least to fall as knights with honour.' At least that is what a chronicler wrote down some time later.

Whatever Sir John actually said, it was enough. His chief rival on the tournament field, Sir Adam Gordon, spurred forwards and shouted 'Indeed, you are the finest knight in Scotland. Let us ride together.' The two young men flourished their lances and spurred down the hill at the English army waiting below. A hundred or so mounted knights followed, surging down the slope.

Seeing the charge, Douglas at last took action. He picked up his lance and ordered a general advance, charging forwards in the wake of Swinton and Gordon.

Seeing the Scots army at last in movement, Northumberland ordered his main body to fall back. But he was not retreating, merely luring the Scots into a prepared killing ground at the foot of the slope. The Scottish knights reached the flat ground first and were instantly deluged with an arrow storm from the English main body as well as from the flanking archers. Their horses killed or wounded, the knights crashed to the ground to be peppered with arrows themselves. The few dozen who remained mounted veered to the right and fled.

Seeing their social superiors effectively wiped out, the Scottish infantry abandoned the advance and ran. They were pursued by English arrows, which cut down more Scots, and then by cheering Englishmen who sprung to their horses to give chase. Most of the Scots got across the River Till, but the Tweed was running high. Many Scots, too tired to face the torrent,

The view from the initial Scottish position down the hill and across the valley of the Till towards Scotland, which so few of them would ever reach.

surrendered. Others dived in. For days afterwards hundreds of bodies were found floating down stream. It is thought that less than half the Scottish army got home.

Aftermath

Once the killing was over, the English moved into the field and up the slopes where the Scots had been mown down by the archers. Most of the heavily armoured nobles and knights were still alive. Thrown by wounded or dying horses and injured by the arrow storm they lay prostrate awaiting capture. The Earl of Douglas himself was hauled from beside his horse with five arrow wounds, including one that cost him his eye. Three other earls were taken together with nearly 100 knights and lesser barons. Even Murdoch Stewart, the king's nephew, was taken alive.

The Percies were jubilant. They had got their revenge for the disgrace of Otterburn and gained great fame. More lucrative, they had a clutch of wealthy prisoners who, according to the rules of war of the time, could be held for ransom.

There was a complex set of rules about the treatment of noble prisoners at this time. In theory the ransom was to be paid to the person who captured the prisoner, but equally the prisoner expected to be kept in the luxury usual for his station. If a humble foot soldier captured an earl, it was obvious such luxury

126

could not be afforded. It was normal, therefore, that a prisoner would be sold on to somebody able to bear the costs of captivity. In this way the man who made the capture would become instantly wealthy, while the nobleman who 'bought' the prisoner would get the eventual ransom, which was usually more than had been paid for the prisoner.

This system was well understood, but in the wake of Homildon Hill it went badly wrong. King Henry IV of England was insecure on his throne and in desperate need of money. He therefore instructed the Percies to hand over the prisoners taken at Homildon Hill and offered them a derisory fraction of the expected ransom in return. The Percies were furious. They argued, they delayed, they pleaded and in the end they rose in revolt and England was plunged into civil war.

Scotland, meanwhile, had its own troubles. Robert III died in 1406 and left the throne to his infant son James I. The nobles fell to squabbling, taking power that rightfully belonged to the crown. It was not until James III became king in 1488 that internal peace came to Scotland. James III was too busy repairing the damage caused by the years of civil strife to feel the need to go to war with England. The English, meanwhile, were bleeding themselves white in the bloodbath known as the Wars of the Roses.

There were, of course, border raids. Some of them led to substantial fights such as that at Wark in 1435. The Earl of Northumberland was driven off by the Earl of Angus and another English defeat, this time at the hands of the new Earl of Douglas, in 1448. But these were relatively small affairs. Both nations were far too busy with their internal troubles to put a large army in the field.

The lower slopes of Homildon Hill. The original Scottish position was behind the line of trees, which did not exist at the time of the battle. It was down this slope that the Scots charged in the later stages of the battle.

Visiting the Battlefield Today

On a fine day Homildon Hill, now known as Humbleton Hill, is a joy to visit. In less kind weather the rain-lashed slopes are better avoided. The battlefield lies astride the A697 just west of Wooler, which has more than enough in the way of food, drink and shops to keep the visitor supplied.

On leaving the small town of Wooler, you pass a narrow turning on the left signposted to Humbleton and, half a mile further on, a large lay-by on the left which offers convenient parking. Walk back along the main road to find the Battle Stone in a field to your left. If the field has standing crops, the five feet tall boulder may be difficult to spot and impossible to reach. This field is where the English line ended up after its slow retreat and is where most of the Scots met their deaths. The hill on the other side of the main road is the slope down which the Scots attacked. Unfortunately a modern line of trees about 100 yards up the slope cuts off the view to the original Scottish position.

To reach the Scottish position you need to return to the narrow lane signposted to Humbleton and go up it until it turns sharp left and an unmade bridleway goes straight on. If you walked from the Battle Stone, you will have completed a tough uphill walk of 500 yards and will appreciate the bench thoughtfully placed here by the Council. If you drove, this is where you park.

Walk on up the bridleway until you pass through a gate. Here a second bridleway turns right over a stile and out on to the open moorland. As ever in sheep country, be careful to shut gates behind you and if you have a dog, keep it on a tight lead. The bridleway runs along the shoulder of the hill. Soon a gulley or ravine opens up on the right. This is almost certainly where the Scots placed their baggage train as it is the only place on the hill which matches contemporary descriptions of the baggage train being hidden or concealed. The bridleway divides, so take the right hand fork to the end of the ravine where the path goes over a stile and emerges on what was the left centre of the original Scottish position. The line of trees is visible downhill, masking the Battle Stone and the final English position in the field beyond. The public bridleway continues across the moorland and eventually reaches Flodden, scene of another Scottish defeat some generations after Homildon Hill.

Chapter Twelve

FLODDEN 1513

Introduction

King James IV of Scotland is known to history for two things. The first is that he married Margaret, daughter of King Henry VII of England, ensuring that the English crown eventually passed to the Scottish kings. The second is that he led one of the greatest Scots army ever mustered to disaster on the field of Flodden.

The early success of Home and Huntly in sweeping away the English right wing encouraged King James to launch a frontal assault, leaving his own right wing exposed to a sweeping flank attack by the resourceful Lord Stanley.

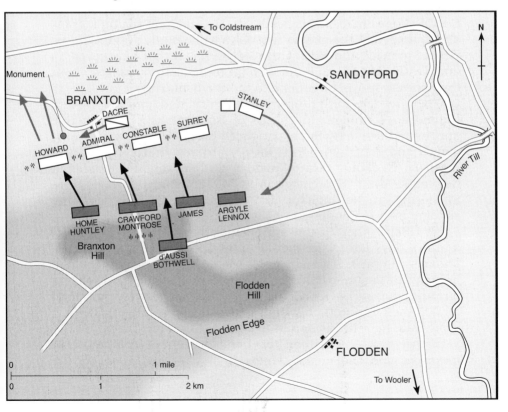

In 1513 Spain went to war with France. The King of Spain called on his young son in law, King Henry VIII of England, for support and Henry took an English army to France. The King of France in turn called on his ally, King James IV of Scotland. James declared that England would be 'guarded by millers and priests' and set about raising a mighty army to invade England and draw English troops and supplies away from France.

On 11 August James officially declared war and crossed the border at Coldstream. His army was drawn from many sources. The bulk of the men were Lowland Scots who spoke a dialect of English, but there were many thousands of Highlanders who spoke Gaelic and a sizeable contingent of French, few of whom spoke English. Language and discipline were potential problems and affected James's conduct of the campaign.

Having crossed the border, James was in no hurry to push south. This was not an invasion or a raid, but a deliberate attempt to drain English forces away from France. To achieve that, James needed to lure the English as far north as possible. He spent the next few weeks calmly capturing once impregnable border fortresses such as Etal Castle and Ford Castle, using his new cannon to smash the walls to rubble. Having captured Ford Castle, James made it his headquarters and kept the bulk of his army camped in the nearby meadows while raiding and scouting parties rode far and wide. Later legend has it that he enjoyed an affair with the Lady of Ford, who promptly sent messages about the Scottish King's intentions to the English army.

When he left for France, King Henry had put his Queen, Katherine of Aragon, in charge of England. Queen Katherine appointed the elderly but experienced Earl of Surrey to face King James and sent him north. Surrey ordered that every man in northern England, able to wield a weapon, should muster at Newcastle by 1 September. The Midlands, meanwhile, were mustering at Nottingham and the southern counties were sending men to London.

On 1 September, Surrey and his northern army left Newcastle and two days later were met at Alnwick by the Earl's son, Lord Thomas Howard. Thomas was Admiral of England. He had brought his fleet north and now led a force of sailors and soldiers on land, having stripped his ships of men. Surrey now had 26,000 men and, although he was unsure how large the Scots', army was, he sent his herald to James with a challenge.

In true chivalric fashion the heralds exchanged honourable messages and challenges. James at first refused to accept the challenge on the grounds that he was a king and Surrey was only an earl. After much toing and froing it was agreed that a battle would be fought on or before 9 September.

James, therefore, moved his army from the meadows around Ford Castle and drew them up on Flodden Edge, a steep hill commanding the surrounding countryside. He dug emplacements for his cannon and sat back to await the arrival of Surrey and the English army.

When Surrey arrived at Flodden, on 7 September, he took one look at the prepared Scottish positions and decided it would be suicide to attack. He sent his herald back to James complaining that the challenge had been to fight on level ground where both sides would have an equal chance. Whatever the spirit of the chivalric challenge, James knew the agreement said no such thing and replied that he would 'take and keep his ground at his own pleasure'.

Surrey called a council of war with his senior commanders, including his son, Admiral Howard. It was decided to try to get behind the Scots by marching in a sweeping curve to the north–east, thereby attacking from the rear and avoiding the entrenched artillery and other defences. At dawn on 8 September, the English army marched off.

From on top of Flodden Edge, James saw the English leave, but heavy rain stopped him from seeing where they were going. Rather than abandon his strong position and follow the English, James sent out a number of mounted scouts to find the enemy. Throughout the long day there was no definite news. But on the morning of 9 September Scottish scouts brought in news that the English army was crossing the River Till at Twizel Bridge north of Sandyford and was heading for the Scots rear.

The view from King James's position on top of Branxton Hill towards the English right wing. The Scottish Borderers charged down the slope from the left and won a sweeping victory over the English right wing, pushing them back in confusion over the undulating ground. It was this which prompted James to order a general advance.

James ordered his army to about face and march across the Flodden plateau to draw up on the crest of Branxton Hill. This hill was not as commanding as Flodden Edge, nor did the Scots have time to dig entrenchments, but it was still a formidable defensive position. A short distance to the north was a marshy stream called Pattins Burn. The English crossed the stream in two divisions, Admiral Howard's men to the west over a bridge and Surrey's men to the east across a ford. At the ford there was some confusion which resulted in Surrey's rearguard under Sir Edward Stanley being held up for almost an hour.

The rest of the English army advanced as planned and drew up for battle just south of the village of Branxton facing towards the Scots. The English drew up on a slight ridge with a mound known as Piper's Hill just behind their right wing. To their front the ground dipped before climbing up the steep slope to the Scottish position. It was mid-afternoon.

The Opposing Armies

King James had taken great care to call out almost the entire fighting force of Scotland before invading England. Some of these men were left to guard castles and towns, but the majority marched south. It is thought that something between 40,000 and 45,000 men crossed the border and that the vast majority of these were present at the battle.

The key fighting element of the Scots army were the 25,000 heavily armoured Lowlanders under the command of the Earls of Crawford, Montrose and Bothwell and of James himself. These men were much better equipped than had been earlier Scottish infantry. They wore plate armour and helmets hammered from steel and shaped into graceful curves and ridges. The armour was designed to deflect arrows, thus neutralizing the key advantage of the longbow which had won the English so many battles.

In the weeks leading up to the invasion these men had been put through a training programme by the French Count D'Aussi. The men had been re-equipped with Swiss-style pikes in place of their traditional spears. The pikes were over sixteen feet long and had stouter staffs than the shorter, traditional Scots spears. This made them clumsier to wield, but more effective if used correctly.

As well as the Lowlanders, James had with him some 7,000 Borderers and several thousand Highlanders. Both groups of men were equipped in traditional fashion and fought in their own way, not having been equipped with pikes. The Borderers had helmets and shields, and some had mail or light body armour. They fought with swords or axes and preferred to form in a line with interlocked shields. The Highlanders were more lightly equipped and only chiefs had armour of any kind. Equipped with daggers, axes and broadswords, the Highlanders were better at swooping charges and ambush than at fighting in fixed formations.

The English army was smaller than the Scots, having about 26,000 men, and only about half were professional troops. To make up numbers, Surrey had collected a quantity of garrison troops and older men who, although well trained, had not been considered good enough to go to France. He also had a collection of younger men who fancied a go at the Scots and who had been given rudimentary training at the mustering grounds and on the march.

As with the Scots, the key element of the army were heavily armoured infantry. The English, however, were not armed with long pikes but with bills. Being only nine feet long the bill had a much shorter reach than the pikes, which put the English at a disadvantage. But the bills had a chopping edge as well as a thrusting point and many had a vicious hook on the back as well, which made the bill a more flexible weapon in close quarter fighting. The English heavy infantry, like the Scots, carried swords and axes to use if their pole weapon broke. Some of the English lacked plate armour and fought in mail or leather jackets.

As well as their infantry, the English had a number of cavalry under the command of Lord Dacre. It is not clear how many mounted men were present, but there seem to have been less than 2,000. Most were armoured and fought with lance, backed up by sword or mace.

Both armies had artillery on the field of battle. These early cannon were heavy and cumbersome. Once they were in position at the start of a battle they tended to stay there all day. Compared with later guns, the cannon of the early sixteenth century were slow and inaccurate. Gunners thought they were doing well if they managed to get a shot fired every five minutes and hitting a building at anything over 600 yards was considered good shooting. As a result many historians tend to discount the impact of these cannon on the battlefield. This, however, is a mistake.

Cannon could throw solid balls of stone over 1,500 yards, much further than any other weapon. Even if the aim was highly

This English billman is typical of the men who fought at Flodden, and made up as much as forty per cent of most English forces at the period. He is dressed in a cheaper, bulk produced version of the plate armour that would have been custom made for the lords and knights of the period. He has an open-faced metal helmet which gives good vision and breathing, though at the loss of some protection. His breastplate is all of one piece and would have been matched by a solid backplate. The lower arms are protected by plate armour gauntlets, the upper arms by mail. The vulnerable lower body is covered by flexible strips of plate armour over mail. His primary weapon is the bill, a short, stout pole weapon with a thrusting point, a chopping blade and a spike for crushing armour. He carries a sword and a dagger for close quarter work or if his bill breaks.

erratic, this range was impressive and often caused consternation to men who thought they were safe. The noise of the guns could have a great effect on morale. Without motorized transport or amplified music, the fifteenth century was a very quiet place. The loudest noise the average person was likely to hear was somebody shouting or a tree falling, neither of which was any preparation for the ear-splitting roar of cannon.

Finally, there was the effect a cannon ball had on the human body. Soldiers were accustomed to the brutal effects of sword and axe on their colleagues. Men could be cut in half, disembowled or beheaded by swords and pikes, but a man hit by a cannonball would simply cease to exist. Arms, legs and bones were flung about as the body disintegrated in a fountain of blood and flesh. These early guns were terrifying.

Tactics

Both sides at Flodden were intending to use broadly similar tactics. The artillery would open fire first in an attempt to demoralize the enemy troops and to disrupt their formations. The heavy infantry would then be deployed to engage in hand-to-hand fighting with the opposing heavy infantry, and decide the battle. The light troops would be used to pursue a defeated enemy or cover the retreat if disaster threatened.

Moreover, both Surrey and James believed that their best chance of victory was to stay on the defensive. Surrey did not trust his hastily formed army to engage in any complicated manoeuvres, while James held a virtually impregnable position. Of the two, James had more faith in his army's offensive abilities because of the training received in Swiss tactics from D'Aussi.

The tactic D'Aussi taught the Scots was to form up in a dense column some twenty ranks deep and fifty men wide. The front five ranks held their spears horizontally forward and the rear ranks held their pikes angled up and forwards. The pikes of the rear ranks served to deflect arrows while those at the front did the killing. When this column was set forward at a brisk walk or trot it gained a formidable momentum. Few formations could stand against a charging pike column, so long as it kept its tight formation and did not slow down.

The English billmen, by contrast, were trained to form up in less dense formations some eight men deep. They fought standing still, hacking and thrusting at the enemy with their bills and moving forward only when a gap in the opposing line opened up. Being less massive, the English formation was more flexible in retreat or manoeuvre, but lacked the momentum of the Scottish columns.

It was with these tactics in mind that Surrey and James drew up their men. James put his heavy infantry in the centre in two divisions. The right hand division was under his own command and that on the left under Crawford and Montrose. A third division of heavy infantry was put under the command of Bothwell and placed in the rear as a reserve. This reserve included Frenchmen led by D'Aussi. On the left James placed the Borderers under Lord Home while the right wing was held by the Highlanders under Argyll and Lennox.

Surrey also put his best troops in the centre in three divisions. He, himself, led the left wing, Sir Marmaduke Constable held the centre and Admiral Howard commanded the right. Further to the right, holding the ground beyond Piper's Hill was another son, Edmund Howard, in command of 3,000 relatively untrained men from Cheshire. Edmund's task was not to take part in the main fighting, but to guard against a flank attack. In the rear was posted Dacre with his cavalry. Sir Edward Stanley with another 3,000 men was due to take up position on the left, but he had not arrived by the time the battle began in the late afternoon.

The Battle

As planned, the battle opened with an exchange of artillery fire. Both sides were hampered by the squalls of rain that lashed the ground and by having to take account of the steep slope when setting the trajectory of their shots. The English got the range first and their cannon balls slammed into the Scottish infantry

135

with bloody effect.

The Borderers on the Scottish left were unaccustomed either to artillery fire or to working as part of a large army. Disobeying orders to stand firm, Home led his men in a sweeping charge down the hill. The charging Scots crashed into the Cheshire men of Edmund Howard who, after a short fight, fled. Some of the Borderers raced on to pursue and cut down the fleeing English, others got down to the serious business of looting the dead and looking for rich wounded men to capture. Home tried to gather his men together to attack the now exposed flank of the English centre, but the Borderers were too busy to listen.

Up on the hill, King James saw the success of Home and assumed that the Borderers would shortly attack the flank of the English centre. Sensing victory, he ordered the Scottish heavy infantry to advance down the hill. Marching in their closely packed columns bristling with Swiss pikes, the men came down the slope, crossed the dip and climbed up to crash into the English line. The impact of the charge had all the momentum the French training had given them and the English centre gave way.

Meanwhile, on the Scottish left, Home was gathering his forces and getting them into formation. It was at this moment that Lord Dacre charged with his cavalry. The Borderers were scattered by the English attack. Dacre wisely did not pursue as his men were heavily outnumbered. Instead he drew back to Piper's Hill where he stood between the Borderers and the right flank of the main English army. Home gathered his men again, but dared not attack. The two forces eyed each other warily, but neither moved.

On the Scots right wing the Highlanders of Argyll and Lennox

The hill down which the Scottish pikemen advanced, seen from the centre of the English position.

had not moved. The Highland lords were watching a body of English troops advancing steadily towards the foot of Branxton Hill. These men were the delayed rearguard under Stanley. Carefully skirting the main battle raging in the centre, the English troops deployed for the attack. Argyll and Lennox decided to await the English on the hill crest.

It was now over an hour since the fighting had begun and the sun was nearing the horizon. The steady advance of the Scots centre had been halted in front of Branxton Church by the English, but the English line was dangerously thin. James judged it was time for his reserve. He sent back a runner to call forward the men of Bothwell and D'Aussi. From the hill top the reserve could see that their King's division was holding its own but that the left wing division under Montrose and Crawford was beginning to give way. They therefore marched down hill, veering to the left to support the weaker force.

As the last of the heavy infantry marched off the hilltop, the Highlanders got a nasty shock. The English troops advancing up towards them turned out to be a feint. Stanley had led the bulk of his men up a hidden ravine on the Scottish right. Emerging from this fold in the land, Stanley let loose a storm of arrows which inflicted heavy casualties on the startled and unarmoured Highlanders. A charge by Stanley completed the work and the Highlanders fled.

Stanley now found himself in command of the original Scottish position on the hilltop. Resisting the temptation to plunder the Scottish camp, Stanley reformed his men into line of battle and set off down the slope after the men of Bothwell.

From his position on Piper's Hill, Dacre saw Stanley's victory and his advance down the hill. Taking the risk that Home's Borderers would not attack, Dacre left only a token force to face them and led his main body in a charge which hit Bothwell's men in the flank just as Stanley attacked their rear. The fight was vicious, but brief. The Scots were slaughtered.

Elated by victory, Stanley and Dacre surged on to take the remaining Scots in the rear. James refused to surrender and chose to try to fight his way out of the closing English trap. James and his men thew aside their pikes, now useless in such close quarter combat, and reverted to their traditional swords and axes. The English were surprised by the sudden determination of the Scots and drew back, but by now they so outnumbered the King's division that the result was not in doubt. As the sun set on Flodden, King James died along with

The entrance to the narrow gully which was used by Stanley to hide his men as they marched around the Scottish right flank to launch the surprise attack which won the day for the English.

his leading nobles and their followers.

Aftermath

During the night the surviving Scots rallied under Lord Home who led an organized retreat to the Tweed. The English had not eaten since breakfast and were too exhausted to face another battle. They let the Scots go.

At dawn the English searched the field of the dead. They found the body of King James, embalmed it and sent it to London for burial. The bodies of twelve earls, thirteen barons, five heirs to titles, three bishops and two abbots were among the more than 10,000 Scottish slaughtered that lay on Flodden Field. Casualties had been highest among those who were near the King and there was not a family of wealth in Scotland that did not lose someone in the battle.

The English had suffered too, though not so badly, having lost about 4,000 men. Surrey sent news of his victory hurrying south with a messenger who carried with him James's bloodstained tunic. Queen Katherine hurriedly sent the dispatch and the tunic to Henry in France. When news of the battle reached them, the French offered terms which Henry, with autumn fast approaching, was only too happy to accept.

The town of Selkirk sent over a hundred men to join the invasion of England. Three days after Flodden a single man, badly wounded and mounted on an exhausted pony, rode into the town square. His name was Fletcher and he was the only survivor. He had, however, managed to capture an English banner during the successful Borderers' charge which he waved before collapsing on to the cobblestones. Each year the people of Selkirk hold a recreation of the return of Fletcher and sing a ballad entitled 'The Flowers of the Forest' which mourns the losses of Flodden.

> *We'll hear nae mair lilting at the ewe-milking*
> *Women and bairns are heartless and wae*
> *Sighing and moaning on ilka green loaning*
> *The Flowers of the Forest are all fade away.*

Visiting the Battlefield Today

The battlefield at Flodden is relatively large and spread out, but can be visited easily by car, or on foot by the more energetic. The original Scottish position can be viewed from the B6352 to the west of Flodden hamlet itself. The first lane running north from the B road runs through the centre of the Scots first position. It was from the line of the B6352, west of Flodden, that Surrey surveyed the Scots position and decided against attack.

The battlefield itself lies around the monument, signposted from the A697. Unfortunately, parking consists of no more than a grass verge in a narrow lane and the path to the monument is unsurfaced. Once at the monument, however, you receive a splendid view of the battlefield as it stands on Piper's Hill. If you face south towards Branxton Hill, the fields where the Borderer's swept away the English are to your right, and the line taken by Dacre's charge is behind you. In front of you is the slope down which Montrose led his men while to your left is the slope down which King James advanced. It is thought that the Scots pushed the English back from their original position to the field just south of the churchyard before being halted. It was here that King James died.

The impressive monument on Piper's Hill which is dedicated to the dead of both nations who fought at Flodden.

Return to your car and drive through Branxton Village to emerge on to the A697 and turn right. Shortly beyond the left turn to Crookham is a footpath to the right. This path follows, fairly closely, the route of the flank attack made by Stanley. If you follow the path you emerge on to the top of the hill beside a wooded ravine. Argyll and his Highlanders were drawn up just on the other side of the ravine, from which Stanley and his men emerged. Again there is little provision for parking, so it is best to find a lay-by nearby if you intend to

follow this footpath.

Several other sites linked to the battle are worth visiting. Ford Castle, where King James stayed before the battle, was modernized in the eighteenth century and is now used as a conference centre. Etal Castle stands in ruins, as does Norham Castle, but both are open to the public and much remains to look at. Twizel Bridge is today bypassed by the modern bridge on the A698 and a small car park on the east bank of the Till allows the visitor to walk over the old bridge or to pass through the metal gate at the back of the car park and walk up the narrow footpath to the ruins of Twizel Castle. Further afield, Selkirk has a statue of Fletcher, the sole survivor of the Selkirk men who marched to battle, and a museum preserves the flag he captured as well as the sword used at Flodden.

Unfortunately neither Flodden nor Branxton have anything much to offer the visitor in the way of food, drink or even a postcard. However, Coldstream is not too far to the north up the A697 and it boasts facilities in plenty.

The statue in Selkirk of Fletcher, the sole survivor of the men of that town who marched to disaster at Flodden.

Ford Castle, where King James whiled away the days waiting for the English army to arrive. The castle is now a conference centre and is not open to the general public.

Chapter Thirteen

SOLWAY MOSS 1542

Introduction

The fight on Solway Moss was really little more than a skirmish, but its consequences were immense. Some have argued that this little fight was more important in the long run than the great battle at Flodden.

The conflict grew out of the continental ambitions of England's King Henry VIII. Keen to play a part in European affairs, Henry did not want a hostile neighbour in his rear. He therefore set out to settle the outstanding differences between himself and his nephew Scotland's James V. Henry decided on a policy of bullying mixed with charm and tempting offers. He thus encouraged his northern barons to launch a series of raids over the border while at the same time sending James gifts and inviting him to a meeting in York in September 1541. Henry, of course, denied he had anything to do with the raids and claimed the meeting was a chance to sort out the mutual differences.

James agreed to travel to York, not least because he was in a difficult position at home and was desperate to stop the border raids. The Scottish nobles had never taken to King James V, still less to his domineering queen, and truculently refused to pay taxes or obey laws that they did not like. At the last moment James refused to go to York after being told by a Scottish bishop that Henry planned to kidnap him.

Henry was furious. He ordered the English ambassador to Scotland both to ask James awkward questions and to stir up the nobles as much as possible. He also told his own border nobles to increase their raids and in February gave secret instructions to the commanders of his border fortresses to help the raiders in any way possible.

Sir Thomas Wharton, Governor of Carlisle, responded by sending a galloper to Henry informing him that James was at Dumfries with only a small guard. Wharton asked permission to take his troops over the border to kill or kidnap James – rather ironic in light of James's concerns over the meeting at York. Henry asked his council of nobles for advice. They were shocked and advised the king to avoid a scheme which would not only inevitably lead to war but would also put England in a very bad light on the European diplomatic scene. Wharton, they said, should concentrate on Carlisle, not Dumfries.

In August 1542 a force of English raiders pillaged deep into Teviotdale and acquired a large quantity of plunder. On the way back the English were ambushed by the Earl of Huntly at Haddon Rig. The English fled, but the less nimble horsemen among them were captured and one of these was Robert Bowes, Governor of Berwick. No longer could Henry claim the border raids were nothing to do with him. In October another English raid burnt Kelso and Roxburgh, this time the regular English army was involved.

By the start of November James had managed to calm his nobles to the extent that he could raise an army of 18,000 men and march south towards England. He declared that he was to invade down the east coast past Berwick, but then set out on a forced march to the west coast to take the English by surprise.

Unfortunately, James fell sick on the march and took to his bed at Lochmaben. He handed command of the expedition over to Lord Maxwell, Warden of the Western Marches, but kept half the army at Lochmaben to guard against any kidnap plots by the English. Maxwell marched into England, but as soon as he was

The view that Sir Thomas Wharton, the English commander, had from his position on the wooded ridge across the Solway Moss towards the route being followed by the Scottish army.

over the border Lord Oliver Sinclair announced that the Warden's jurisdiction did not extend beyond Scotland and that he, Sinclair, was now the army's commander.

The Scottish army came to a halt while the nobles tried to sort out who was in command. Sinclair was the King's favourite courtier, so some nobles sided with him in the hope of gaining royal favour. Others recognized that Maxwell was the better soldier and backed him as they wanted an experienced commander when invading England.

At this point a force of English horsemen appeared on the scene commanded by none other than Wharton, Governor of Carlisle. Wharton's plan was to shadow the Scots army, taking every opportunity to ambush patrols or steal supplies. Meanwhile he gave orders for the northern garrisons and nobles to muster their forces at Carlisle ready for a battle. By 24 November he had followed the Scots to Solway Moss.

The Opposing Armies

The Scottish army on Solway Moss was about 9,000 strong. Although most, possibly all, of these men were mounted on the march, they would have fought on foot. After the disaster at Flodden, the Scots had abandoned the long pike and gone back to their traditional spears, swords and axes. They were, however beginning to field an exciting new weapon – the musket. In 1540 these were big heavy weapons which took over a minute to reload and were accurate to little over fifty yards. It is not clear how many Scots were carrying firearms, but they were in a minority and were interspersed among other troops rather than formed as units of their own.

The English fielded about 700 cavalry men. Very few, if any, of these men would have had pistols and most relied on lances or swords for weaponry. Some of the wealthier men wore plate armour, but most were light cavalry equipped with helmet and leather jerkin.

The Battle

On the morning of 24 November the Scottish army was straggling across the bleak Solway Moss. Seeing the chance for a hit and run attack, Wharton led his men in a fierce charge. Maxwell gave orders for the Scots to take up a defensive formation. Sinclair countermanded the orders. The Scots milled about in confusion, many of them simply sat down and refused

The wooded ridge on which the English cavalry appeared at the start of the battle. It was the arrival of the English which caused the final breakdown of discipline in the Scottish army.

to move. The nobles shouted insults at each other, blaming the incompetence of Sinclair or the treachery of Maxwell. Officers ran to join the argument, leaving their men leaderless.

Wharton wheeled his highly disciplined men back and reformed them. Seeing the utter confusion among the Scots, he decided to launch a real charge. As the English horsemen thundered forwards in well-ordered ranks, the Scottish army simply disintegrated.

The astonished English could not believe their luck and plunged into the running mob that the Scottish army had become. About a hundred Scots were killed and over a thousand captured. Wharton had to call off the pursuit simply because he could not guard the men he had captured. The English had lost just seven men.

Aftermath

The fleeing Scots carried the news of their defeat to the sickly James at Lochmaben. The King seemed more concerned about his favourite than his army. James eagerly asked the fugitives 'Is Oliver fled? Is Oliver taken?' In fact the favourite had escaped, but took some days to reappear.

A few days later more messengers arrived to give James the happy news that his Queen had been delivered of a healthy first child, a daughter. This news gave James fresh cause for depression. Referring to the fact that the Stewart family had inherited the Scottish crown through a woman James remarked 'It came with a lass; it will pass with a lass'.

Then he turned his back on the messengers and on the nobles who had gathered to congratulate him and stared at the wall. Two weeks later he was dead.

The King's death, almost certainly brought on by depression at the news of Solway Moss, meant Scotland had a Queen who was just two weeks old. This young monarch was to become famous as Mary, Queen of Scots. Her minority led to civil strife within Scotland and fresh war with England. Once adult, the Queen followed a path of folly and glory that led to fresh misfortunes for Scotland.

If any skirmish can be said to have decided the fate of a kingdom for decades to come, it was that fought on Solway Moss.

Visiting the Battlefield Today

The battlefield of Solway Moss has not changed much since 1542 and has the advantage to the visitor of being crossed by roads and a footpath. From Longtown, take the A7 south, but turn right beside the war memorial just before the road leaves the town. Follow a narrow lane to a large church on the righthand side of the road and park in the lay-by on the left. A notice board in the lay-by gives information on the battlefield and other local sites of interest. From here you get a good view over the battlefield to the east. The Scots were advancing south along what is now the A7 when they were attacked by the English cavalry who emerged from the wooded hill to your right. Walk through the churchyard to find a public footpath leading across the route taken by the fleeing Scots to the River Esk. If you walk back along the lane towards Longtown for about 200 yards you will find a footpath heading east. This path runs right across the centre of the battlefield, emerging on the A7 and then continuing on beyond the scene of the fighting towards the A6071. You should return to the town of Longtown if you feel in need of anything to eat or drink.

Chapter Fourteen

ANCRUM MOOR 1545

Introduction

Scottish politics during the childhood of Mary Queen of Scots were notoriously complicated and treacherous. Archibald Douglas, Earl of Angus, played a murky and devious part in those years, but on one glorious day in 1545 he vindicated himself and his family with a military masterstroke which made him the talk of Europe.

The Earl of Angus counted himself one of the premier nobles of Scotland. His title, its wealth and lands dated back to before written history as one of the leading chieftainships of the ancient Picts. If the title had descended through women and illegitimate sons, this did nothing to diminish the wealth and power of Angus.

Angus fought and intrigued, both for and against the Regent, the Earl of Arran, spending some time in exile in France and then in England. In 1542 Angus returned to Scotland to support the plans of England's King Henry VIII that his sickly son Edward should marry the young Mary, Queen of Scots. When the

The pretended panic among the Scottish baggage and its guard lured the English army over the crest of the hill into a carefully prepared Scottish ambush.

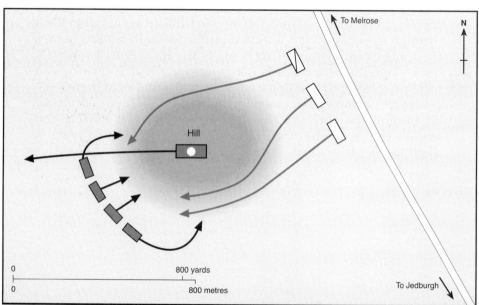

The ruins of Melrose Abbey, ancestral burial place of the Earls of Angus. It was the destruction of the Abbey and the desecration of his family tombs at the hands of the English that prompted the Earl of Angus to lead an army to seek revenge on Ancrum Moor.

Scottish Parliament turned the idea down, Henry sent his army on a series of cross border raids which were intended to bully the Scots into agreeing. It was a time known as the 'Rough Wooing'. Angus intrigued with the various factions at the Scottish court and with English spies. At first Angus was in favour of the English marriage, then slowly turned against it.

The final straw came in January 1545 when a column of English raiders sent from their base at Coldingham Priory struck Melrose. Not content with pillaging the town and abbey, the raiders deliberately smashed the ancient tombs and monuments of the Angus family. The Earl was in Edinburgh when he heard the news and he was furious. He rounded up 300 of his supporters and rode out of the city vowing to take bloody revenge on the English.

Angus may have been a devious courtier, but nobody doubted his skills at war. News that he was marching against the English spread quickly and men flocked to his banner. By the time Angus reached the smoking ruins of Melrose he had well over a thousand men. The survivors of the sacking of Melrose told Angus that the English army, over 5,000 strong, had left marching south-east. Undismayed by the fact he was outnumbered five to one, Angus followed. At Broomhill the Scots heard that the English had burned a towerhouse complete with all its inhabitants, including an old lady who screamed from the roof as she was consumed by the flames. Angus also learned the English force was led by Sir Ralph Eyre, a man known for his cruelty, and that it included a number of German mercenaries.

On 11 February a group of English scouts came across the small Scots force, and rode off before they could be intercepted. Later that day Sir Norman Lesley of Rothes arrived to join Angus, bringing with him some 1,200 men. As a result Angus had about twice as many men as the English thought he did. On the afternoon of 12 February scouts reported to Angus that the English were camped on Ancrum Moor. Angus led his small force up on to nearby Palace Hill from where he could look down on the enemy camp and where he could be seen. The battle he wanted was about to begin.

The Opposing Armies

The Scottish force at Ancrum Moor was a mixed one and details are sketchy. Lesley's men were drawn from his and neighbouring estates far to the north in Aberdeenshire. Many of his men were cavalry and the remainder infantrymen, armed with spears and pikes. The cavalry seem to have been equipped with a form of half-armour, lightweight plate or scale covering their bodies and arms, but the legs left free. This gave some protection against arrows and swords, but was light enough to allow for fast manoeuvre.

The men already with Angus came from different sources, but were mostly infantry. They were equipped with spears and pikes, some up to eighteen feet long, as well as with swords and axes. Most of the Scots infantry wore helmets and many had breastplates, but few had any other armour, as extensive armour was rapidly falling out of favour. The English no longer fielded large numbers of archers, partly because few men were willing to undergo the long years of training and partly because the new firearms were replacing the longbows. These firearms were cumbersome and slow, but their use could be learned by recruits in a short space of time and the bullets smashed through light armour.

More is known about the English army. Eyre had with him 1,500 English Borderers mounted on quick, sure-footed ponies and equipped with lances and swords. The main bulk of his army was made up of 3,000 mercenaries lent to King Henry by the Holy Roman Emperor Charles V, who wanted Henry's help against France. The remainder of Eyre's force was made up of some 700 renegade Scots borderers, equipped much like their English counterparts.

Tactics

The Scottish army was made up of various small contingents which had come together only in the previous day or two. The

Earl of Angus had had no time to train his men in any complex plans, and did not even know how well many of them would fight. He therefore decided to rely on traditional, even old-fashioned, tactics that he was confident his men would know and understand.

Angus placed his infantry in deep formations with spears and pikes bristling forward to form an impenetrable hedge of points to hold off horsemen. The same formation could be used to push forward against infantry, rolling over less disciplined troops. Those men with guns were spread along the line to pick off the enemy. The cavalry were to be kept in the rear with orders to pursue the enemy if the infantry won the main battle, or to cover a withdrawal if they lost.

In contrast, Eyre was preparing to use the most modern weapons and tactics of the day. For this he relied on his mercenaries. Many of these men were the dreaded *landsknechte* who dominated the battlefields of central Europe at the time. A full unit of *landsknechte* was about 1,000 men strong and composed of some 300 men armed with heavy muskets, 200 armed with powerful two handed swords or bills and 500 men with short swords and shields. It is not clear how complete were the *landsknechte* units at Ancrum Moor, nor how many of the mercenaries were less disciplined troops.

In battle the front rank was made up of the men with long swords and bills. Their task was to hold off an enemy formation with long thrusts and slashes. The rear rank was composed of the men with guns, shooting past their comrades to kill and injure the enemy. Between the two were huddled the men with short swords. They waited until the guns had disabled enough of the enemy, when they would surge forwards past their own front rank to tear the enemy formation apart. It was a tactic which had proved devastating in Europe against militia and seasoned professionals alike.

Like Angus, Eyre intended to hold back his cavalry for the later stages of the battle. Confident that the mercenaries would swiftly deal with what he saw as a rabble, Eyre gave his borderer cavalry orders to hover on the rear of the flanks and wait the chance to join the pursuit.

The Battle

When the Earl of Angus appeared over the skyline on Palace Hill, Eyre sent out his scouts, then called a hurried conference with his officers. The Scots made a tempting target and Eyre was keen to attack, but his men were tired after a full day of marching and plundering. The scouts reported that only some 500 Scots were on the hilltop. This was even fewer than Eyre's scouts had reported the previous day. Perhaps some of the Scots had deserted overnight. While the officers considered what to do, they saw the Scots begin to move off towards the rear. Convinced the Scots army was breaking up, Eyre gave the order to attack.

The *landsknechte* formed up in their attack lines and marched forward. Dressed in multi-coloured tunics and hose, topped by extravagantly plumed hats, the Germans were a bizarre and daunting sight. Steadily the mercenaries tramped up the hill, the Borderers riding to their sides and rear. The Germans stopped just out of range of the waiting Scots and indulged in their traditional pre-battle ceremonies. The men knelt down and recited their prayers. Then, at a given signal, they suddenly leapt to their feet screaming savage defiance at the enemy and brandishing their weapons. The Scots promptly fled back over the crest of the hill.

The mercenaries surged after them, up and over the crest running at full speed. Not wanting to be left out of the killing and plundering, the Borderers put spurs to their horses and followed at the gallop. As they topped the crest, the pursuing army found themselves hit by the full glare of the setting sun. And instead of the fleeing 500 Scots they expected, Eyre and his men found over 2,000 Scots drawn up in strong battle formation and bristling with weapons.

The cavalry hit the Scots first. Horses and men were impaled on the Scottish pikes and spears, the men cut down by swords and axes. The remaining horsemen, wheeled off and fled. Meanwhile, the *landsknechte* had lost all formation in the chase. Instead of ordered ranks of swordsmen and gunmen, they were a confused mass of individuals. Angus gave the order to his men with guns to fire. The gunfire cut down many Germans, and the belching smoke, tinged red by the setting sun, blinded those that

The view the English army had towards Palace Hill where a small force of Scots appeared as dusk drew in on 12 February 1545.

The rear slopes of Palace Hill where the main Scottish forces waited to ambush the advancing English army. The structure on the hill crest is a modern mausoleum.

still stood. Then the disciplined ranks of Scots infantry moved forward at a steady march. The German mercenaries were pushed back, many being cut down and the rest pulling back in total disorder.

Eyre tried to rally his men on the crest of the hill, but without effect. He tried again half way back down the slope, but was killed. At this point those renegade Scots on the English side promptly changed sides. Throwing aside their English badges, they cheerfully joined the charge of Angus's cavalry in cutting down the fleeing mercenaries and Borderers. The local villagers now joined in the attack and the English army collapsed into a fleeing mob scampering across the moor in search of safety. Darkness came quickly, mercifully halting the killing.

In all about 800 men from the English army had been killed. Next day over a thousand lost and bewildered mercenaries wisely concluded that the war between England and Scotland was not their battle and surrendered. Scottish losses were small, barely a hundred having been killed.

Aftermath

The death of Eyre and the destruction of his army spelt the end of English raiding over the border. For a while some raiding parties tried to cross into Scotland, but all were beaten back with ease. It had been made clear to Henry that his 'rough wooing' had failed. If the Scots were disunited over the future of their kingdom, they were at least united in wanting it to remain a kingdom, not become a province of England.

Henry pulled back from Scotland to consider his next move. He decided on a new strategy of invasion and occupation, but never had the chance to carry it out. In January 1547 Henry VIII died and left his kingdom and his invasion plans to his son, the new King Edward VI. But Edward was only nine years old.

Visiting the Battlefield Today

The battlefield of Ancrum Moor is easy to find for it lies astride the A68 just north of the village of Ancrum. Visiting the battlefield is another matter entirely for no public footpaths are in the area and some forthright signs make it clear the landowner does not welcome visitors. However, a good idea of the ground can be had by viewing from the public highway.

Driving north from Ancrum, park in the lay-by on the right immediately past Lilliardsedge Caravan Park. From here you can look north towards the position of the English army when they first spotted the Scots. The English were on the crest of the hill, near to the edge of the woodland. If you have a good pair of binoculars you should be able to see the pale bulk of Lilliard's Stone on the edge of the wood. This is said to mark the spot where one Scot gained a very personal revenge. In the course of the earlier pillaging one English Borderer had killed a young Scotsman at Lilliard. The young man's girlfriend had seen the murder and had been craftily tracking the English army ever since, waiting for a chance to get at the murderer. In the pursuit that followed the fighting, the girl snatched up a sword from the field and chased after her lover's killer. The stone was set up to mark the spot where she killed the man. Or so it is said.

The A68 is a busy main road with speeding traffic and heavy trucks thundering along it. Sadly it has no paths alongside it, so walking along this road is not recommended. Better to drive further north until you pass over the crest of the ridge and glance to your left. A large mausoleum about 400 yards away marks the position of the Scots when the English first saw them.

To view the area of the main fighting, turn around and drive back south along the A68 past the caravan park. Take the first lane to the right, signposted to Longnewton. After about half a mile the mausoleum will come into view again, this time to the right of the road. From this vantage point it is easy to see the steep slope into which the English stumbled and where the main Scots army was hidden in ambush.

Chapter Fifteen

PINKIE 1547

Introduction

The defeat of the English at Ancrum Moor forced King Henry VIII to adopt a new strategy for dealing with the Scots. Instead of launching border raids and trying to pressure the Scots into marrying their child queen, Mary, Queen of Scots, to an English prince, Henry decided on a purely military option.

A reorganization of the English army was mistaken for confusion by the Scots, who crossed the river to meet disaster.

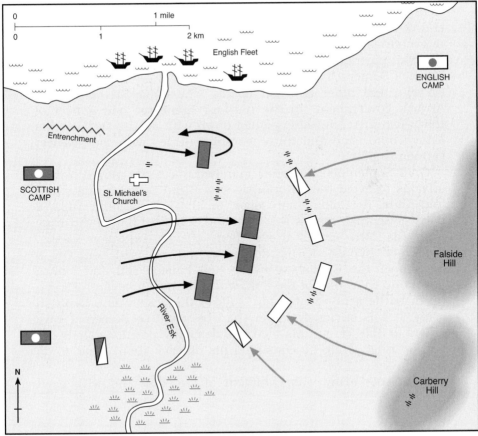

The new war plan envisaged a large English army marching into Scotland to capture key towns, cities and fortresses. These were to be garrisoned with strong bodies of English troops and supplied from the sea by the newly powerful English Royal Navy. There would be no attempt to rule Scotland or to occupy its more rugged areas. Instead, the English-held strongpoints would disrupt attempts to muster an army while English money would be used to bribe the various factions of nobles into continuing their disputes.

In this way Henry hoped to keep Scotland in turmoil and unable to invade England. Henry died in January 1547 and left the plan to his nine year old son, the boy-king Edward VI.

As Edward was unable to rule the kingdom, Henry had put a Regency Council in control, led by the Duke of Somerset. Somerset was King Edward's uncle, being his mother's brother. He also had plans to usurp the powers of the Council and become sole Protector of England. To do this he needed prestige, and he looked for a military victory in Scotland to give it to him.

Declaring he was merely carrying out the dying wishes of Henry VIII, Somerset called a muster of English soldiers for the end of August in Berwick. Then he hired a force of European mercenaries, who could be relied upon to be loyal to himself as the man paying them, and marched north to take command. At Berwick Somerset met up with the Earl of Bothwell, the Earl of Cassilis and other Scottish nobles who opposed the Earl of Arran's government. In the harbour Somerset had a fleet of thirty-two merchant ships laded down with all the supplies his army would need and thirty warships armed with the heaviest cannon available.

On 1 September, Somerset marched north. He moved slowly, anxious to avoid the notoriously successful Scottish ambushes and raids. At Coldingham Moor, on the Lammermuir Hills, a party of Scottish scouts was seen and Somerset halted the army until his own scouts drove them off. At Tantallon Castle, Somerset bypassed the defences and pressed on. On 8 September the English army crested Falside Hill and looked down into the valley of the Esk, with Edinburgh beyond. Drawn up in battle array on the far bank of the river was a Scottish army. It was obviously larger than his own, so Somerset gave orders to halt. He put his men into defensive positions along the Falside ridge while he consulted his officers about what to do next.

The Scots army was confident of success, and with good

reason for, despite their internal differences, Scotland had rallied to face the invader. The Regent, the Earl of Arran, had persuaded the majority of the nobles to bring their men to the mustering in front of Edinburgh. The Earl of Huntly had brought the Highlanders, Lord Home had brought the Borderer light cavalry and the Earl of Angus, victor of Ancrum Moor, had come with all his men.

The Opposing Armies

The Scottish army under the Earl of Arran was a large one, probably about 28,000, though exact numbers are not recorded. The main bulk of his army, some 20,000 strong were the armoured levies from the Lowlands. There were around 3,000 Highlanders and another body of 2,000 Borderer cavalry and a few hundred more heavily armed cavalry. Arran also had some artillery.

The Lowland infantry were the main force in the Scottish army. The way in which these men were raised and trained had not changed much since the reforms of Robert Bruce two centuries earlier. Every man aged sixteen to sixty was expected to own weapons of war, graded according to his wealth, and to be ready to fight for the kingdom at a moment's notice. Over the years the actual weapons had changed somewhat, but the basic concept of a nation in arms, with men serving alongside others from their own villages and towns was unaltered.

The men that marched to Pinkie were those whose lords had passed on the muster order and who had had time to reach the banks of the Esk. They came largely from the eastern Lowlands. They came equipped with shield, helmet and mail jacket, the richer men having plate armour of various types. Most carried a long spear or pike, between twelve and eighteen feet long, and had a sword or axe as a back up. Some came equipped with bows of various types. The equipment was generally of a good quality, but the very mixture of weapons made the armoured infantry difficult to handle at the tactical level.

The Lowland infantry also came equipped with hand guns – generally a form of matchlock musket or arquebus. Only the richer men, or the vassals of wealthy nobles, could afford these weapons and it is estimated that some 1,000 of them were at Pinkie. The hand guns were slower to fire than a bow and had a shorter range, but the bullets could punch through armour and had the weight to stop a man even if he was only lightly wounded.

The Highlanders wore much less armour and many fought with only a shield as a defence. They had axes, swords and a few came with bows, but pikes were not part of a Highlander's equipment. The borderers were also lightly equipped having little armour and carrying swords and short lances. They rode nimble ponies able to scamper over the border hills and bogs with ease. The few heavier cavalry Arran had, came from the Lowlands. They wore plate armour over their bodies and arms, but it was lighter than in previous centuries to allow for more speed on the battlefield.

The Scots artillery was heavier and better served than it had been at Flodden. Arran had about forty cannon of various shapes and sizes with him. These were, by now, all mounted on the familiar carriage with two large wheels and a wooden tail that remained the norm until the later nineteenth century. These guns could be moved more easily around a battlefield than could the earlier bombards, but they were still pulled by oxen and the gunners walked on foot, so a speed of two miles an hour would have been good going.

The guns that Somerset had with him were of a broadly similar type to those of the Scots, but with two clear advantages. First he had twice as many of them and second the English gunners were more adept at moving their pieces about by manhandling them or hitching them to horses.

Most of the English army, like that of the Scots, was armoured infantry. Some 10,000 men came equipped with helmets, armour, bills or bows much as had the men who fought at Flodden – in many cases using their father's equipment. Only about 400 of these men had matchlocks or arquebus. Like the Scots, Somerset had about 2,000 Borderer light cavalry, but he also had some 2,000 armoured cavalry, all led by Lord Grey. About 500 of these men were drawn from the notoriously tough garrison of Bolougne which, like Calais, was an English city on the coast of France.

Among this fairly traditional English army Somerset's mercenaries stood out clearly. The more colourful were the German infantry, clothed in multi-coloured jackets and hose. Somerset had hired over 2,000 of these men, most of whom were at Pinkie. There was also a force of some 300 mercenary cavalry from Spain led by Pedro da Gamboa. They wore light plate armour and carried pistols or short-barrelled arquebus. Somerset had also hired the famous Italian mercenary chief, Malatesta. No longer a young man, Malatesta did not bring many troops with him, but his advice was invaluable.

Tactics

The general tactics of the two armies were similar to those of previous battles. Crucially neither Arran nor Somerset really appreciated the firepower of their artillery, though Malatesta tried to impress this on Somerset. Not until the battle was well under way did the destructive power of field artillery become evident.

The Scots relied upon their spears and pikes to hold off English cavalry attacks, and formed up in dense columns to surge forward with massive momentum and simply roll over opposition. Archers and gunmen were spread among the infantry to shoot down the enemy as opportunities arose. The Highlanders had no pikes and so had no place in the main body of infantry. Arran believed they were useful for ambushes and raids, but had little faith in the chieftains promises of sudden, devastating charges on the field of battle. He viewed them as second rate troops to be used in unimportant areas.

The heavy cavalry could most effectively be used in a charge to break up enemy formations, but Arran had so few that they could not realistically be directed to this purpose. He placed these men to his left rear where they could be activated if any opening presented itself. The light Borderer cavalry were more numerous but again were not thought of as crucial to the main battle. Their role was to pursue a beaten enemy or to cover the withdrawal if the Scots were being defeated.

With these considerations in mind, Arran drew up his army. His task was to block the English advance on Edinburgh and so he was planning a defensive battle. Arran drew his army up on the hills to the west of the River Esk. The centre was held by the armoured infantry with the majority under his own command, but with flanking columns under the Earl of Argyll on the left and the Earl of Angus on the right. The Scottish left flank rested on the coast. Here Arran placed the Earl of Huntly and the Highlanders. They were to guard against any landing by English sailors or marines. Not wanting to be exposed to gunfire from the ships, Huntly ordered his men to dig entrenchments. The right wing was more exposed to attack by ground troops and it was here that Arran put his light cavalry. They would be able to ride quickly to halt any English attempt to outflank the Scots and delay the attackers long enough for the infantry to redeploy.

Like the Scots, the English had not greatly changed their

tactics in the years since Flodden. The armoured infantry were again seen as the key to the battle, with the cavalry reduced to a pursuit role. The English infantry, however, were trained to stand in small formations which could be moved more nimbly than the Scottish columns, but lacked the Scots momentum and impact power.

The mercenaries, however, had quite different tactics. The German infantry were experts at the combined use of firearms and cold steel and had won famous victories in Europe. They put men with long swords or pole weapons in the front rank to hold the enemy troops at a distance, while the arquebusiers behind mowed them down with gunfire. When the enemy formation was disrupted, the infantry would storm forward to destroy them and put them to flight.

The Spanish cavalry were trained in an even newer and more deadly tactic known as the *caracole*. This involved the cavalry forming into a column a dozen men deep. Having ridden at speed to where they were needed, the column trotted up to the enemy troops. The front rank fired their guns, then wheeled aside and trotted back to the rear of the column. Meanwhile the new front rank trotted forwards to fire, before wheeling aside. By the time the original front rank had worked its way up to the front again they had had time to reload and were ready to fire. In this way a continuous rolling fire was kept up, while the smoke, dust and speed of the cavalry made return shots inaccurate. The impact of the *caracole* was great and the swiftness of the cavalry meant it could be moved about the battlefield at high speed. If Somerset was unaccustomed to the potential of these men, Malatesta was not.

Arriving on Falside Hill on 8 November, Somerset was faced by the strong, almost impregnable position of Angus. The following day, Somerset sent mounted scouts out to his left and fast ships went up the coast to view the Scots flank and rear. He could find no way forward. The English army was drawn up on the ridge of Falside Hill, and Carberry Hill to the south, more or less as it had arrived. With no battle plan in mind, Somerset had no reason to deploy his men in any particular way.

The Battle

Soon after noon on 9 September, Lord Home grew tired of waiting. He asked Arran for permission to take his Borderer cavalry across the Esk. He planned to launch a series of hit and run attacks to goad the English into advancing against the

The beautiful parkland which runs alongside the River Esk in the area where the Scots waded across the shallow river to attack the English.

impregnable Scots position. At first Arran refused, preferring to sit safely behind the river. As the hours ticked past and neither army moved, however, Arran himself grew impatient. He gave Home permission to cross the river.

The Borderers splashed over the river and formed up on the level land beneath Falside Hill. For a while they galloped about, shouting insults at the English. The English artillery fired a few shots, but otherwise there was no response. The Scots came nearer to the English line, which was exactly what Lord Grey had wanted. He sent his own Borderers galloping at speed around the rear of Home's men while leading his heavy cavalry in a crushing charge into the Scots front. Hundreds of Scots were killed or wounded, including Home himself, and many others were captured. The few Scots cavalry who got back across the river were badly shaken and leaderless. Some slipped away to return home. The furious Arran moved his heavy cavalry to the right to guard the flank exposed by the Borderers' defeat.

It was at this point, late on the 9th, that an idea was put to Somerset, probably by Malatesta and the English gunners. The gunners had noticed that there was a small hill just on the English side of the river, topped by St Michael's Church. This hill stood in a bend of the river and would give the English artillery

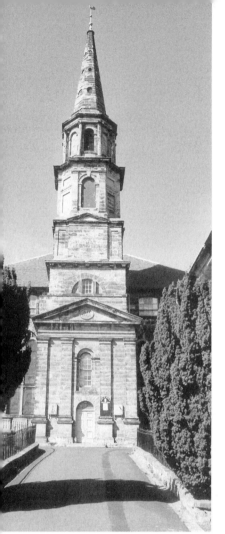

The Church of St Michael at Inveresk, where the English were digging artillery emplacements when the Scots attacked. The spire was added to the church some years after the battle.

just the elevation they needed to enfilade the left wing of the Scots position. To reach it the English artillery would have to cross the stretch of open ground between Falside Hill and the church. With Home's Borderers waiting to charge this would have been impossible, but now it was feasible.

Somerset spent most of the evening thinking about the plan. He did not particularly like it as he did not trust the guns to do great damage to the Scots. There would still be the need for a hazardous infantry attack over the river and up the hill. It was, however, the only plan Somerset had and since his ambition to be Protector of England depended on victory, he decided to follow it.

At dawn on 10 September, Somerset gave his orders. Engineers swarmed forward to build gun emplacements around the church, while the artillery was made ready to follow. Meanwhile, the mass of the infantry were to move to the right and form up for an advance. The infantry moved first, the guns still loading their ammunition as the men marched off to the right.

Arran, of course, saw these movements. It is unclear whether he correctly guessed the English plan. He may, just as plausibly, have thought the English were moving to a better defensive position on their right where they would be close to the English fleet if anything went wrong. What was definitely the case was that the English infantry were strung out on the march along the slopes of Falside Hill and were becoming separated from the artillery and cavalry.

Arran saw his chance to attack, ordering his men over the Esk. The lightly armed Highlanders moved first, pulling out of their

The view from the English left flank on Falside Hill towards the Esk. The level land in the foreground is the area where the fiercest fighting took place. The hill in the distance is Arthur's Seat in Edinburgh.

entrenchments and flowing down the hillside to the bridge that crossed the Esk near the sea. Here they came under heavy cannon fire from the English fleet. Casualties mounted alarmingly. The Highlanders recrossed the Esk to gain the shelter of the entrenchments.

The armoured infantry, meanwhile, had got moving and were over the river. As they marched forwards the English fleet, no longer having the Highlanders as a target, began firing long shots at the Lowlanders. The fire was ineffective, but it did cause Argyll's column to move to the right and merge with that of Arran. The Scots, left and centre, had become one massive column of armoured infantry moving forwards at a brisk pace.

Somerset, seeing the unexpected Scottish advance, was worried. He immediately sent orders that his infantry was to abandon their attack column and redeploy in a defensive line. The artillery, having just finished attaching their guns to horses and loading their ammunition, now had to unload the ammunition and get their guns back into firing position. All this would take time, and the Scots were advancing rapidly. If the Scots reached Somerset's men before the English had time to reform, Arran would have a spectacular victory.

At this point the laird of Falside Castle threw off his pretence at friendship to the English and opened fire on Somerset's rear.

It was a decision he would soon regret.

Somerset decided it was time for the cavalry. He sent his heavy horses forward to charge the Scottish heavy infantry. They did not stand a chance of success, but that was not their job. The cavalry were being sent forward to slow down the Scots and give Somerset's infantry and artillery time to deploy. The cavalry charged, came to a crashing halt against the pikes, turned and charged again. It was bloody work; the Scots were forced to halt each time the cavalry charged home, then were able to march forwards again as the English pulled back. The Spanish mercenaries did magnificent work, their *caracole* of rolling fire tearing into the Scots to their front. Angus, worried by the Spanish, brought his right flank division to an effective halt.

Still the majority of the Scots formation marched forwards. They caught Sir Andrew Flammack who was bearing the Royal Standard of the cavalry. In a desperate struggle, the Scots got hold of the flagpole, but Flammack tore the flag itself free and rode off. Lord Grey, commander of the English cavalry received a pike thrust to the face. The weapon entered his right cheek and exited his left cheek, missing the jaw and skull completely. Drenched with blood, Grey rode back to the English lines, hastily drank a quart of ale, washing the blood away, and turned back to lead another charge.

He did not need to do so. With the Scots barely a hundred yards away, the English infantry were formed up and the artillery was ready to open fire. With a thunderous crash the English artillery fired at point blank range. The shot tore massive holes in the packed Scottish ranks. Simultaneously, da Gamboa led his cavalry in a swooping movement on the Scots, firing their guns into the packed ranks, then wheeling, reloading and firing again. The Scottish columns came to a halt. The cannons continued to fire, joined now by those infantry with bows or with guns.

The Scots broke and the infantry began falling back. As the English cavalry advanced they found some of their comrades who had been wounded in the fighting lying with their throats cut by Scottish daggers. Declaring that no surrender would be taken, the English pushed forward in vengeful mood. Scots were cut down, the wounded butchered and those who tried to surrender mercilessly killed. The gunners, delighted to be able to prove their weapons to the sceptical Somerset, continued pouring a storm of iron into the fleeing Scots.

On the Scottish right wing, Angus saw the collapse of the

centre and left. He carefully kept his men in order, pulling back step by step and fending off English attacks until he got over the Esk. There his formation served as a bulwark around which the Scottish survivors could reform. Seeing the battle won and anxious not to risk lives by letting his men pursue so far they might fall into a Scots ambush, Somerset called his men back to their ranks. He then turned on Falside Castle, but the laird and his men had fled, so the English satisfied themselves with looting the mansion.

The English did not bother to count the Scottish dead, only their own. Some 600 Englishmen were killed at Pinkie and the Scottish losses are estimated at between 7,000 and 11,000, though nobody knows for certain.

Aftermath

If Somerset hoped that the victory at Pinkie would lead to English domination of Scotland he was sadly mistaken. According to the plan drawn up by Henry VIII, Somerset planted garrisons in the strategic towns and fortresses of Scotland, but they were not to stay there long.

In July 1548 Mary, Queen of Scots, was sent by ship to France where she married the heir to the French throne. French troops flooded into Scotland, bringing sophisticated continental siege tactics and weapons to Britain for the first time. The English garrisons were gradually overcome or talked into surrender. By 1550 the English had been expelled from the northern kingdom.

Thereafter, the Scots nobles once again fell to their habitual feuding. Mary's French husband died in 1560 and she returned to Scotland to rule in her own right. More feuding and bloodletting followed, as a result of which Mary fled to England to find only captivity and, eventually, death. Her throne was taken by her son, James VI who in 1603 became King James I of England. The two nations were united under one crown, but they kept their separate laws, parliaments and nobility. Peace was not assured.

Visiting the Battlefield Today

The village of Inveresk, little more than a hamlet at the time of the battle, is now a sprawling suburb of Edinburgh. As a result, much of the battlefield has been obliterated by building developments. There is, however, something to be seen.

Leaving the A1 at the junction with the A6094 puts you more

or less in the position where the extreme left wing of the English army was redeployed to face the Scottish attack. Driving north along the A6094 takes you along the position of the front line of the English army. To your right are the hills on which the English army had camped and to the left is the slope up which the Scottish were advancing to the attack. At the junction with the A199, turn left to reach Inveresk. Here you can visit the Church of St Michael which still has the artillery emplacements built by the English engineers on the morning of the battle. The River Esk, which runs through the centre of the small town is bordered by pleasant parks in which to stroll and there are plenty of pubs or cafes offering refreshment.

Falside Castle still crowns the hill above the battlefield, but it is now a private house and is not open to the public.

Falside Castle, whose laird made a catastrophic error on the day of the battle. It is now a private house and is not open to the public.

Chapter Sixteen

NEWBURN FORD 1640

Introduction

Rarely can a single idea have had such a startling effect on the outcome of a battle as did Alexander Leslie's bright idea at Newburn Ford in 1640. So simple and devastating was Leslie's manoeuvre that Newburn Ford is rarely cited as a battle, for the enemy fled before any real fighting took place. Well, almost.

After 1603, England and Scotland shared the same monarch, but they kept their respective armies, parliaments, legal systems and churches. It was the latter that was to cause the outbreak of war in 1639 and again in 1640. King Charles I was more inclined to Catholic doctrine in Church matters than were his

The brilliant siting of a light cannon on the church tower allowed the Scots to force the river crossing and scatter the English army beyond.

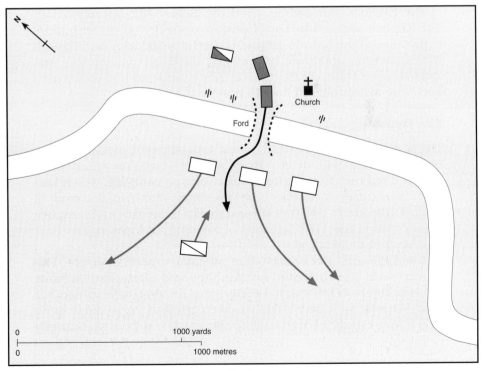

Scottish subjects. When he attempted to impose his ideas, the Scottish Kirk refused to accept them and the mass of the Scottish people, being staunch Protestants, rallied to its defence. In 1639 some early skirmishes led to deadlock and war resumed in 1640.

Scotland managed to muster an army of 25,000 men who had signed the Covenant supporting the Kirk and were known as Covenanters. Led by Sir Alexander Leslie, an experienced mercenary who had risen to be a general in the Swedish army, the Scots headed for Newcastle upon Tyne. Knowing that the northern defences of the city were more formidable than those to the south, Leslie decided to cross the Tyne upstream of Newcastle and attack from the south.

The first crossing point practicable for an army upstream of Newcastle was the ford at the village of Newburn. Leslie reached Newburn late on 27 August. He saw, on the other side of the ford, a series of earthwork entrenchments and an English army well dug in and supported by artillery. The English army appeared to be small, but its defensive works were formidable and Leslie could not be certain how many English troops lurked in the wooded ridge beyond the defences. He decided to wait until his scouts had spied out the land. One of these scouts was dramatically shot dead in front of the Scots army at dusk.

The English, meanwhile, eyed the Scots with apprehension. The English were led by Lord Conway, a cavalry officer with more experience of the parade ground than the battlefield. And though the Scots were uncertain how strong the English army was, the English were painfully aware that they numbered just 6,000 men and were outnumbered four to one by the Scots.

The Opposing Armies

The English army at Newburn Ford was largely composed of raw recruits. They had been raised in the southern counties of England to bolster the levies of the northern counties, which had been so largely ineffective the previous year. By the end of August, the men's pay was several weeks in arrears and supplies were running low. The logistics of keeping an army in the field had been badly ignored.

The 3,000 infantry consisted of pikemen and musketeers. The former wore steel helmets, breastplates and often plate armour over the thighs. They carried pikes some fifteen feet long together with swords or knives. The musketeers had matchlock guns which had a range of over seventy-five yards but were notoriously inaccurate. Furthermore the slightest shower would render the muskets inoperable.

In open battle, the musketeers and pikemen formed up in mixed units. The pikemen fended off enemy cavalry or pikemen while the musketeers sought to shoot the enemy down with organized volleys. When rival infantry bodies met, the struggle could descend into the 'push of pike', a sort of vicious scrum in which brute force at pushing counted for more than dexterity with the weapon.

Conway also had some 2,500 cavalry. These men were equipped with swords as the weapon of choice, though some still carried lances. Their armour was made up of tough leather jackets with long skirts and high boots. Able to deflect most sword blows, the leather was vulnerable to a determined thrust so heavier cavalry wore metal plate armour. All wore helmets.

Cavalry could do little against a tight formation of pikemen, but were otherwise a devastating weapon. If they caught infantry when disorganized, cavalry could inflict appaling casualties, and even against well formed enemies the horsemen could be effective by riding up to discharge pistols at short range and then riding off again.

Finally, Conway had twelve cannon which he had removed from the city defences of Newcastle. Built into the earthworks, these guns were well sited and could sweep the ford with a devastating fire. If Conway were to hold the ford at Newburn, it was the cannon that would do the work.

The far larger Scottish army fielded some 19,000 infantry and 2,500 cavalry. Equipped in a similar fashion to their English enemies, the Scots were fully paid and had adequate supplies of food and ammunition. Leslie had with him only ten cannon. These were relatively light pieces and at least four were of the type known as 'leather guns'. These were light copper cannon which were bound with tough boiled leather and could be dragged about by half a dozen men with ease. They were really intended to support infantry units on the field of battle but, short of cannon, Leslie had to bring what was to hand.

The Battle

The night of 27 August was spent by the English infantry in their earthwork emplacements while the cavalry camped on the wooded ridge behind them. The Scots, however, were all activity. Leslie sent forward patrols to keep the English distracted while he got nine of his cannon hidden in the dense undergrowth

The church tower on top of which the wily Alexander Leslie mounted a light gun to dominate the English defences on the other bank of the river.

which lined the north bank of the River Tyne either side of the ford. It was then that Leslie pulled his masterstroke. He got one of his leather guns mounted into a sling and hoisted it up to the top of the tower of Newburn Church. From there the light gun was able to hurl cannonballs to plunge vertically down into the English defences, making the earthworks useless.

At dawn the Scottish cannon opened fire with a deafening crash. The guns on the river banks swept the field on the south bank with a hail of shot, while the gun on the church tower inflicted heavy casualties on the English infantry behind their breastworks. Under cover of this heavy fire, a troop of Scottish horse got over the ford and lined up in the shelter of the high bank on the southern side. They were soon joined by a mass of infantry. At Leslie's order the Scots surged up over the river bank and stormed towards the English defences.

The English infantry did not wait. Already reeling from the fire from the church tower and faced by a horde of screaming enemy, they simply turned and fled. The jubilant Scots surged over the abandoned defences and gave chase across the open field beyond.

Conway ordered his cavalry forward. Charging out of the woods, the English cavalry came as a nasty surprise to the Scots. Finding the enemy infantry in disorder, the English cavalry at first inflicted heavy casualties. However it was not long before the Scottish calvary counter-attacked and the infantry got into

The site of the ford from the south bank. The ford has now been replaced by a modern bridge of steel girders a few yards downstream.

formation. Knowing the battle was lost, the English cavalry soon joined their colleagues in retreat to the south.

Aftermath

As the English army fled southwards, Leslie marched on Newcastle. The city fathers saw little point in holding out and surrendered on 30 August. A few weeks later the Scots signed an agreement with King Charles under which the religious dispute would be referred to a new English Parliament to meet in London. Meanwhile, the Scots were allowed to occupy Northumberland and Durham and were paid £850 per day from the Royal funds.

The English Parliament met in November and one of its first acts was to refuse Charles funds to fight the Scots, who were allowed to run their Kirk as they liked. The Parliament soon began to make other demands and these, in time, led to the English Civil War, which swiftly spread to Scotland and engulfed both nations in a struggle based as much on religion as on loyalty to King or Parliament.

Visiting the Battlefield Today

The battlefield at Newburn is, in some ways, much altered since 1640, but it is still easy to follow the outlines of the fighting and most of the area is easily accessible.

The buildings in the village of Newburn are little more than a century old. They do not, however, extend much beyond the boundaries of the village as it was in 1640 and do not impinge on the scenes of the battle. The church still stands on its prominent knoll above the river and the Norman tower on which the Scots mounted one of their light cannon stands almost unaltered. An imposing Victorian porch has been added to the south, but the gun was probably hauled up by rope on the west face of the church, over the now blocked up Norman doorway.

An ugly modern steel bridge has now replaced the ford, but the original position of the ford can be made out by the shallow margins and broken down banks. East of the bridge, on the ground covered by the English right wing, a large electricity sub station has been built and the land is inaccessible. West of the bridge, however, a public footpath runs along the river bank offering excellent views of the north bank where the Scots cannon were positioned and the field to the south, now under crops, where the English entrenchments were located.

The lane down which the English cavalry advanced is open to the public and is known as Peth Lane. It can be accessed from the battlefield via a foot level crossing over the railway. Likewise a view across the land covered by the English cavalry charge can be gained from this same level crossing. The road along which the English retreated climbs the steep ridge south of the battlefield and now runs through suburbs of Newcastle.

The field in which the English infantry formed up to dispute the Scottish crossing of the river. The wooded ridge beyond hid the English cavalry, which charged too late in the day to affect the outcome of the battle.

Chapter Seventeen

PRESTON 1648

Introduction

In the wake of the Battle at Newburn Ford, King Charles had been forced to summon a Parliament in England. Conflicts and disputes between King and Parliament led to the Civil War which broke out in August 1642 and rapidly engulfed all of England and Wales. Both sides in the dispute looked to Scotland for money and support, with the inevitable result that that nation too fell into civil strife, though with less damaging effects than in the south.

By 1646 the Royalist armies were everywhere defeated. The King surrendered to Parliament and was placed under house arrest in the royal palace of Hampton Court. Charles, however, had not given up hope. Parliament was not a united force, but was riven by local and religious disputes which had been put aside to defeat the king. Now these disputes were resurfacing and Charles hoped to exploit them, but first he needed a new army. Charles turned to Scotland. The northern kingdom had never been as hostile as the southern and Charles was able to gain its support by promising religious concessions. On 8 July 1648 the army of Scotland crossed the border and invaded England.

Leading the invading army was the Duke of Hamilton. This gallant soldier was experienced and brave with a secure grasp of tactics that he displayed time and again in the heat of action. Unfortunately, he was utterly incompetent when it came to staff work and logistics, with the result that the Scottish units were almost continually short of food and often received conflicting orders.

Despite these shortcomings, the invasion began well. The Scots captured Carlisle without a fight and moved on to trounce an English force under John Lambert at Appleby. Lambert retreated eastwards, blocking the passes over the Pennines. Hamilton pushed on south into Lancashire, where he met up with strong reinforcements from Ulster. More reinforcements were expected in southern England from Royalist forces mustering in Colchester and elsewhere. Hamilton had to link up with them before marching on London and facing down Parliament.

Lambert was by now in Skipton and it was there that he met the brilliant soldier Oliver Cromwell, who had led an army on a forced march to reach Lambert in time to launch a joint attack on the Scots. Cromwell knew from his scouts that his forces were heavily outnumbered, so decided to attack when the Scots were crossing the River Ribble and their army would be divided by that rapid, deep flowing stream.

Hamilton decided to cross the Ribble at Preston, where a good bridge would be able to carry his guns and the few supply wagons he had thought to bring with him. Hamilton knew that Lambert was to his east, but not that Cromwell had joined him. He sent a force under Sir Marmaduke Langdale to the east of Preston to watch a ford at Ribchester and forbid it to Lambert.

The Opposing Armies

Both the armies at Preston were fairly typical of the Civil War era as regards their equipment and tactics, but they varied greatly in terms of numbers, experience and training.

The Scottish army was the larger and better equipped of the two forces. By the time he reached Preston, Hamilton had in his army 13,500 infantry and 6,000 cavalry. Some of these men were on detached duties, but most were with the army. Hamilton also had some artillery with him, but these appear to have been fairly light pieces and took little part in the fighting.

The Scottish cavalry was absent for most of the day and took little part in the fighting until evening on the 17th. The troopers were equipped with straight swords with three foot long blades and sharp points. Some men carried a pair of pistols, others had a single carbine. All wore body armour of one type or another.

The old bridge over the turbulent waters of the Ribble at Preston, which was almost entirely rebuilt after the battle.

Tough leather coats with long skirts to cover the upper legs were common, as were metal helmets with long neck flaps. Some men also wore metal breast and back plates.

Infantry was formed into regiments and companies, usually based on where the men had been raised. As a result the regiments varied enormously in strength from as few as 200 to as many as 1,200 men. Whatever their size the regiments had a similar composition being made up of roughly equal numbers of pikemen and musketeers. Some officers preferred to have more musketeers than pikemen, but shortage of weapons made this the exception in the Civil War era.

The pikemen wore leather coats and metal helmets, some men having metal breastplates. The pikes were officially eighteen feet long, but many men cut them down to around twelve feet to make them easier to handle. The musketeers were unarmoured and were armed with matchlock guns. These took up to a minute to load and it was the slow rate of fire which made the pikemen necessary as a defence while the musketeers reloaded.

Cromwell and Lambert had men equipped similarly to those of the Scots, but in different proportions. Between them they had

173

about 8,000 men, of whom 1,500 were cavalry. The English troops were, therefore, outnumbered but they were veterans of several campaigns in the Civil War while the Scots were largely newly raised formations. Moreover, Cromwell was famed for his efficient staff work and supply systems. As a result his men were well fed and fully supplied, unlike the Scots.

Tactics

In set piece battles, tactics were highly formalized at this time. It took a brave commander of skill to break this tradition. Cromwell was one, but in this battle the royalists lacked either Prince Rupert or the Earl of Montrose who had proved themselves masters of warfare.

It was usual to draw up the infantry in the centre, where the battle would be decided. The commander who managed to end the day with his infantry in physical possession of the battlefield would be the victor. Cavalry were placed on the wings and given the task of trying to outflank the enemy infantry or, conversely, protect their own infantry from being outflanked. Artillery was placed among the infantry and was usually well spread out to provide support along the whole line.

The cavalry were notoriously unreliable and ill disciplined. Often they would sweep away the enemy cavalry and then go off in search of plunder instead of attacking the enemy infantry. Cromwell had, by this later date, formed cavalry units with an iron discipline and which could be counted on to stay in the fight and obey orders. All cavalry carried firearms which were useful when skirmishing or plundering, but by 1648 these had fallen out of favour on the battlefield. It was more usual for cavalry to form up in ranks six men deep and charge home with cold steel.

The infantry in action mixed their pikemen with the musketeers. The pikemen formed up in a dense mass eight or ten men deep. They stood steady while the musketeers did their work. The musketeers formed up on either side of the pikemen in lines known as 'sleeves'.

When facing infantry, the musketeers would fire steadily at the enemy. When the commander felt the moment right, he would launch his pikemen forward to drive the enemy from the field. When called upon to charge, the pikemen moved forward at a brisk walk taking great care to maintain their solid formation. If successful, the momentum of the advance would smash the enemy formation, but if not the two masses of pikemen often became locked together in 'push of pike', a vicious scrum in which numbers and muscle power counted most. If cavalry threatened, the pikemen formed a wall around the musketeers, using their pikes to hold the horsemen at a distance.

Whichever infantry formation broke first would be pursued by the enemy for as far as possible and casualties were often heavy. However, the pursuit was rather less brutal than it had been in earlier times and surrendering was a real option which many men took.

The Battle

It was on the morning of 17 August that Langdale led his 3,000 infantry east from Preston towards Ribchester and the ford over the Ribble. He never reached it. He was still marching up the narrow lane to Longridge when he ran head on into the English army marching west. Langdale quickly deployed his infantry into defensive lines among the hedgerows on either side of the lane. It soon became clear to Langdale that he was facing a much larger force than expected and that he was hopelessly outnumbered. He sent a messenger to Hamilton asking for support.

Hamilton, meanwhile, had got his cavalry over the Ribble and sent them galloping south to scout out the land ahead. He was now marching his main body of infantry across the bridge and organizing his artillery, which were still north of Preston, to cross later that evening. When he received the message from Langdale, Hamilton thought it meant only that Langdale was skirmishing with the expected English attempt to take the ford. He ignored the request for help.

By mid afternoon, Cromwell's cavalry had managed to get around the flank of Langdale's position. A few isolated units rode forwards to reach Preston while Langdale began to fall back rapidly.

By this time the Earl of Callander, who had fought Cromwell before, had convinced Hamilton that the fight to the east was no mere skirmish but a determined attack. Hamilton pushed a small force up the lane towards Longridge, but they merely arrived in time to join the retreat. More productively, Hamilton organized a defensive perimeter on the open ground that then lay between Preston town and the river. He also sent riders south with orders for the cavalry to return at once.

It was now that Hamilton proved his courage and tactical skill. The English army, fresh from its victory over Langdale, surged through Preston and then on towards the bridge. Hamilton drew his sword and personally led a series of brilliantly successful charges which disordered the English and threw them back into the town. This gave Hamilton time to get all his infantry and many of his guns over the bridge. It was dark by the time the Scots were across the river. Both sides had lost about 2,000 men.

Leaving his campfires burning and organizing a few men to stay by the bridge and fire the odd shot, Hamilton now led his army off to the south. Having successfully driven off the English attack and cunningly convinced Cromwell that he was still on the river bank, Hamilton was proving himself a leader of stature. It was now that his failings took over.

Hamilton led his infantry on the wrong road south and completely missed his cavalry who were returning north along the Wigan Road as ordered. Not until they reached Preston and ran into English scouts did the Scottish cavalry realize they had missed Hamilton and returned towards Wigan. This, of course, alerted Cromwell to the fact that Hamilton had gone, so the English army was roused and set off south in pursuit.

At dawn the next day Hamilton's failings became even more obvious. The wagons containing almost the entire Scots stores of gunpowder had been left behind in Preston. and the overnight rain had dampened the powder the men carried with them in their pouches and packs. Despite the strong defences of Wigan, the Scots had to march on south.

By the next day the powder was dry and Hamilton decided to make a stand at Winwick. Hamilton again made brilliant tactical use of the defensive possibilities of the ditches, banks and hedges around the church and drove off the English attacks launched by Cromwell.

Despite this success, Hamilton was a deeply worried man. He was almost completely out of ammunition and had received no news at all of the expected English royalists marching to join him from the south. He ordered his infantry to fall back on Warrington where the defences would reduce their need to use ammunition. Then he divided his cavalry and led one section himself and put another under Langdale. Langdale rode south and Hamilton into Wales, both of them looking for news of the reinforcements.

There were no reinforcements, for the English and Welsh royalists had been outmanoeuvred and forced to surrender. Within days Langdale was surrounded at Nottingham and Hamilton at Uttoxeter. The poor Scottish infantry had been left in Warrington without their two commanders, without food and without ammunition. Despite holding out bravely for some time, they eventually surrendered.

Aftermath

Having defeated the Scottish army, Cromwell marched north into Scotland. He used his military muscle to ensure that a new government under the Duke of Argyll was installed which could be relied upon not to intervene again in England. Then he marched south once more to mop up any royalist sympathizers holding out in fortresses such as Pontefract.

The victory at Preston secured for Cromwell the undisputed leadership of the more radical wing of Parliamentarian opinion in England and ensured that it was this more radical wing which gained dominance. After Preston, Cromwell and the army commanders read Charles's letters to the Scottish government and to Irish nobles. They were appalled by the duplicity of the King who had been debating a way forward with the English Parliament while secretly making very different agreements with his Scots and Irish subjects. Cromwell and the army concluded that Charles had committed treason against England. They wanted him put on trial.

Although in a dominant position, Cromwell could not persuade all of Parliament to agree with him. After months of discussion, debate and argument, Cromwell acted on 6 December 1648. When MPs arrived that morning to take their seats they were met at the doors by Colonel Thomas Pride, a former brewer who was now one of Cromwell's most trusted men. Pride had with him a large squad of tough soldiers and a list of MPs. Of the 180 MPs who arrived that morning, Pride arrested or expelled nearly 100. The minority who made it into the chamber were those who agreed with Cromwell. They voted to the put King Charles on trial for treason.

In doing so, they set in train the events that would lead to another war between England and Scotland.

Visiting the Battlefield Today

Lying close to a large town, it is hardly surprising that most of the battlefield of Preston has now been covered by the spreading sprawl of the Preston suburbs. The area between the river and the city walls was engulfed in Victorian building, while the fields around the land to Longridge vanished in the 1930s and 1950s. Sadly, the small fields north of the B6243 and west of

Grimsargh, which saw the earliest fighting between Langdale and Cromwell's advance guard, were covered in industrial estates in the 1990s and the few remaining fields are not easily accessible.

The original Preston Bridge was rebuilt after the fighting and it gives a good idea of the bridge that the Scots infantry defended so well. It spans the river on a number of piers and has a distinct hump at its centre. The carriageway is cobbled and barely wide enough for a farmcart to cross. It is now closed to traffic and serves as a footbridge connecting a maze of Victorian terraced streets on the north bank to the aptly named Bridge Hotel on the south bank.

Although little remains to be seen at the main battlefield at Preston, the village of Winwick where the skirmish was fought between the retreating Scots and the pursuing English offers more to the visitor. The village is now surrounded on three sides by modern roads as part of the M6/M62 complex. However, the churchyard is almost unaltered, as are the fields north of the village where fighting took place.

The church at Winwick around which the Scottish infantry made a final stand before being forced to surrender by a lack of ammunition.

Chapter Eighteen

DUNBAR 1650

Introduction

After 1603 England and Scotland had been two different kingdoms ruled by the same king. Their legal systems, parliaments, nobility and other state systems had remained quite separate, but the personal union of the kingdoms in the

The English dragoons managed to pin down the bulk of the Scottish army while the vast majority of the English army launched a devastating attack on the exposed coastal flank of the Scots.

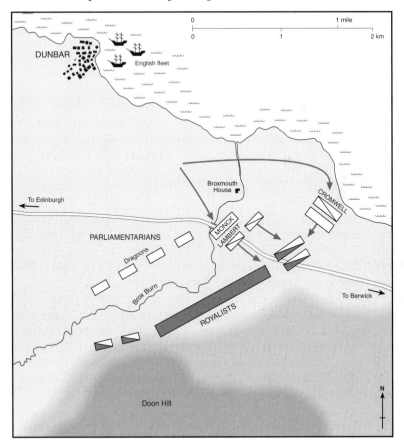

body of the same king appeared to be firm.

Then in 1649 the English tried King Charles I for treason against England, found him guilty and chopped off his head. This man was also the King of Scots and the Scottish people did not take kindly to having their King executed. England declared itself to be a republic under Parliament, but Scotland opted to remain a kingdom and hailed the eldest son of the executed king to be their King Charles II. It was unclear if the two nations would go their separate ways as in the past or if they would again unite. The question led to the Battle of Dunbar.

Almost as soon as Charles entered Edinburgh, the English gave their army orders to march into Scotland and expel the nineteen year old prince they termed 'Mr Charles Stuart'. The English believed that Charles would not be content to rule only Scotland but would, sooner or later, make a play for England. They decided to strike first.

Inevitably it was Oliver Cromwell who led the English army, He took with him Lambert who had fought at Preston, and the remarkably able George Monck. On 22 July Cromwell crossed the border with 20,000 men, supported by a fleet cruising off the coast. Cromwell was determined to crush the Scottish army, capture Edinburgh and force the Scots to get rid of Charles.

Facing Cromwell was David Leslie, victor of the Battle at Newburn Ford. As a professional soldier, Leslie had been fighting in the Swedish army while Cromwell was still a farmer in East Anglia. Leslie had an army of some 16,000 men, most of them raw recruits. Realizing he could not face Cromwell in open battle, Leslie opted for a grinding summer of attrition. His first move was to strip the countryside bare. People, livestock and supplies were packed into the cities and fortresses so that the English could not get at them.

Then Leslie turned to his army's one true strength. If his men were inexperienced at fighting, they were experts at marching. When Cromwell attacked Edinburgh from the east he found himself faced by strong defences manned by Leslie's Scots. When he marched on Leith, Leslie got there first and manned the defences. When Cromwell marched far to the west in a feint then came back to attack Edinburgh, the Scots again got there first.

By the end of August, Cromwell had had enough. His army was footsore and hungry. Supplies were running out and disease was rampant. Barely half of Cromwell's army was fit for service. On 1 September Cromwell retreated to the fortified harbour of Dunbar, unloaded his remaining supplies from the fleet and

The harbour which on the morning of the battle was crammed with English ships, waiting to evacuate the depleted English army.

allowed his troops a day of rest and full rations. Then he gave the order to march out of Dunbar and head south towards England.

Again, Leslie had got there first. The entire Scots army was drawn up on the formidable Doon Hill, blocking the road south.

The Opposing Armies

By the time the two armies met at Dunbar on 4 September after weeks of marching and countermarching they were both very different from the forces which had begun the campaign in July. From being the larger and better equipped army, the English were now the smaller and more exhausted.

On the morning of battle Cromwell had about 11,000 men fit for duty. These men were largely from the famous New Model Army with which Cromwell had beaten the Royalist forces in the English Civil War. The 4,000 cavalry were each equipped with a pair of pistols and a sword three feet long. For armour they wore tough leather coats with a helmet and breastplate of steel strong enough to stop the low-velocity bullets of the day.

The English infantry were very different from those that had fought at Newburn or Preston in terms of both equipment and tactics. They retained the division into musketeers and pikemen, though there were now about twice as many musketeers as pikemen.

A cavalry trooper from Cromwell's army. Troopers carried a heavy, straight sword and a pair of pistols mounted on their saddles as weapons. The coat of heavy, buff leather was able to turn aside glancing sword blows, while the plate armour of the helmet, breastplate and left gauntlet was able to stop a direct sword thrust and turn aside a pistol bullet. The right hand was protected by the basket hilt of the sword. A charge by a squadron of these men mounted on heavy horses could be devastating against disorganized infantry, a tactic Cromwell used often in his career.

The key improvement in equipment was that most of them had flintlock muskets in place of matchlocks. Instead of relying on a spluttering fuse which could go out in bad weather, the flintlocks had a flint and steel arrangements which struck fresh sparks each time the gun was fired. The new gun was more reliable in action and lighter to carry. Both matchlock and flintlock was accurate to about fifty yards, though the bullets could still inflict injuries at up to 150 yards.

Equally obvious to contemporary eyes was the fact that these men wore uniforms. Earlier regiments had worn whatever the men had brought with them. Sometimes a commanding officer might give his men cloth to use, so that they all wore the same colour, but cut and fit was up to the individual. Cromwell's infantry were dressed in identical red coats and grey trousers. it was an innovation which helped create regimental pride and raised morale.

The Scottish army was more traditional. The 6,000 cavalry were equipped in virtually identical fashion to the English, but the infantry were very different. Most of the Scots infantry conformed to the old division of equal numbers of pikemen and musketeers. And the musketeers had old-fashioned matchlocks with their less reliable firing and slower rates of discharge. Some of the Scots cavalry drawn from among the traditional raiding families of the old border regions, came without armour but carrying long lances.

Both armies had large numbers of light artillery firing a four or five pound shot over 1,000 yards. One or two of these guns were attached to each infantry regiment and operated by men from that unit. The larger guns fired nine pound balls over 1,500 yards. Both types were slow to load and operate, though the lighter guns could get off a shot every two or three minutes. The light guns also had case shot, a large number of small balls packed into the barrel, which operated like a giant shot gun and could inflict dreadful casualties at close range. At Dunbar, neither side had large guns.

Tactics

Leslie's men were largely recruited that spring specifically for the 1650 campaign. They were trained in traditional fashion. This was most obvious among the infantry who fought in the same dense formations as did those who fought at Preston.

These traditional tactics involved the pikemen forming up eight deep in the centre with the musketeers forming sleeves on either flank. When facing infantry, the musketeers would fire as their weapons were ready. As each man fired his weapon, he would step back to go through the complicated process of reloading, stepping forward again when ready to fire. When the opposition was sufficiently damaged, the pikemen would surge forwards in tight formation to inflict a shock effect and drive the enemy from the field. The pikemen were equally useful in warding off cavalry who would shy away from the wicked pike points.

Cromwell's Englishmen used a new tactic for the infantry. The new flintlock muskets could fire twice as quickly as the matchlocks. There was no need to step aside to let others give fire. As a result the musketeers drew up in a line three men deep, not six or eight, and loosed off devastating volley fire on the command of their officers. The crash of a concentrated volley was effective and demoralizing in equal measure.

The cavalry of both armies were trained to charge home with cold steel to exploit the shock effect of armoured horsemen. The pistols and carbines were kept for use when skirmishing or once the enemy formation was broken by a charge. Cavalry formations tended to be six or eight deep to add weight to a charge. Though cavalry could not be expected to break up a dense formation of pikemen, they were highly effective against disordered infantry.

The English had another type of troop that the Scots lacked. These were the dragoons. Mounted on second rate horses and armed with short muskets, the dragoons rode to their position on the battlefield at the trot, then dismounted to form ranks and open fire. They had no need of pike support for, if cavalry threatened, the dragoons simply remounted and rode off.

The Scots, meanwhile, had several thousand Highlanders with them. Armed with swords, daggers and old muskets these men were quick, nimble and able to deliver quite devastating charges. Leslie, however, was wary of their indiscipline and would not trust them in any position of importance.

The Battle

On 2 September the English army stood south of Dunbar and stared up at the much larger Scottish army on Doon Hill. The Scottish position was impregnable and attack was hopeless. Cromwell was beginning to think about loading his men on to the ships and scuttling back to England in disgrace. Then, using the new-fangled telescope he had with him, he saw the Scots begin to move.

Up on Doon Hill, Leslie had come under intense political pressure. With his army he had large numbers of devout Presbyterian clergy. Officially these men were there to minister to the spiritual needs of the army and to raise morale with regular sermons and preaching. Unofficially, they were the agents of the strictly Presbyterian government. Many dozens of junior officers had lost their positions through being insufficiently devout – or by arguing with the clergyman attached to his regiment. Now Leslie was put on the spot.

Why, the clergy demanded, was Cromwell being allowed to escape by sea. 'The Lord hath delivered the Antichrist into your hands and like Gideon you should descend on them and sweep them away before you,' loudly proclaimed one. Fearing for his job if he refused, and in any case convinced the English were a starving remnant about to retreat, Leslie obeyed. He marched his army down from the heights of Doon Hill to occupy a new position on top of the ridge just south of Brox Burn.

It was this movement which Cromwell watched through his telescope. As the Scots redeployed on the ridge, obviously to launch an attack next day, Cromwell called a meeting of his officers at Broxmouth House. They decided on a daring and risky plan. The entire English army was ordered to redeploy at night ready for an attack before dawn. It was hoped the movements would go unnoticed and the attack come as complete surprise.

The basic plan was for the dragoons to use their speed and mobility to keep up a demonstration of force along the front and left wing of the Scottish army where it faced the steep ravine of the Brox Burn. Meanwhile the main English force of cavalry

The level ground where the Scottish right wing was attacked by Lambert and Monck, the precipitous slopes of Doon Hill lie beyond.

under Lambert would charge the Scottish right wing cavalry to sweep it from the field. Behind Lambert was Monck and the main body of infantry who would move up to turn the right flank of the Scots infantry. Cromwell held a small reserve force under his own command behind Monck. Cromwell had some eighty per cent of his men on his left wing.

As the first cold grey light seeped over the horizon, Lambert led his cavalry charge up the gentle slope and crashed into the Scottish cavalry. The Borderers recovered from their surprise first and fought Lambert to a halt. The English brought up more cavalry, as did the Scots. Monck now brought up his infantry, attacking to the right of Lambert and pinning down the Scottish infantry.

For an hour the two forces hacked and shot at each other. The Scottish army was holding its own, but Leslie was having difficulty pulling men from his centre to strengthen the right. With the Brox Burn ravine to his front and the steep slope of Doon Hill behind him, Leslie did not have much room to manoeuvre. The English dragoons were darting here and there to pester the Scots front ranks. His efforts were further hampered

The area in front of Doon Hill where the English dragoons kept the majority of the Scottish army tied down while Cromwell delivered his decisive flank attack to the east.

by the Presbyterian clergy who insisted on giving sermons to inspire the men while the officers wanted to get them moving.

An hour after dawn the situation changed dramatically. Cromwell had led his reserve force of cavalry far out to his left and along the coast. Turning to his right under the cover of a small hillock, Cromwell then charged into the already disordered right flank of Leslie's cavalry.

The sudden attack by Cromwell's men destroyed the Scottish cavalry, who fled eastward, disrupting the formations of their own infantry. Into the newly disordered Scots surged Monck's infantry who pushed forward with the pike and thundering volleys of musket fire to roll up the Scottish line from right to left. First to go were a body of Highlanders who stood and fought until wiped out, then Monck moved on to the Lowlanders.

Less than thirty minutes after Cromwell's charge the battle was effectively over. Cromwell halted his men to sing the 117th psalm 'O praise the Lord all ye nations, praise him all ye people. For his merciful kindness is great toward us and the truth of the

186

Lord endureth for ever. Praise ye the Lord.' Then he let his men loose to continue the killing.

Aftermath

In all some 3,000 Scots and over 1,000 English had been killed. The Scottish army was broken and some 10,000 men surrendered before nightfall. These unfortunates were herded south to Durham with little in the way of food and no shelter from the driving rain which set in. Hundreds, perhaps thousands, of them died before they reached Durham. They later ran riot and, firm Presbyterians that most of them were, did much damage to the ornate Durham Cathedral.

Leslie, meanwhile, had managed to extricate about a third of his army and march off in good order towards Stirling. As he fell back, Leslie made certain that the extremist Presbyterians in government got their full share of the blame for what had happened. The disgraced officers were returned to their commands in the army and with them came a large number of new recruits and old veterans to increase the Scottish strength.

The newly resurgent Scottish force could not stop Cromwell capturing Edinburgh a few days after the battle, but they were sufficiently organized by December to stop him advancing any further. On New Year's Day 1651 young Charles was crowned King of Scotland at Scone with all the pomp and pageantry he could muster. More recruits flooded in to join his army. But both he and Leslie knew that, come the spring, they would have to face Cromwell again.

Visiting the Battlefield Today

Much of the battlefield of Dunbar remains effectively unaltered from how it appeared in 1650 and the town of Dunbar still offers plenty of refreshment to the visitor. Unfortunately the crucial area occupied by the Scottish right wing where Cromwell launched his flanking attack has been buried beneath a concrete works, a quarry and other industrial constructions. As a result, the monument to the battle now lies beside the A1087 just south of Dunbar instead of alongside the A1 in the heart of the battlefield. Its inscription – 'Here took place the brunt or essential agony of the Battle of Dunbar' – is not entirely inappropriate, however, as it now stands to the front of the Scottish right wing where some fighting did take place.

Crossing the new A1 dual carriageway from the A1087 takes

The monument at Dunbar, moved in recent years when a quarry was opened up on the site of the fiercest fighting.

you along a lane off which is an unmade road signposted to Little Pinkerton. The road peters out at the strangely semi-derelict village, but if you are feeling energetic you can walk the rough bridleway along the foot of Doon Hill and along the line of the position taken up by the centre and left wing of the Scottish army.

Ignoring the turning to Little Pinkerton, the lane continues to a second turn on the right signposted to Doon Hill. This narrow lane becomes increasingly poorly surfaced, but eventually emerges on to the hilltop on the site of a Dark Age chieftain's hall which was destroyed during the English invasions at the time of the Battle of Degsastan. This site is well signposted, and is surrounded by the open fields where Leslie camped his army before the battle.

If you return to the A1 and drive north you can turn left down a lane signposted to Spott. This lane twists and turns, then crosses a narrow stone bridge. It was here in 1296 that the English army brushed aside a Scottish force on its way to the Battle of Stirling Bridge.

Chapter Nineteen

WORCESTER 1651

Introduction

On New Years Day 1651 the youthful King Charles II was crowned in Scone Abbey as King of Scotland. But an army from the English republic was occupying Edinburgh and its leader, Oliver Cromwell, was determined to oust Charles from his northern kingdom. Charles, however, planned to regain England as well as Scotland.

Charles's experienced but cautious commander, David Leslie, mustered his army at Stirling, but by July the troops from the north and east had still not arrived. Forestalling the union of the Scottish armies, Cromwell shipped his men across the Forth and marched north to capture Perth. He hoped the Scots would retreat into the Highlands where they could be penned in and starved to submission.

Charles was not the man to fall in with Cromwell's plans. Instead of going north, Charles marched south and invaded England. It was a daring, but not foolhardy move. Charles had Royalist supporters in various parts of England, especially the south-west, and in Wales with whom he was in regular contact. He hoped that these men would rise in his cause.

As Charles and the Scottish army marched south they took Carlisle with ease and found the gates of Penrith opened to them. At Warrington they caught up with Cromwell's cavalry, under the famous commander John Lambert, guarding the river crossings. A prompt and spirited attack by Charles scattered Lambert's men. It was just the morale booster the Scots needed.

The defeat of Lambert meant the road to London was open, and some urged Charles to march on the capital. Leslie was, as usual, more cautious. He pointed out that an English army was gathering at Coventry while Cromwell was coming south through Yorkshire. To march on London risked being caught between these two forces. Much better, it was said, to continue down the west of England to gather in the expected recruits from the south-west and Wales before turning to face the English army.

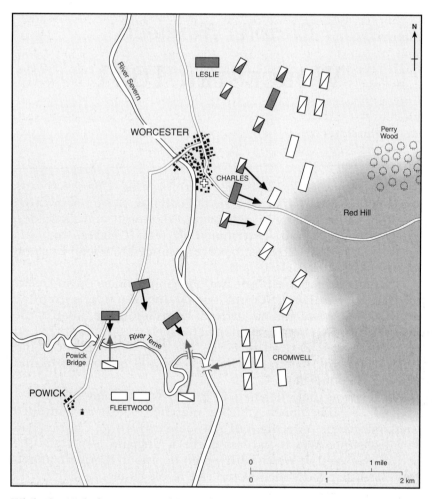

While Scottish forces around Powick Bridge tied down the main English forces under Fleetwood and Cromwell, King Charles launched an attack on the denuded English centre. The attack faltered when Leslie refused to advance the left wing cavalry.

So the Scots marched on Worcester, a fortified city with excellent road connections to the recruiting grounds. Charles entered the city on 22 August. He raised the Royal Standard of England and sent out messengers asking for recruits to his banner to overthrow the republican government of England. Ironically it was nine years exactly since his father had raised the Royal Standard in Nottingham at the start of the English Civil War. With even greater irony that very day saw Cromwell and his army march through Nottingham on their way south.

Charles waited in Worcester for a week. His men busily repaired the defences, which had suffered during the English Civil War and scouts rode out to look for the expected recruits and for the gathering English army. The city of Worcester stands on the east bank of the Severn and was surrounded by cannon-proof walls. Charles built a new fortress, dubbed Fort Royal, outside the Sidbury Gate which faced towards London and where the English attack was expected to fall. He also gave orders that the bridges over the Severn north and south of the city were to be blown with gunpowder. Also blown up was Powick Bridge across the River Teme, which flowed into the Severn south of the city.

The house in Worcester where King Charles lodged in the days before the battle. The building is now a restaurant.

Royalist sympathizers there were in plenty, but very few came to join Charles. The most significant were a body of sixty Worcestershire men under Lord Talbot. The others were waiting to see how the Scottish army fared before declaring themselves. Exasperated, Charles realized he had to win a victory before his faint-hearted supporters would rally to him. His plan was to lure the English under Cromwell into a futile attack on the defences of Worcester, then launch a counter-attack and sweep them from the field.

Cromwell, meanwhile, was laying his own plans. By the end of August he had about twice as many men as Charles and was camped around Evesham. He knew the defences of Worcester were strong, and getting stronger. So Cromwell decided to attack as soon as possible. He intended to launch his main force against the Sidbury Gate, while a diversionary attack was made across the Teme on the west side of the Severn. To keep communications open between the two forces, Cromwell decided to build a pontoon bridge over the Severn and another over the Teme.

Building pontoon bridges was common practice at the time, but only to aid supply routes in the rear of an army. Constructing one on the battlefield under enemy fire had never been tried before.

The Opposing Armies

Charles had an army of some 16,000 men in and around Worcester, of which about 4,000 were cavalry. Cromwell had in all about 28,000 men including some 9,000 cavalry.

The majority of the cavalry on both sides were equipped in almost identical fashion. They wore tough leather coats with long skirts. These were able to deflect most sword cuts but not bullets, so many men had steel breastplates as well. All wore steel helmets with neck guards and open visors.

The infantry on both sides were equipped with pikes or with muskets. The Scots were equipped mainly with matchlock muskets. Many English troops had matchlocks as well, but a substantial number of Cromwell's best troops were equipped with flintlocks.

Both armies had some artillery, but not as much as had been common in the English Civil War. Most infantry regiments had one or two small cannon able to fire a four or five pound ball over a range of 1,000 yards. In Fort Royal and elsewhere on the city ramparts the Scots had some larger cannon firing nine pound balls over 1,500 yards. The advancing English had a number of even larger cannon which they intended to use if they had to batter down the city walls. In the event, these heavy siege guns were not used.

In addition to these troops, the English fielded several thousand dragoons. These men rode on horses or ponies to where they were needed, then dismounted and fought as musketeers. Their combination of speed and firepower made them formidable on open battlefields.

The Scots had some Highlanders with them at Worcester. These men were lightly equipped, often having only swords and daggers as weapons. They were, however, quick and nimble and famed for their savagery in battle as well as for the effectiveness of their wild charges.

Tactics

The cavalry were the main shock attack weapon. Although they were equipped with pistols or carbines for skirmishing, the cavalry were trained to charge home using their swords during battle. The shock of a cavalry impact could be enough to sweep enemy formations from the field.

Pikemen, however, could easily withstand a cavalry charge if they kept their formation tight and their pikes levelled at the advancing enemy. The pikemen were also used for infantry attacks, when they would march forward at a brisk walk and use the momentum of their massed ranks to roll over enemy formations.

The light field artillery was pulled about the battlefield by men from musketeer units and added their fire to that of the musketeers. With rates of fire as low as one shot every two minutes or so, this artillery was of more use against a static target a long distance off than it was at close range against moving targets.

The Battle

The fighting around Worcester began on 28 August, twelve miles to the south. Cromwell had sent a strong force of dragoons and cavalry under Lambert to try to find a crossing over the Severn

The tower of the church at Upton, the main part of which was burnt down in the fighting of 28 August when Cromwell established an English force on the west bank of the River Severn.

south of Worcester. Such a crossing was essential if Cromwell was to implement his plan of a two pronged assault, one either side of the river.

When Lambert arrived at Upton on Severn he saw, as expected, that the bridge had been blown up, one span lay in ruins in the river. However, a stout plank of wood had been placed over the broken span. Clearly a Scottish patrol was somewhere on the east side of the Severn and the plank was there to enable them to cross back.

Taking a gamble, Lambert dismounted a troop of his dragoons and instructed them to walk nonchalantly down to the bridge and over the plank. This they did, the 700 Scots in Upton making no attempt to stop them. As soon as the English dragoons were over the river, they barricaded themselves into the church, which offered sweeping fields of fire up the village high street and across the approaches to the bridge. Lambert then broke cover and dashed forwards with his main body.

Edward Massey, the Scots commander, belatedly realized what was happening, but could not get to the bridge because of the dragoons in the church. Massey ordered the church set on fire to drive out the dragoons, but it was too late. By the time the Scots had recaptured the church, Lambert had got enough men over the river to outnumber the Scots and drive them back. Massey, a veteran of many campaigns, was badly injured in the fighting and his men retreated north to take a stand in Powick village, standing on a ridge south of Worcester.

Hearing that Lambert was over the Severn, Cromwell marched his main body out of Evesham. On the night of 29 August the Scots mounted a raid on the advancing English, but Cromwell kept on coming. By 2 September the main English army was camped east of Worcester behind Red Hill, while some 12,000 men were on the west side of the Severn under General Charles Fleetwood, who also had the boats for the pontoon bridges.

Soon after dawn on 3 September, the anniversary of Dunbar, Charles left his lodgings and climbed the cathedral tower. There was no sign of any English troops, but Charles for some reason thought an attack was imminent. He rode south to Powick to talk to Colonel Keith, who had taken over from the wounded Massey. Then he cantered back to Worcester, crossed the bridge and inspected his guns on Fort Royal. Finally he rode north to the meadows beside the river where Leslie was camped with the cavalry. Satisfied that his men were ready for battle, Charles returned to his lodgings for lunch.

Powick Bridge, where the Scots put up such a savage resistance that Cromwell had to move troops from his centre to strengthen the attack.

Cromwell, meanwhile, had been having trouble getting his pontoon boats into position. He had intended to attack about mid-morning, but the boats were not ready until well after noon. The attack then opened when Fleetwood ordered his cannon to bombard the Scots troops in Powick. The cannon fire was unusually intense for the period and before long Keith retreated down the hill and crossed Powick Bridge on wooden planks, then pulled the planks away and waited behind the formidable River Teme for the attack.

Charles had heard the gunfire and ran back up the Cathedral Tower. From there he saw Keith fall back and estimated over 10,000 English troops were coming down the Powick ridge to attack Keith's 700 men on the river. Charles ordered 2,000 infantry under Colonel Montgomery to march down to the River Teme and support Keith. A body of 1,000 Highlanders was put between Powick Bridge and Worcester as a reserve.

At this point, Cromwell's main artillery force opened fire on Fort Royal. This was merely a diversionary tactic to distract the Scots attention from the engineers feverishly building the pontoon bridges over the Severn and the Teme close to their confluence. The ruse succeeded and by 3 p.m. the pontoon bridges were completed.

Worcester Cathedral. It was from the top of this tower that Charles watched the battle unfold and planned his counter-attack.

Cromwell now ordered his main body over the crest of Red Hill and towards the Sidbury Gate, bringing them into view of the Scots in Worcester for the first time. Before committing them to the attack, Cromwell wanted to ensure Fleetwood was over the Teme and advancing on Worcester from the west. But Fleetwood had been halted by the determined resistance of the Scots along the Teme. So Cromwell led his best units away from Red Hill and over the pontoon bridges to attack these Scots on the flank.

The Scots under Keith and Montgomery at once fell back from the river, but mounted a determined defence as they retreated. In this area the ground was broken into many small fields fringed by dense hedges, each of which was made into a makeshift defence until outflanked.

Meanwhile on the Cathedral tower, Charles watched the battle unfold. He saw a large body of English leave the main army and cross to the west bank of the Severn where they seemed bogged down in the hedgerow fighting. Meanwhile the main body of the English was standing around on the lower slopes of Red Hill doing nothing. Charles guessed Cromwell was on the west bank of the Severn with what seemed to be his best troops. He realized he had been given a magnificent opportunity to win a spectacular victory. Trusting Montgomery to hold up the English advancing from Powick, Charles gathered all his remaining infantry, some 9,000 men and surged out of the Sidbury Gate. He sent orders to Leslie to bring up the cavalry to attack the English right wing while he attacked the centre.

Charles personally led the Scottish infantry forwards, giving orders to his men in his loud booming voice. The Scots marched up and began firing their matchlocks into the stationary English formations. Sensing that he was facing relatively untried troops, Charles ordered his pikemen to advance. The massed ranks marched resolutely forward, driving back the enemy formations. Charles then unleashed his remaining Highlanders, who swept through the English centre. But Charles could not see Leslie or the Scottish cavalry anywhere.

Mystery still surrounds the actions of Leslie during the critical half hour that Charles's infantry attack was driving back the English centre. He received more than one order from Charles to attack, but did nothing. He kept the Scottish cavalry stationary in the water meadows north of the city. One account says that he sat silently on his horse 'like one amazed'. Another says Leslie refused to advance saying he wanted to keep his men to form a rearguard to cover what he saw as the King's inevitable retreat. Whatever the reason, Leslie's inaction meant that Charles's spirited attack went unsupported at the critical moment when victory was possible.

Cromwell, on the other hand, was not a man to hesitate. As soon as he heard of the Scottish attack he realized his danger. Telling Fleetwood to do the best he could, Cromwell gathered up all the English cavalry on the west bank and galloped at high speed over the pontoon bridges. Pausing only long enough to form his men into orderly ranks, Cromwell launched a crushing charge at the right flank of the advancing Scots. The time was about 4 p.m.

The English cavalry hit the Highlanders first and swept the lightly armed men from the field. As the Highlanders fell back they disorganized the pikemen of the Lowland regiment next to them, and they too gave way. Seeing his attack faltering, Charles dashed back to Fort Royal and directed the cannon to give covering fire to the retreating infantry. He then rushed off again to make a final appeal to Leslie to join the fighting. But the streets of Worcester were a seething mass of Scottish troops some going one way, others another and all being hampered by the panicking citizens. Charles could make no headway and the situation got even worse when the English infantry burst through Sidbury Gate and the street fighting turned savage.

At this point Lord Talbot got hold of Charles. Talbot and his men knew the back streets of Worcester. They guided Charles to the north gate of the city where they put him on a horse and advised him to flee. They then returned to the fighting and barricaded themselves into the Guildhall, being among the last to surrender as darkness fell. In all some 3,000 Scots had died in the fighting and another 10,000 were captured as Worcester fell. Leslie and the cavalry made no attempt to mount a rearguard, but simply fled northward towards distant Scotland. None of them made it, though isolated units got as far as Lancashire before being captured.

Aftermath

The Battle of Worcester made Cromwell secure as the virtual dictator of England, and his orders ran throughout Scotland as the Scottish government was in no position to defy them. Scottish prisoners were rather unfairly treated as rebels against the English government and sentenced to seven years slave labour. Some were put to digging drainage ditches in the Fens of Cromwell's own East Anglia – the New Bedford River being the largest of these – others were sent to the American colonies. The lesser officers were exiled abroad, the more important were held prisoner in London.

But for many weeks there was a mystery which absorbed Cromwell and most of Europe. Nobody knew what had happened to King Charles. The last known sighting of him was when Lord Talbot had put him on a horse at the north gate. He had not been captured and nor had his body been found. Where was he?

In fact, as he rode out of the city, Charles had met the Earl of Derby who happened to know the Worcestershire gentry from previous visits. He advised Charles to make for Boscobel, the home of Richard Penderel. This well-to-do farmer had not joined Charles, but Derby knew he was a Royalist. However, Charles and Derby were then caught up in the mass of Leslie's retreating cavalry. 'I couldn't get these fellows to join me this afternoon,' complained Charles. 'Now I can't get rid of them.' It was after dark before Charles and Derby got away from the fugitives and rode for Boscobel. It turned out to be a wise choice for not only was Penderel willing to hide the King, but he was also in touch with a number of other secret royalists in the western counties. Derby rode off to try to rally Leslie's men. He failed and was quickly captured. Derby kept secret where Charles had gone and was one of the few men to be executed for joining his King.

Charles stayed at Boscobel for some days while Penderel made secretive contact with his friends and relations. Henry Wilmot, another fugitive from Worcester, joined the King and together they embarked on a six week adventure to get out of England. Passed from royalist to royalist, the two men donned disguises and hid in attics, cellars and – famously – once in the branches of an oak tree while Cromwell's men tried to find them. After lengthy journeys and several hair raising escapes, the two men got on board a coal barge called *Surprise* at Shoreham and sailed to France.

In hindsight it was the experiences of Charles in his weeks on the run that may have had the most enduring results of the battle at Worcester. Charles was forced to live like a peasant or a poor farmer and he came into close and intimate contact with the humblest of his subjects, who were risking their lives to help him. Some believe that the habitual affability to social inferiors that thereafter marked Charles, dates from this period. Certainly Charles never forgot those who helped him. After he was invited to become King of England again in 1660, he bestowed annual payments on all those who had been his friends in time of need and he gave handsome dowries to their daughters when they married. Wilmot was made Earl of Rochester.

The frivolity and happiness of the reign of the 'The Merry Monarch', as Charles was to become, may be traced back to the Battle of Worcester.

Visiting the Battlefield Today

Much of the battlefield of Worcester has been built over. The lands east of the River Severn, including the scene of the most intense fighting which took place during the Scottish attack, has now vanished beneath Victorian and modern housing estates.

Some of the buildings in the city centre, however, remain. The house where King Charles had his headquarters still stands in New Street. The Cathedral Tower, from which he watched the battle and planned his counter-attack still dominates the city and can be visited. The Guildhall, where the final fighting took place, was badly damaged in the fighting and was replaced after Charles's Restoration in 1688. The entrance features a fine statue of the King.

Fort Royal is clear of buildings and now forms a pleasant park complete with children's playground. The earthwork defences have crumbled somewhat since 1651, but their outlines can be

The memorial erected in 2001 beside Powick Bridge.

traced without too much difficulty. The sharp angles of the southern bastion, in particular, can be made out. The park is off Wylds Lane, which branches off the A44 just south of the Commandery, a building which stood here when the fighting took place and which is now a museum, dedicated to the battle and its times.

Powick Bridge was repaired after the fighting and remains much as it appeared at that time. It is now bypassed by the main road which crosses the River Teme on a modern bridge, but a convenient car park just south of the river can be used. The steep banks of the Teme and nearby meadows can be visited along a signed footpath from the bridge. There is a memorial to the Scots who fought here. From Powick Bridge, the tower of Powick Church can be seen on top of the hill to the south about a mile away. It is a steep climb up the hill to the church, which still bears the scars of cannon balls and musket fire.

The village of Upton, twelve miles south, was the site of the preliminary skirmishes and is worth a visit. The old bridge has vanished, but the church tower, where the English dragoons held off the Scots, still stands and the old houses of the main street are little changed since the fighting.

The marks left by English cannonballs and musket bullets on the stone work of Powick Church, where fighting began on 3 September, the day of the main battle.

Chapter Twenty

KILLIECRANKIE 1689

Introduction

The Battle at Killiecrankie was the first conflict in the fifty year struggle known as the Jacobite wars. In many ways it set the pattern for the rest of the conflict, for it began with a magnificent and overwhelming Jacobite victory, which soon turned to defeat and despair.

The underlying cause of the Jacobite wars was the decision in 1688 to expel King James II of England and VII of Scotland from his dual thrones. Unlike his elder brother, Charles II, James had failed to realize that England and Scotland had changed as a

After hours of waiting and some skirmishing on the western edge of the field, Bonnie Dundee led his Highlanders in a downhill charge which won the battle in minutes.

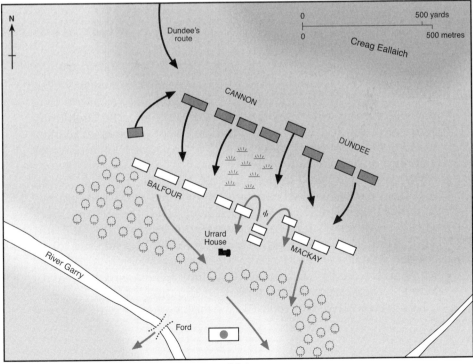

result of the Civil Wars of the 1640s. James attempted to rule as an autocratic king acting by divine right, and his subjects resented it. His open Catholicism made him even more unpopular among the predominantly Protestant English and the Lowland Scots. In 1688 he was expelled and his Protestant daughter Mary installed in his place along with her husband William, Prince of Orange.

Many felt that James had been unfairly treated and called for his return. These people were given the name of Jacobites, from Jacobus, the Latin version of the name James. In Scotland the most prominent Jacobite was John Graham, Viscount Dundee of Claverhouse, whose good looks and charming manner won him the name of Bonnie Dundee, while his career as a mercenary in the French and Dutch armies made him highly respected as a commander. In March 1689 Dundee attended a meeting of the Scottish Parliament in Edinburgh, but stormed out when a vote went in favour of William and Mary.

Dundee fled the capital and rode hard to his home at Dudhope Castle, Dundee. His dramatic departure became the subject of the words written by Sir Walter Scott to the Highland tune 'Bonnie Dundee', with its rousing chorus,

> *So its ho for the West Port*
> *And let us gae free*
> *And we'll follow the bonnet*
> *of Bonnie Dundee*

When a warrant for his arrest was issued, Dundee left Dudhope and sought refuge among his wife's clan at Glen Ogilvy. From there he called for the return of King James and set off on long journeys through the Highlands to rally support. The Highlands were staunchly Catholic and Dundee found a ready audience. Assured of support, Dundee called for an army to muster at Lochaber on 18 May.

The response was impressive as the MacDonalds, Appin Stewarts, MacNeils, MacLeods and many other clans brought out their fighting men. Inverness, Ruthven and Dunachton were quickly captured. Dundee now wanted the Murrays to come out, but their chief, the Marquis of Atholl, refused. Messages reached Dundee that if he could reach the Murray stronghold of Blair Atholl it would be surrendered to him by clansmen loyal to James – the Marquis being absent at the time.

Dundee reached and took Blair Atholl complete with its store of weapons and supplies. In July, Dundee's men reported meeting, near Blair Atholl, a forward patrol of the army the new government of William and Mary had raised. The patrol was chased back to the mouth of Killiecrankie Pass, but there it halted and held off the pursuing Highlanders. Dundee guessed that the enemy commander, General Hugh MacKay, was coming to take Blair Atholl. Dundee had a quick conference with his clan chiefs, and decided to ambush the enemy as it emerged from the pass. Next day, Bonnie Dundee and his Highlanders set out for Killiecrankie.

The Pass of Killiecrankie through which the Government army was passing when the Jacobites under Bonnie Dundee learned of their advance.

The Opposing Armies

The army which MacKay was bringing up from Dunkeld towards Blair Atholl was a strong one. It was drawn from both England and Lowland Scotland, having regiments from the official armies of both kingdoms. He had with him some eight battalions of regular infantry and two squadrons of cavalry together with several hundred militia.

The infantry were equipped almost exclusively with flintlock muskets. These guns could be fired twice a minute by trained men and were accurate up to around sixty yards, though the bullets remained able to injure at 150 yards. In addition to the muskets, the men had bayonets which plugged into the end of the barrel rather like a cork in a bottle. The bayonets largely replaced the pike of earlier years, being able to hold cavalry at a distance so long as the men kept in tight formation. Some officers still preferred to arm a few of the men with pikes.

One company in each battalion was armed with grenades in addition to their muskets. The grenades were rarely used in open battle, being a weapon of siege and entrenchments. This company was habitually the elite unit containing the toughest, bravest men. They were distinguished by having a tall, conical hat in place of the wide-brimmed hat of the other soldiers. This gave them greater freedom to use their arms in an overhead throwing action.

Horsemen were universally armed with a long, stout sword and with either a pair of pistols or a short musket. They could skirmish with their firearms, but on the field of battle were expected to charge home with their swords as shock troops. Among the cavalry there was an increasing tendency to discard armour as it became increasingly ineffective against firearms. Breast and back plates remained in general use, however, as they gave good protection against the swords of enemy cavalry.

MacKay had in his army several hundred dragoons. These men rode horses or ponies to the battle, but when they went into action they dismounted and fought as infantry. The dragoons combined speed of movement with heavy fire power. Their horses made them extremely useful for raids and scouting in the rugged Scottish Highlands. As a result, MacKay had all his dragoons out on patrols and missions of various kinds, so he had none with him at Killiecrankie. Finally MacKay had nine small cannon. These were light pieces which could be dragged along the mountain tracks by a horse or half a dozen men. They fired balls of about three or five pounds over some 1,500 yards with a fair degree of accuracy.

Dundee's army was very different from that of MacKay. In place of the regular troops which would be recognized across Europe, Dundee's men were Highlanders raised by their clan chiefs and equipped with traditional weapons that had seen action for generations. Each unit consisted of the men of the clan, led by their chief or his son, so a clan 'regiment' might be a few dozen men or several hundred strong.

The front rank of each clan was made up of the wealthier men who carried a musket, a sword and a small shield known as a targe, often they had an axe or dagger as well. Some of the richer men carried a huge six-feet long sword which needed to be used double-handed. This was the dreaded 'great sword' or *claidaemh mor* in Gaelic. The name became claymore and was later given to the basket-hilted, single-handed broadsword which became more common later. The poorer clansmen made up the rear ranks. They came armed with swords, daggers or axes as they saw fit, though most had the targe. Some carried the so-called Locahaber axe, a ferocious weapon with a six-feet haft and broad cutting blade. The clansmen fought almost exclusively on foot, so Dundee had only a few dozen cavalry with him and these were lightly armed.

The Highlanders came to war not only with their own distinctive weapons, but also with their dress and music. Bagpipes were played by clansmen on the march and in battle, adding their wild notes to the noise of fighting. Dressed in blue bonnets and wrapped in the tartan plaid, the Highlanders looked savage and wild to the eyes of the Lowlanders and the English.

Tactics

As might be expected, given the very different armies led by MacKay and Dundee, the two commanders relied on quite different tactics.

MacKay's men were trained in the tactics of mainland Europe. His infantry stood in lines three deep, from which they would deliver united volleys of musket fire at the enemy. In Europe opposing regiments would fire at each other until one side gave way or until cavalry appeared on the scene. Sometimes bayonets would be fixed to pursue a defeated foe, but otherwise it was a case of fire, reload and fire again.

It was usual for battalions to form up their companies so that about one third of them were in a second line thirty yards or so behind the front line. This would allow the rear companies to plug any gaps that occurred or to cover a retreat as proved necessary.

At Killiecrankie, MacKay changed the usual order of musket fire. It was customary to march to within effective range, about sixty yards, before opening fire. But MacKay knew the Highlanders would want to get to hand-to-hand fighting. To deter this he ordered his battalion commanders to open fire with one company while Dundee's men were still 100 yards distant, then to fire with each successive company as the Highlanders advanced. He hoped to inflict high casualties and to deter the Highlanders from closing. Because the various companies would fire at different times, MacKay reasoned he did not need to hold any in reserve. Instead he placed all the companies in a continuous line. It was a good plan but, with few exceptions, MacKay's men were not trained well enough to give this sort of rolling fire and most battalion commanders ignored the order.

In contrast, the Highlanders' tactics were brutally simple. They would advance to within effective musket range of the enemy and deliver a single volley by those men with muskets. Even while the heavy white smoke of musket gunpowder still hung in the air, the clansmen threw aside their guns and charged forward with cold steel. Falling on the enemy in a ragged column some six or so men deep, the Highlanders had great momentum behind them. If they could break the enemy line, they would turn the battle into a hand-to-hand struggle, in which the swords, axes and dirks would have a clear advantage over the muskets and bayonets. Success depended on reaching the enemy line before they had time to reload their muskets and fire a second volley at point-blank range into the charging Highlanders.

The Battle

When MacKay led his men out of the Pass of Killiecrankie into the wider valley west of Killiecrankie village, he saw Bonnie Dundee's scouts hanging about the track leading to Blair Atholl. The scouts showed no signs of activity, so MacKay decided to wait at Urrard House until his entire army was out of the pass before moving forwards. It seems he expected to meet Dundee coming down the path.

In fact, MacKay was still awaiting his rearmost battalion, the English 13th Regiment of Foot, when Bonnie Dundee himself came into sight. He was not advancing down the road, but was leading his lightly armed infantry over the steep slopes of the mountain Creag Eallaich.

The battlefield of Killiecrankie as seen from the left wing of the Government army. The Jacobites occupied the ridge on the left while the Government troops were drawn up approximately along the modern line of the fence on the right of the picture.

MacKay was an experienced soldier and at once realized that if Dundee got on to the ridge of rugged high ground on MacKay's right he would be in a dominating position. Hurriedly, MacKay realigned his infantry so that they faced north, with the river at their backs, and ordered them up the hill. MacKay's men reached the crest of the ridge first, but were horrified to discover that it was not the top of the hill, but merely a fold in the land. The main ridge was some 300 yards further on and it was already swarming with Highlanders.

MacKay realized he would have to fight a defensive battle, for the ridge was too steep for him to take it with infantry. He therefore redeployed his men to occupy the whole length of his position, with the lately arrived 13th Regiment on the extreme right. This involved spreading the infantry even more thinly than he had intended, and relying on his two squadrons of cavalry to hold the centre of the line. He put the left wing infantry under Brigadier Balfour, and kept the cavalry and right wing infantry under his own command.

Watching these movements from above, Dundee also extended

his line. Unable to get the Highlanders to form in thinner lines than tradition demanded, he simply placed the clan units further apart. Aware the far right flank would be out of reach of his shouted orders, Dundee put it under command of an Irish mercenary named Cannon. Dundee had the strong July sun straight in his men's faces, for the sky was cloudless. He decided to wait until the evening when the sun would have swung to the west and sunk towards the horizon. MacKay unaware of the reason for the delay, tried to goad Dundee into attacking by opening fire with his light cannon. The gunners had trouble aiming up hill and most of the cannonballs fell harmlessly in the heather. When one of the guns blew up, the gunners stopped firing.

Meanwhile, Dundee wanted to raise the morale of his own men by retaliating in some form, so he pushed a group of men from Clan Cameron down the hill from his right wing. Once within range of the enemy, the Camerons opened a sporadic fire from their hiding places in the heather and among the rocks. MacKay's left hand battalion returned fire. There were few casualties on either side and, after a while, the Camerons returned to their clan.

By now it was just an hour before sunset and the sun had lost its fierce heat and glare. Dundee gave the order to advance. The

Dundee's view across the battlefield. The Government army was drawn up near the bottom of the slope, where the modern road runs from left to right.

clans came down the hill towards MacKay's men. Only the 13th Foot on MacKay's far right and some companies of the adjacent Leven's Regiment opened fire early as ordered. This caused the Clan MacDonald, which faced them, to swerve to their right and merge with the Clan MacLean.

When the Highlanders were fifty yards from MacKay's men their lead ranks lifted their muskets and fired a volley. The balls inflicted few casualties, but caused the return fire to be ragged and to some extent badly aimed. Then the screaming clansmen were charging forward with drawn swords. Some of MacKay's officers gave orders to reload muskets, others ordered their men to fix bayonets. They were all too late, for the Highlanders were upon the infantry in seconds.

Hacking with their terrible swords and axes, stabbing with dirks and daggers, the Highlanders quickly cut down the front rank of their enemies, at which the remaining infantry turned and bolted down the hill towards the river. At this point, MacKay drew his sword and ordered his cavalry to charge into the flank of Clan Glenmoriston. Although he did not realize it at the time, none of the horsemen followed him, but instead turned and joined the rout. MacKay charged forward and the clansmen drew aside to let the lone horseman through. Thus MacKay found himself in the rear of the entire enemy army which was rapidly disappearing downhill in pursuit of his own fleeing men. He was utterly alone on the heather slope. MacKay then saw a cloud of musket smoke and concluded that at least some of his men had stood firm, so he galloped to join them. These were the men of the 13th and Leven's Regiment who had not been hit by the initial charge.

Taking command, MacKay ordered an orderly and phased withdrawal up over the hills towards Weem Castle which he knew to be held by a Menzies chief who was hostile to Dundee. He picked up scattered bands of fugitives as he marched, and several others also made for Weem.

The bulk of the government army, meanwhile, was running back to the Pass of Killiecrankie. One soldier escaped his pursuers by leaping the ravine of the River Garry – clearing eighteen feet in a single bound – a place now known as Soldier's Leap. Most were less fortunate and were killed. At the river a small group rallied and delivered a volley. Dundee rode over to organize his men to crush the resistance and was hit by a musket ball just under his breastplate. He fell to the ground.

Aftermath

Three days after the battle, MacKay arrived at Stirling Castle with about 600 men. He found another 500 or so who had made their own way back. The remaining 3,000 men of his command lay dead on the heather at Killiecrankie, or were being held prisoner by the Highlanders.

The news of Killiecrankie spread fast and the people began preparing for war. Most clansmen expected their chiefs to call them out to join the thriving Jacobite cause of Bonnie Dundee. Swords were sharpened and muskets cleaned across the Highlands. In the Lowlands, people hid their valuables and braced themselves for the onslaught.

The victory was not all it seemed. Among the dead was Bonnie Dundee himself who had died of his stomach wound sometime after sunset. The clansmen wrapped his body in a tartan plaid and carried it to the old kirk at Blair Atholl for burial. As the charismatic leader and military brains of the Jacobite cause in Scotland, Dundee was a serious loss for the Highlanders.

The government army had effectively ceased to exist, as only the dragoons and one regiment of infantry had escaped disaster by not being present at Killiecrankie. These men, under the

Weem Castle to which the fugitives from the battle fled for safety.

command of the noted poet William Cleland, prepared to meet the full wrath of the Jacobite army. They would not have long to wait.

Visiting the Battlefield Today

Killiecrankie has more than most battlefields to offer the visitor. Not only is the battlefield relatively easy of access, but there is a visitor centre and numerous local sights relevant to the fighting.

To find the battlefield, take the B8079 north from Pitlochry, which soon plunges into the Pass of Killiecrankie. About three miles from Pitlochry the Killiecrankie Visitors' Centre and an ample car park are on the left. Refreshments are on offer here, and there is a path to the Soldier's Leap and the wide footpath which served as a road through the Pass at the time of the battle.

If you are feeling energetic, you can explore the battlefield on foot from here, but others may prefer to let their car take the strain of otherwise extensive walking and some steep hills. Leave the Centre on the B8079 heading north, passing through the area where MacKay camped part of his army while waiting for the rest to finish coming through the Pass. The heather-topped hill to your right is Creag Eallaich over the left shoulder of which Dundee and his army appeared. The ridge to which MacKay led his forces is now occupied by the A9. The land between the A9 and the river is where the pursuit and most of the killing took place. The spot where Bonnie Dundee was shot is marked by an upright boulder in an open field to the north of the B8079 a mile or so from the Visitors' Centre.

To reach the slopes down which Dundee launched his attack, you need to take the unsignposted lane which turns right off the B8079 just north of a prominent sign instructing drivers not to overtake due to a blind summit and before Garry House. This road passes under the A9 and emerges into open fields at the left flank of the position taken up by General McKay. The slope down which Dundee and his Highlanders charged, is to your front and right. The lane winds across the hillside to reach a number of farms and cottages and gives magnificent views across the battlefield. However, all the branches off the lane are dead ends or peter out into footpaths so, if you are driving, be prepared to reverse back down the hill.

The battle was fought for control of Blair Atholl Castle, which lies just off the B8079 about two miles north of the battlefield. This castle is open to the public and is one of the most impressive castles in Scotland. The Menzies Castle at Weem, to

211

which the surviving government troops fled after the battle, is also open to the public and boasts among its exhibits weapons used by the Clan Menzies at Bannockburn, Sheriffmuir, Prestonpans and Culloden. The bedroom in which Bonnie Prince Charlie stayed in 1746 has been preserved and is now furnished much as it was then. The small church where Bonnie Dundee was buried is now ruined, but his tomb remains and can be visited. Follow the B8079 north from the battlefield, turning right to Old Blair just before Blair Atholl Castle. This lane twists about before reaching a crossroads, where you turn left and find the entrance to the chapel on your left as the lane takes a sharp right turn.

The stone erected by the clansmen to mark the spot where Bonnie Dundee was shot from his horse.

Chapter Twenty-One
DUNKELD 1689

Introduction

The Battle of Dunkeld was a savage affair in which neither side asked for nor showed any mercy. It ended with the total destruction of the town of Dunkeld and the collapse of the first Jacobite uprising.

On 27 July the Jacobite army of Highlanders had routed the army of English and Lowland troops which was supporting the new Protestant monarchs William and Mary against the ousted Catholic King James II of England and VII of Scotland. At the moment of victory, however, the Jacobite commander, Viscount Dundee, was killed. His place was taken by Colonel Cannon who had been chosen by Dundee as his second in command because of his formidable organizational abilities.

Unfortunately for the Jacobites, Cannon had none of the charisma of Dundee nor did he have the trust of the various clan chiefs. Precious days were lost in arguments over who had precedence over whom and which clan would be given what duties. It was not until 16 August that the Jacobite army marched out of Blair Atholl towards Perth and the Lowlands.

The Protestant government had not been idle. Desperate pleas were sent south asking for new regiments of English troops to come north to oppose the Catholic forces of the exiled King James. Unaware of the disputes in the Jacobite camp, the government daily feared that the Highland clans would burst into the Lowlands. Hurriedly the only complete regiment to hand was sent to hold the road south at Dunkeld.

This regiment was the 26th Regiment of Foot, which had its own peculiar ways. The regiment had been originally raised in the Lowlands from fanatical Presbyterians. Their religion was frowned upon in official army circles, so the regiment held their Sunday Services away from whichever barracks they were in and with sentries posted to keep more conventional Christians at a distance. The tradition of posting sentries outside religious services continued with the 26th Regiment until it was

The hills north of Dunkeld over which the Jacobite army came marching.

disbanded in 1969. Moreover, while most regiments took the name of their colonel, the 26th was named the Cameronians in honour of the preacher Richard Cameron who had been their first clergyman.

As the 26th marched towards Dunkeld they were led by twenty-eight year-old William Cleland. Young Cleland had gained plenty of military experience in Europe, but he was better known for his evocative poetry. To amuse his men on the march, he wrote a series of abusive verses about the Highlanders. Arriving in Dunkeld, Cleland ordered his men to erect breastworks around the Cathedral and the home of the Marquis of Atholl and to barricade the streets. A force of English dragoons and cavalry arrived soon after and Cleland set them to scouting the surrounding hills. The citizens of Dunkeld, who were more friendly to the Jacobites than to Cleland, were bundled out of their homes and told to find shelter as best they could.

On 18 August a small group of Highlanders arrived bearing a message from Cannon which read: 'We, the gentlemen assembled, desire whether ye come for peace or war, and certify you that if ye burn any one house we will destroy you.' Cleland sent the messengers back without a reply. Three days later, on 21 August the entire Jacobite army came down to attack Dunkeld.

The Opposing Armies

Cleland's force was composed only of the 26th Regiment on the day of battle, for the cavalry and dragoons had been ordered off to Perth to deal with trouble there. The regiment was up to full strength of 1,200 men equipped with muskets, bayonets and swords. The men were relatively inexperienced in battle, but were superbly trained at musket firing and could loose off two rounds each minute with ease. Cleland's plan was simply to stand behind his defences and hope to hold off the expected attack.

The Jacobite army led by Cannon was about 4,000 strong. The men were armed and equipped in typical Highland fashion as was the army that had fought at Killiecrankie. The problem Cannon faced was that the battle-winning charge his men favoured would be difficult to pull off against the heavily entrenched positions they faced at Dunkeld.

Dunkeld Cathedral. The final redoubt of the government troops was built around these massive stone walls.

The Battle

Despite the tactical problems that Cannon expected, the Jacobite attack began well. The clansmen surged down the valley and into Dunkeld town. They quickly overran the barricades in the outer part of town and pursued the retreating infantry through the alleys and streets. When the fight reached the Cross, the Highlanders came across a particularly high barricade which held them up for some time. When the officer in command of the Cross, Lieutenant Stewart, was killed, his men gave way and the clansmen surged on.

Emerging from the narrow alleys of the town, Cannon and

215

The narrow streets of Dunkeld in which the early stages of the battle took place. The houses shown here were built in the 1690s to replace those burned down during the fighting.

his Jacobites reached the open ground around the cathedral and Atholl's house. They attempted to charge, but the heavy and regular fire of the 26th Regiment drove them back. The leading clansmen broke into the houses facing the defences around the Cathedral and opened fire on their enemies. Cleland was hit in the liver and turned to get to the first aid post, but was then shot in the head and collapsed.

For over two hours the musket fire continued until the desperate defenders were out of bullets and firing lumps of lead torn from the Cathedral roof. Captain Munro, who now commanded the Regiment, gathered together a band of volunteers. He dashed across the open ground with each volunteer carrying a burning torch. The few who reached the houses set fire to their thatched roofs. As the houses caught light, the clansmen were forced to pull back. Soon the entire town was ablaze.

For some hours the two sides held back as the town burned to ashes. Cannon wanted to renew the attack when the fires had died down, but his clansmen were having none of it. Their traditional tactics had not worked against the entrenched enemy and losses had been heavy, perhaps over 250 men. And they were led by the Irishman Cannon, not their beloved, but deceased, commander Bonnie Dundee.

The clan chiefs declared that they were taking their men home to gather in the crops and prepare for winter. They would, they promised Cannon, come out again for the Jacobite cause the following spring. As the Highlanders streamed out of smouldering Dunkeld towards the mountains, the surviving

The Haughs of Cromdale where the Jacobite clansmen were scattered a few months after the Battle of Dunkeld.

Protestants began to sing psalms.

Aftermath

In the spring of 1690 the exiled King James sent Thomas Buchan to raise the clans in his cause while he himself led a French army to Ireland to help a Jacobite rising there. But without Bonnie Dundee to lead them, most of the larger clans refused to come out and only 1,500 men gathered at Cromdale. In May the government forces for once acted more quickly than the Highlanders. A force of dragoons and cavalry launched a surprise attack at Cromdale and scattered the clansmen back into the mountains. In July King James was badly beaten at the Battle of the Boyne in Ireland. He returned to exile in France.

Although James himself would never return to Britain, his cause was not dead. The Jacobite Wars would go on.

Visiting the Battlefield Today

The charming town of Dunkeld lies a short way off the A9 where the A923 towards Dundee branches off eastwards. The Cathedral is largely ruined, though the choir now serves as the parish church, and is well worth a visit. The town was burnt down during the battle, but most of the houses built in the immediate aftermath still stand and follow the same street plan as existed at the time of the battle. The town today boasts plenty of watering holes and can easily entertain the visitor for an hour or two.

Cromdale, where the clans were scattered the following spring, lies on the A95 west of Aberdeen, just east of the junction with the A939. To find the battlefield, take the lane which runs south from the A95 beside the public house and follow it up the hill for about half a mile. Turn right down the track signposted to Lethendry Farm. A couple of hundred yards along this track a large information board put up by the local Council marks the battlefield and gives a good outline of events which took place here. The tracks and lanes across the battlefield are narrow and rough, better suited to off-road vehicles than modern saloon cars, so the area is best explored on foot.

Chapter Twenty-Two

SHERIFFMUIR 1715

Introduction

The second of the major Jacobite wars was to become known later as 'The 15' to distinguish it from 'The 45', the uprising in 1745 which was led by Bonnie Prince Charlie. Unlike 'The 45', 'The 15' began in both England and Scotland, though it was in Scotland that its fate was to be decided.

'The 15' was raised in favour of James Edward Stuart, known

The right wings of both armies were successful, but the battle ended as a stalemate.

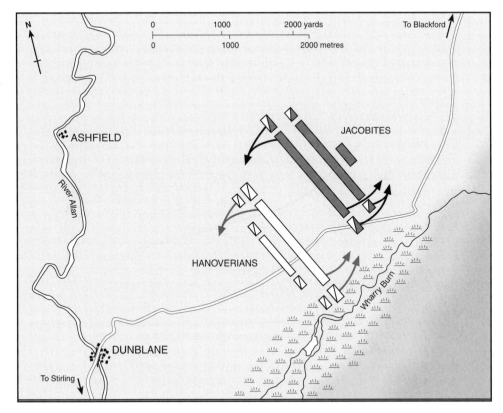

to his supporters as King James III of England and VIII of Scotland and to his opponents as 'The Pretender'. This prince was the son of the ousted King James II and VII who had been expelled in 1688, whose throne had been taken first by his daughter Queen Mary and her husband William of Orange and then by his second daughter Anne.

By 1713 it had become obvious that Queen Anne would die without producing a surviving heir and the noblemen and politicians of Britain had to consider the possible claimants. By far the strongest claim was that of James Edward who was, after all, the legitimate monarch. A delegation went to France to talk to the exiled prince. They offered him the joint thrones of England and Scotland on condition that he renounce his Catholic religion and promise to respect the democratic constitution brought in under Mary and Anne. But James Edward was a devout Catholic and was convinced of his right to rule. He refused the conditions.

So when Anne died in 1714, the two crowns were offered to a remote German cousin, George, the Elector of Hanover. George spoke no English and had no knowledge of British customs or ways. Though a useful figurehead, George was neither well-known nor popular. This was especially the case in Scotland and northern England where economic depression was blamed on the government. Supporters of the exiled James Edward, known as Jacobites, stirred up trouble and promised that if only the Stuart line was restored all would be well.

In August 1715 the leading Scottish Jacobite, John Erskine, Earl of Mar, left London in disgust at the behaviour of the new King George. He sent out invitations to all the Scottish noblemen and clan chiefs whom he believed to be Jacobites to join him on his estates for a 'hunting trip'. When they arrived, on 6 September, Mar dramatically unfurled the Royal Standard of the Stuarts and 'The 15' had begun.

Mar had good reason to hope for success. The Earl of Derwentwater had promised to raise the north of England in the Stuart cause and was already mustering his forces. In France, James Edward had the support of King Louis XIV who had already lent him 6,000 crack troops. Within three weeks over 5,000 clansmen had joined Mar at Perth. Three weeks after that Mar's army had more than doubled. It was time to move.

The news from England was promising, Derwentwater had raised several thousand men from the north-east and had marched over the Pennines into Lancashire with the government troops retreating before him. Events in France were less encouraging. Louis XIV had died and the ministers who ran the country in the name of the five-year-old Louis XV, were not too keen on stirring up trouble with Britain. The French troops had been taken back. Still, James Edward had promised to come to Scotland to join Mar's army and was trying to find a captain willing to risk running the gauntlet of the British Royal Navy.

By the end of October, Mar had over 10,000 men and controlled all of Scotland, north of the Tay. He knew he had supporters in the Lowlands, but to reach them he had to get past John Campbell, Duke of Argyll, who held Stirling with a force of 3,000 government troops.

Mar's first move was to detach forces to cross the Forth and draw Argyll out of Stirling. Mar then marched his main body straight at the fortress to capture it while Argyll was busy elsewhere. Argyll, however, had been using his fast moving dragoons to scout out the roads and keep an eye on Mar. He marched out of Stirling, but not to chase the detachments. He moved on Dunblane to block Mar's advance. It was a bold move for an outnumbered force, but Argyll commanded professional soldiers and believed himself able to defeat Mar's army of clansmen.

Mar, meanwhile, was equally confident of victory. The two armies continued to advance and

The statue of Rob Roy Macgregor in Stirling. The famous outlawed clan chief of the Macgregors fought on the Jacobite side at Sheriffmuir. The statue gives a good idea of the basic equipment of the clansmen who fought in the Jacobite wars. He carries a targe and broadsword and wears the kilt, plaid, shirt and bonnet of the period.

on 13 November met each other on the bleak, damp moorland of Sheriffmuir.

The Opposing Armies

The armies that met at Sheriffmuir were similar to those that fought at Killiecrankie in 1689. Mar's army, like that of Dundee, was made up almost entirely of clansmen from the Highlands. These men came and fought in their clans, so that a 'regiment' might number anything from 50 to 1,000 men. They wore the traditional highland dress of blue bonnet, with eagle feathers for chieftains, and heavy tartan plaid wrapped around their bodies into a kilt and over the shoulder to cover the shirt. All the clansmen carried swords or axes and dirks, but the richer men had muskets and pistols. In battle, the men with firearms formed the front rank. Unlike Dundee, Mar had a few hundred cavalry drawn from the rich lands around Aberdeen.

Argyll, in contrast, had a force of regular army soldiers. He had drawn in his dragoons and had almost 1,000 with him. These men were mounted on small horses or ponies which they rode to battle and on the march. The dragoons carried short muskets as their main firearm, but usually had swords as a back-up weapon.

The bulk of Argyll's army comprised some 2,200 infantry. These regiments, from England and Lowland Scotland, wore red coats and were armed with muskets and bayonets. Unlike the earlier plug bayonets used at Killiecrankie, these men now had socket bayonets which fitted around the muzzle of the musket and allowed the gun to be fired with the bayonet fitted.

One company from each regiment was made up of elite grenadiers. They did not use grenades except in siege works, but they were the tallest and toughest men in the regiment. The infantrymen had been drilled for hours in the use of the musket and could fire at least twice each minute. They were also able to form and reform from line into column and back again on all sorts of terrain. These English infantry were fast becoming the terror of Europe.

Tactics

Mar was not an experienced commander, but his clan chiefs knew what their men were capable of doing. The clansmen had only two tactics. The first was to stand and fight, the other was to attack. In attack the clansmen performed what is known as

222

the Highland charge. They would advance to within effective musket range, about fifty yards, then halt. The front rank would fire their muskets,then hurl them aside and join the rest of the clan in a charge with cold steel. The impact of the shrieking, screaming Highlanders, backed by the skirl of the bagpipes could be devastating.

The regular infantry under Argyll were used to fighting a quite different sort of battle. On European battlefields there were cavalry in large numbers, and tactics had to take this into account. The infantry had bayonets which could be used to deter cavalry charges, but only if the infantry kept in tight formation. A charge would disorder the infantry and lay them open to cavalry attack. So the men tended to march in dense lines to within musket range, then fire volley after volley at the enemy until one side or another retreated. A retreating enemy might be followed up with bayonets, but at a steady pace not in a wild charge.

Dragoons were usually expected to dismount once battle was joined. They would then deploy into line and act as regular infantry. The horses were kept close by, however, in case the men needed to mount up to escape a superior enemy or move to another part of the battlefield. By 1715 there was a tendency for dragoons to be equipped with cavalry-style swords, so they could deliver a mounted charge in favourable circumstances.

The Battle

It was the Duke of Argyll who reached the undulating moor of Sheriffmuir first. He placed his men in a long line from the banks of the Wharry Burn to the top of Kippendaive Hill, blocking the road. Argyll had the majority of his infantry drawn up in the front line with small units of dragoons on each flank. Learning the lesson of Killiecrankie and bearing in mind what a Highland charge could do to unsupported infantry, Argyll had a second line. This was made up of around 600 infantry and the main bulk of the dragoons, again on either flank. Believing he had done what he could to make both flanks secure, Argyll awaited the arrival of the enemy whom he could see approaching in the distance like the shadow of a cloud moving over the landscape.

Mar halted his men beside Black Hill, where they were out of sight of the enemy. There he harangued them with a speech which fired them up so much that the massed ranks burst out into a roar of anger and defiance. The troops waiting on Sheriffmuir heard the shout and wondered what was coming at

The bleak moorland of Sheriffmuir across which Mar and his Highlanders advanced to the attack.

them. Mar then lined his men up, put the few cavalry he had on the flanks, kept a reserve back under his personal command. Then he ordered the advance.

As the Jacobites came up on to the moor they were just 500 yards from Argyll's men. Mar realized the right wing of his line overlapped that of Argyll, but his left was in danger of being outflanked by the dragoons. He sent orders to the Appin Stewarts, the Camerons and the Robertsons on the far left to extend out towards the marshy banks of the Wharry Burn as they marched forwards. Argyll saw at the same time that his own left was in danger of being outflanked and likewise ordered his men to extend the line. Then he rode over to his right wing to try to take advantage of the very obvious confusion being caused on the Jacobites' left wing.

The Jacobite left was preparing to deliver a traditional Highland charge when it was met by disciplined volley fire from Argyll's line. Confused deployment was causing the Jacobites even more trouble, and when the mounted dragoons came up, it proved too much. The clansmen began to fall back. Argyll looked across the battlefield. On the left he saw his men also delivering volley fire and the Highlanders hesitating to attack.

Argyll moved forward with the infantry of his right wing,

driving the clansmen back along the Wharry Burn. It was no rout, however, for the Highlanders were staging a fighting withdrawal towards another stream, the Allan Water where they intended to make a stand. For over two hours the fight went on, with Argyll ordering his infantry to fire volleys while the dragoons tried to get into position for a charge, and all the time the clansmen held formation and fell back.

Meanwhile the action elsewhere was not going as Argyll thought it was. He had seen his men on the left wing open fire and the clansmen hesitate, and had thought his disciplined men were victorious. In fact the infantry had opened fire early while the clansmen were out of effective range and had inflicted few casualties. The hesitation had been because one of the few men killed was the Chief of Clanranald, one of the most respected fighters in the Highlands. The Clanranald and MacDonalds came to a halt.

The situation was saved for Mar by the Chief of Glengarry who ran forward shouting 'Revenge. Revenge. Today for revenge. Tomorrow for mourning.' The Highlanders followed him forwards and delivered a crushing charge. Though far superior in numbers, the left and centre of Argyll's line collapsed in the face of the clansmen's fury. Even the dragoons fled, not stopping until they reached Stirling.

It took Mar some time to gather together his victorious clansmen. They had chased the enemy for over a mile, slaughtering all those they could reach, and now were spread out looting the dead in traditional fashion. Eventually, Mar got the majority of the clans formed up and marched back to find out what had happened on his left wing where, last he had seen, the Camerons and their neighbours had been staging a fighting withdrawal.

When Mar and his men arrived at the battlefield, it was utterly deserted. Only the dead and wounded were to be seen. Uncertain what to do, Mar drew his men up on Kippendaive Hill and sent out scouts. They reported that his left wing was now two miles away at Kinbuck on the Allan Water and that Argyll was returning to the battlefield with his victorious right wing of some 1,000 men. As Argyll and his column came in sight, they saw the large mass of clansmen on Kippendaive Hill and hurriedly formed a defensive line behind some farm walls.

For some reason that he never later explained, Mar did not attack. The short autumn day drew to a close with the two sides staring at each other across the bloodstained heather. After dark

The Allan Water at Kinbuck. It was here, where a steep ridge backs the stream, that the retreating clansmen of Mar's left wing finally halted the English advance.

fell, Argyll led his men to shelter in Dunblane to await the dawn attack they all expected. But Mar had given the orders to fall back on Ardnoch where he could gather his defeated left wing.

The battle had ended with Argyll in control of the battlefield. He had, however, lost about 500 men to Mar's 140 casualties. It was, effectively, a draw.

Aftermath

A few days after Sheriffmuir, news arrived that the English Jacobites had surrendered at Preston following a short fight and a long period without supplies. Mar fell back again on Perth. He had failed to break into the Lowlands and there was now little point in trying to march on northern England. On 22 December, James Edward arrived from France and at once announced that he intended to be crowned at Scone.

By this time Argyll had been massively reinforced with troops from England and was marching north. In January the government army took Scone and moved on towards Dundee. At Montrose, James Edward realized that all hopes of victory were gone. Mar persuaded him to take a ship immediately on the grounds that, with the Pretender gone, the clans would be able to make better terms for surrender. On 4 February James Edward set sail, having spent just six weeks in his ancestral kingdom.

Instead of seeking terms of surrender, Mar himself then fled abroad. The army, now led by the clan chiefs, staged an orderly withdrawal into the mountains. Once in the safety of the Highlands, the army broke up, each clan returning to its own territory. The government troops moved into the Highlands and rounded up some leaders for prison terms. In 1717 an Act of Pardon was passed by the British government in London granting an end to 'The 15'.

In Europe, James Edward found himself suddenly unwelcome in France. He moved to Rome as a guest of the Pope. In 1718 war broke out between Britain and Spain. James Edward hurried to Madrid and the Spanish sent a small army to Scotland. 'The 19' Jacobite uprising was under way. It ended almost before it began when the majority of the Spanish fleet was delayed by storms. The few Jacobites who had gathered before the Spanish arrived, were defeated near Loch Cluanie on 9 June and 'The 19' fizzled out.

The curious Battle of Sheriffmuir was perhaps best summed up by the words of the song composed soon after:

> There's some say that we won
> And some say that they won,
> And some say that nane won at all.
> But one thing I'm sure
> That at Sheriffmuir
> A battle there was, that I saw, man
> And we ran, and they ran,
> And they ran, and we ran,
> And we ran, and they ran awa, man.

Visiting the Battlefield Today

The battlefield of Sheriffmuir is well signposted and served by both roads and footpaths. If you are considering using the footpaths, be warned. This is wild moorland which becomes very wet after even light rain so you will need stout boots and would be well advised to have dry footwear to change into after your walk.

From the Dunblane Bypass, B8033, take the unclassified road signposted to Sheriffmuir. The road climbs up to the moor, turns

The monument of the Clan McRae erected at Sheriffmuir to commemorate the brave deeds of the clansmen at the battle.

sharp left and after a mile or so reaches two monuments. The larger of the two was erected by the Clan McRae in 1915 to mark the sacrifice of the clansmen from Kintail and Lochalsh who fell here. The smaller monument was erected later by the 1745 Association. From beside the McRae Monument a footpath leads through the woods (which did not exist in 1715) to the Gathering Stone on the summit of Kippendaive Hill. These two monuments stand just behind the right centre of the English army, so continue on along the road to find the main scene of action.

At a T-junction you can turn right to find the Wharry Burn which marked the southern edge of the battlefield. If you turn left, however, you reach the very welcome Sheriffmuir Inn which offers bar meals and, appropriately enough, both Scottish and English beers. Beyond the inn the moorland stretches unbroken to the north-east and it was over this area that the Earl of Mar led his men to the attack.

Chapter Twenty-Three

PRESTONPANS 1745

Introduction

The final battles fought between the English and Scottish belong to the great event known as 'The 45' – the rising led by Bonnie Prince Charlie, which aimed to restore the Stuart kings to the thrones of Scotland and England.

A march undertaken at night put the Jacobites on the English flank at dawn and in a position to launch a decisive charge while their enemies tried to reform their line.

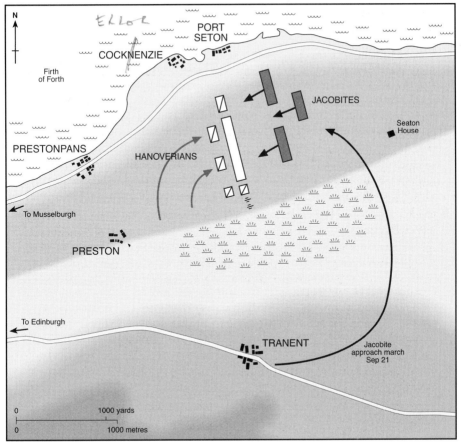

James Edward Stuart, the supposed King James III of England and VIII of Scotland, had kept in touch with his supporters in Britain after the failure of the Jacobite risings in 1715 and 1719. He knew from these contacts that the new German kings, George I and then George II, were unpopular with large numbers of people in England and even more so in Scotland. He also knew that the British Army was a formidable organization and that any armed uprising was likely to succeed only if it had professional military support from one of the other European powers.

During his long years in exile, James Edward brought up his two sons, Charles and Henry, to be princes groomed in royal, military and administrative affairs in case the Stuarts ever regained their lost thrones. Of the two young men it was the elder, Charles, who took the business of regaining the thrones most seriously. He became known in Britain as The Young Pretender, in contrast to his father, The Old Pretender.

In 1744, the twenty-four-year-old Charles left the family home in Rome to go to Paris. France was at war with Britain, Holland and Austria and, James Edward hoped, might be willing to send troops to Britain to lead a Jacobite uprising. When Charles arrived he was hailed as the heir to the British throne by the French government.

King Louis XV told Charles that France would provide troops for a Jacobite uprising, but only if Charles could first obtain written promises from his supporters in Britain that they would join the rising. Such letters would, of course, have been treason, so the Jacobites in Britain were understandably unwilling to sign them. Without such written promises, Charles had only verbal pledges of support. Louis told him that such pledges were valueless and that France would not send men, though he would give Charles money and weapons. Charles remained in Paris pestering French government officials, but receiving only the same promises.

Then, on 11 May, the Battle of Fontenoy resulted in a defeat for the British army on the continent. In response, George II ordered almost all the troops left in Britain to join him in Germany. When Charles heard this news he was jubilant. Britain was stripped of her professional army. He believed that there was now a chance that a Jacobite rising might succeed, even without professional help. He made do with the French promises of money and weapons only and set sail in a French warship. Charles took with him the exiled Duke of Atholl, who knew Scotland well, and a mercenary named John O'Sullivan who was to command the army. He left a message begging Louis to send more money and weapons – and perhaps men – as quickly as possible.

Charles landed in Scotland on 24 July. He was met almost at once by Alexander, the chief of the MacDonalds of Boisdale, the local clan. The MacDonalds were one of the most powerful clans and were well-known Jacobites. Prince Charles expected their support, but Alexander MacDonald told him bluntly that as he had not brought an army with him, he should go back to France at once.

The French captain agreed to stay anchored for two weeks while Charles contacted the clan chiefs. They came to speak to him and inspect the French weapons he had. Some chiefs agreed with MacDonald and told Charles to go back, others said they would rise if others did. Not until the great Donald of Lochiel agreed to raise the Cameron clan did any give real promises of support. Other Camerons did not want to come out, but Lochiel said he would do his best.

It was enough for Charles, who sent away the French warship. He was now committed to the rising. Charles wrote letters to all the clan chiefs inviting them to come with their men to join him. On 19 August, Charles took the Royal Standard of the Stuarts to Glenfinnan. He had with him 150 men of Clanranald. The time for the clans to arrive came and went, but nobody arrived. Then the sound of bagpipes was heard in the distance and over the hill came Lochiel with the full fighting strength of the Clan Cameron, some 700 fully armed men. The rising was under way.

Over the next few days clan after clan came to join Charles. Even the MacDonalds changed their minds and marched to the rallying point. One of the most important single men to arrive was Lord Murray. Murray was a tough professional soldier who had fought in 'The 15' and 'The 19', but had since won a pardon from the British government. Now he was marching again and was put in command of the growing army. Unlike Charles, Murray could speak Gaelic and had a fine appreciation of the abilities, and shortcomings, of the clans in battle. Undoubtedly a good commander, Murray was not overendowed with tact. Disputes between himself and the mercenary O'Sullivan were to cause problems in the coming months.

Other clans remained ominously absent. The McLeods stayed at home and the powerful Clan Campbell prepared for war, but did not march to join the Jacobite army.

The few government troops in Scotland were commanded by

Sir John Cope, a courageous officer who, unfortunately, was inexperienced in command. Cope first gathered his forces at Inverness, hoping to advance into the Highlands and catch Charles before the Jacobite army had grown too large. But Murray slipped past Cope and raced to Edinburgh.

Charles and his Highland army paraded through the streets of the capital. There were cheering crowds, but most citizens were lukewarm to Charles and some openly hostile. Lowland Scotland was settling down under the new Hanoverian regime and the economy was doing well. The Jacobite uprising was looked upon as a dangerous and unnecessary gamble which would gain Lowland Scotland little, even if it succeeded. Moreover, the Highlanders were seen as violent barbarians who lived by a strange code of laws, spoke a foreign language and were dirt poor and dishonest to boot. Charles, however, let loose his devastating charm on Edinburgh and before long some recruits and money were raised for his army.

Cope, meanwhile, had sailed his army to Dunbar and was now advancing on the city. When he approached the twin villages of Preston and Prestonpans on 20 September, Cope brought his army to a halt and drew it up in a strong defensive position. He placed his men on a slight hill with a marsh to his front. The Jacobite army came up in the afternoon and halted on the far edge of the marsh at Tranent while Murray sent scouts to spy out the land. He realized Cope was in a strong position and hesitated to launch an attack.

As evening fell a local gentleman, Robert Anderson, came to see Prince Charles. He offered to show the Prince a path around the marsh which would put the Jacobite army on Cope's flank. At 3 a.m. Murray gave the order for the Jacobites to move. The Camerons were sent off to attack Cope's baggage train while the rest of the army followed Anderson. When dawn came it was to reveal the Jacobites in their new position. Cope hastily reformed his army to face them, but had not finished when the battle began.

The Opposing Armies

The army that Cope had with him at Prestonpans was the entire strength of the government in Scotland – 2,300 men with six 1-pounder guns and six mortars. It was a small army, and the men were inexperienced, as the veterans had all gone to Europe.

Of Cope's army, some 2,000 were redcoated infantry armed with musket and bayonet. The muskets were, by this date, flintlocks which were reliable and could be loaded and fired twice each minute. The muskets were accurate up to about sixty yards, but the balls would carry for over 150 yards and were capable of inflicting injury even at that range. The bayonets were of the socket-type. The men were organized into seventy-man platoons under a captain. Ten or more platoons would make up a regiment.

It was usual for individual platoons to be detached for garrison duty or to guard supplies. As a result Cope did not have any full regiments with him at Prestonpans, but twenty-four platoons from four different regiments. These were the 6th, 44th, 46th and 47th Regiments of Foot, all of them English.

The remaining 400 men were dragoons. These men were mounted on horses, but were equipped in a similar fashion to the infantry. Cope had no true cavalry with him, which was a serious disadvantage. Cavalrymen were mounted on large horses and armed with a long, heavy sword as well as a pair of pistols. Most of the dragoons were raised in England, though they had some Lowland Scots in their ranks. The morale of the dragoons was not helped by the fact that their commander, Colonel Gardiner, had announced that he had dreamed he was about to die.

The Jacobites had about 400 men more than did Cope, though they were convinced that the government army outnumbered them. The overwhelming majority of the Scots were Highlanders who marched and fought on foot. There was no standard uniform or equipment for the clansmen. They came in their everyday clothes and each man brought whatever weapons he could afford. Most had a round wooden shield, or targe, together with a sword or axe. The wealthier men had muskets as well as cold steel. The men marched and fought in their clans under the command of their clan chief. The size of each unit varied depending on the size of the clan, being as small as a few dozen men or as large as a thousand.

Tactics

Cope's infantry were trained to form up in precise formations and to deliver massed volleys of musket fire, reload and fire again.

Officially the dragoons were infantrymen who rode horses to battle. They used their greater speed to get to where they were needed quickly, then dismounted to fight on foot. By 1745, however, the dragoons were equipped with long cavalry swords and had received training in the mounted charge. They were not as effective as heavy cavalry, but could deliver a useful charge on disordered infantry. They would form up in solid masses thirty men wide and two ranks deep, then advance at the trot while keeping formation exactly. Only at the last minute would the formation speed up before hitting the enemy.

Clan tactics consisted of the Highland charge. If the Highlanders could reach the enemy infantry while they held empty guns, the swords and axes proved more effective in hand to hand fighting than a musket and bayonet.

The Battle

As Cope desperately tried to get his forces moved round to face the Jacobites, he put his infantry in a long line from the edge of the marsh reaching towards the coast. The infantry did not stretch quite so far as the coast, so to stop his position being outflanked he put his dragoons out on the left wing, with some held in the rear in reserve. Unable to move his guns far in the time available, Cope had them on the right wing up against the marsh and protected them with a small force of dragoons. The guns were commanded by Colonel Whiteford.

The view Murray had across low lying ground north from Tranent towards the English army drawn up on the wooded rise beyond. In 1745 the flat field was boggy marsh and almost impassable.

The view from the position of the English artillery as it tried to turn around at dawn on the day of battle. The Highlanders came racing across this field screaming their war cries and being played on by the bagpipes as the sun rose behind them.

Lord Murray had drawn his clansmen up in three divisions. He put the right wing under command of the Duke of Perth and the left wing under his own. Prince Charles was in charge of the small rearguard and given firm advice to stay put.

The battle began as the sun's first rays fell on the battlefield. Perth and Murray led their men forward to conduct a typical Highland charge. On Cope's right the artillery men did not bother waiting for any firing to take place. When they saw the solid mass of the Cameron Clan bearing down on them, they turned and ran. Left alone, Colonel Whiteford fired off the guns one by one, but was unable to reload them. The guns fell silent.

Not much else was silent on the battlefield. The clansmen closed in, fired their muskets then charged forward yelling their war shrieks as the bagpipes played them on. Gardiner ordered his dragoons to charge the flanks of the clansmen, but they did not move. Gardiner was still trying to urge his men forward when the Highlanders hit his unit. He was among the first to be killed. The redcoat infantry managed to get off one volley before they were overwhelmed by the Highlanders. The front rank of redcoats went down before the swords and axes, then the rest fled.

Caught by surprise at the speed with which his army collapsed, Cope rode off after the dragoons. He persuaded some of them to halt on the far side of the marsh to act as a rearguard, but as soon as the clansmen came up, the dragoons rode off. Cope checked his watch. It was just fifteen minutes since the Highlanders had begun to advance. The battle over, Cope rode off south.

He left behind him 300 men dead. About 700 had been wounded and, along with 900 uninjured, were now captives. Only the dragoons and a few dozen infantry escaped to follow Cope to Coldstream and England.

The evening after the battle, Prince Charles found himself faced with an unexpected duty. He had to sit and listen while the clan chiefs brought forward their best warriors to give accounts of what they had done in the battle. Most of the tales had to be translated from Gaelic to English for Charles to understand. One boy of fourteen was brought forward and claimed to have killed twelve Englishmen, including an officer whose skull he had sliced in two. The young prince, unaccustomed to such gleeful savagery, was rather taken aback.

Aftermath

The victory of Prestonpans made Charles the master of Scotland. He set about establishing the government in the name of his father, King James VIII. For six weeks Charles stayed in Edinburgh while he raised taxes, appointed officials and gathered fresh recruits to replace those clansmen who had slipped off to take their loot home.

Early in October four French ships put into the Firth of Forth. They brought an ambassador to the newly independent Scotland in the person of the Marquis d'Eguilles. More practically they brought a healthy shipment of money and weapons. Charles was disappointed that there were still no French troops, but the Marquis promised they were on their way.

With such proof of French support, the Lowlands began to turn out for the charming young man who had been dubbed Bonnie Prince Charlie. Lord Ogilvy came to Edinburgh with 600 well trained infantry raised from his estates and armed with muskets. The Earl of Kilmarnock also declared for Charles and brought the men of his estates. Soon Charles had 5,000 men under arms and the promise of many more. It was, he decided,

The monument to the Battle of Prestonpans, which stands beside the modern road from Prestonpans towards North Berwick.

time to regain his father's other throne. On 1 November the Jacobites marched out of Edinburgh and headed south towards England.

Visiting the Battlefield Today

As befits the first victory of Bonnie Prince Charlie, Prestonpans boasts much to show the visitor. The visit should start at the Prestonpans Viewpoint at Meadowhill. This is signposted from the A198 south of Prestonpans village and, despite at first looking like an industrial estate, has its own large car park. The Viewpoint is a large artificial mound on top of which is a viewing platform equipped with metal plates engraved with information about the main points of interest in the area.

Near the entrance to the drive leading to the Viewpoint is the old monument and opposite this is the entrance to a well-surfaced footpath which runs across the heart of the battlefield, approximately on the line of the English army as drawn up at dawn to face the Highlanders. The area around the battlefield, including the original position of the English and most of the approach routes of both armies, has been heavily built over. The battlefield itself is, however, free of development.

Chapter Twenty-Four

CLIFTON 1745

Introduction

After victory at Prestonpans, the Jacobite army of Bonnie Prince Charlie swelled to nearly 6,000 men as new recruits poured in. On 1 November the army, under the command of George, Lord Murray and with the Prince at its head, marched out of Edinburgh to invade England.

The invasion began promisingly, a well timed diversionary raid kept General Wade and the English border army in Newcastle while the Jacobite army swooped on Carlisle. The city and castle fell quickly, delivering more supplies and weapons to the Scots. The clan chiefs wanted to fall back into Scotland, luring the English army into hostile territory where they could be starved of supplies, weakened by ambushes and finally crushed in battle. Charles, elated by the victory at Prestonpans and eager to regain his father's throne, refused and ordered the march south to continue.

On 27 November the Scots crossed the Ribble at Preston, then swiftly outmanoeuvred the Duke of Cumberland and his army of English militia to march unopposed into Derby. In Derby on 5 December, Murray and the chiefs confronted Charles.

Charles had promised his followers that the English Jacobites would flock to join their army, but they had not. He had promised them that the news of Prestonpans would prompt the French to land an army in England, but it had not. Even worse, the mounted scouts sent out had reported that Cumberland had a larger army than the Scots themselves. The scouts had also heard that Wade had left Newcastle and was coming south in pursuit and that a third English army was mustering at London.

The Jacobites were far from home, had no support and were in danger of being surrounded by larger enemy armies. Murray and the chiefs demanded that Charles agree to march back to Scotland where the Duke of Perth had been mustering more support. The combined Jacobite forces, they argued, could face Cumberland and the English in Scotland. Charles was furious, for he saw the crown of England slipping away from him. He refused either to give the orders to retreat or to stop Murray from doing so. Next day Murray gave the orders, the march north began.

For two weeks the Jacobite army marched homewards without incident, other than struggling with snowdrifts in Cumbria. They knew, however, that Cumberland with a strong force of dragoons and cavalry was shadowing them and that a larger English army was following them a day or two days march behind.

At about 1 p.m. on 18 November a party of English dragoons attempted a half-hearted charge on the Jacobite rearguard of MacDonald clansmen near the village of Snap. Lord Murray decided it was time to give Cumberland reason to back off. The main army had just passed through the village of Clifton, and this was where Murray decided to take a stand. The village was spread along the main road where it climbed up to a ridge on top of which was an old fortified Peel Tower. To the west was the River Lowther, which secured the right flank. To the left of the Peel Tower, the ridge ran towards the little hamlet of Clifton Dykes which Murray made his left flank. The top of the ridge was covered by small fields lined by hedges and cut by two sunken lanes, but the slope leading up to it was fairly open. He put his men among the hedgerows and settled down to wait for Cumberland.

The ancient Peel Tower, around which Murray formed his men to fight a rearguard action.

The view from the English right wing toward the ridge held by the MacPhersons under their formidable chieftain Cluny.

The Opposing Armies

Only parts of the two armies were engaged at Clifton. Murray had with him a squad of infantry from Edinburgh together with Clan Donald, the Appin Stewarts and the MacPhersons, probably no more than 800 men. He put the MacDonalds on the right between the village and the river, and took command of them himself. The Edinburgh men and the Stewarts were put in the village and around the Peel Tower while the MacPhersons, under their charismatic chief Cluny, were strung out along the ridge to the left. Murray was not proposing to deliver the type of traditional Highland charge which had proved so effective at Prestonpans, but to conduct a purely defensive fight.

Cumberland had with him about 1,500 men, over half of them dragoons. It was dusk by the time he and his main body caught up with the advanced troops who had halted at the foot of the slope. In the gathering gloom, Cumberland was uncertain how many Scots were on the ridge or how they were drawn up. He decided to use his dragoons in their traditional role. They would ride up to the enemy, then dismount and fight as infantry. They would form a line three men deep and deliver crashing volleys of musketry. If they found themselves in trouble, the dragoons

241

The sunken lane up which the English dragoons tried to infiltrate the Scottish position, but without any success

could mount up and gallop to safety.

Cumberland's cavalry were heavy troops, trained to charge home in dense formations. He would not want to risk them among the hedgerows, where their charges would be ineffective.

The Battle

The fighting began in the dusk about 4 p.m. when a force of Bland's Dragoons used the sunken lane to approach the MacPhersons on the Scottish left. They got to within 100 yards of the Scots before emerging into an open field and advancing. The MacPhersons fired off a volley, which was answered by the dragoons. After a few exchanges, Cluny MacPherson leapt from cover and led his men in a charge. There was a brief fight, then the dragoons rode off the way they had come.

By this time it was dark. Clouds scudded across the sky so that the battlefield was alternately bathed in the pale glow of moonlight then plunged into darkness. On his left wing, Cumberland sent forward Cobham's Dragoons to try to work along the river and turn the Scottish flank. The MacDonalds waited until the English were just ten yards away then let fly a volley of musketry which sent the dragoons fleeing. More parties of dragoons came forward in the darkness, but each was driven back in turn.

Around 10 p.m. the English attacks ceased. At midnight,

Murray gave orders for his men to continue their march north. The Edinburgh men left first, then the clansmen with the MacDonalds the last to slip away. Murray stood alone for a while in the moonlight beside the Peel Tower looking down the road towards the English positions. He could see no signs of movement, so he set off down the hill towards Penrith.

Aftermath

The confused moonlit fight at Clifton saw relatively few casualties. The Jacobites had lost no more than a dozen men. The English had suffered worse, losing about thirty-five dead and as many again wounded – most of them lost to the single volley of the MacDonalds. However, the determination with which the Scots had held the ridge and the unexpected nature of the defence had a profound effect on Cumberland. It had been his first brush with the Jacobites and he had been impressed.

Cumberland ordered that his men were not to risk battle or even offer to take part in a skirmish. Cumberland kept his army together and simply followed the Jacobites to see what they would do. Murray had achieved his main objective of driving the English army off, allowing the Scots to march unmolested.

Bonnie Prince Charlie left a garrison in Carlisle Castle, then pushed on towards Glasgow. Cumberland followed steadily. He paused at Carlisle until his heavy artillery came up and, on 30 December, captured the castle. Now that no Scots were left in England, Cumberland had completed the task set him. He halted to await fresh orders.

Visiting the Battlefield Today

Visiting Clifton today, it is easy to envisage the battlefield as it was in 1745 and to trace the course of the fighting, despite the fact that a motorway and a railway have been driven across the area.

The A6 north of Shap climbs a hill to a junction with a narrow lane running east, and it was on this hillside that Cumberland's cavalry first caught up with the Scottish rearguard. The scene has barely altered since then, except for the surfacing of the roads.

At Clifton itself, the Peel Tower that anchored the centre of Murray's line still stands, and is now part of a private farm. To the west of the Peel Tower, the wide lanes of the M6 scar the ridge on which Murray stationed the MacDonalds. The River

Lowther, has not altered, however, and can be seen from the bridge that carries the A6 just north of Clifton. More energetic visitors may care to follow the riverbanks on foot until they reach the position where the Jacobites set their right wing.

East of the Peel Tower the line of the Jacobites is followed, more or less closely, by a bridleway, turning to a footpath, which runs to the isolated farm buildings of Clifton Dykes. From this path a good view south can be had over the small fields and broken hedgerows, across which Cumberland had to push his men forwards as night fell. At one point a narrow sunken lane, probably one of those along which the dragoons tried to approach unseen by the Scots, comes up the hill from the south. It was just west of here that Murray led his Highlanders in a sword charge at the approaching English, across a field that remains open to this day. Just east of this sunken road, the railway line cuts the ridge, though the footpath continues across a narrow bridge to cover the ground held by the lightly defended Scottish left wing where little action took place.

The road north of Clifton, along which the Scots retreated, follows the same route as it did in 1745, crossing the River Lowther and continuing on to Penrith, Carlisle and Scotland.

Chapter Twenty-Five

FALKIRK II 1746

Introduction

The Battle of Falkirk, the second to take place near the town, was the last victory for the Jacobites. The battle was fought in an atmosphere of growing political confusion, but the military victory seemed clear enough.

Having raised the standard of Jacobite revolt in the Highlands in 1745, Bonnie Prince Charlie quickly gathered an army of

The battle began before either army was fully prepared when a charge by the English dragoons was repulsed and the clansmen on the Scottish right surged forward in pursuit.

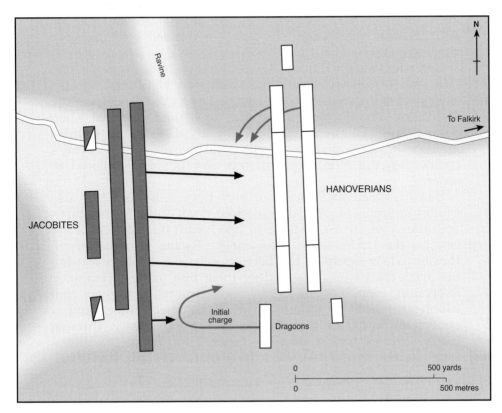

clansmen. At Prestonpans he crushed the English army sent against him and as a result gathered much support from the Scottish Lowlands. His march into England was halted when neither the expected French invasion nor the promised English Jacobite uprising materialized. After fighting a successful rearguard action at Clifton, the Jacobite army arrived in Glasgow on 26 December.

On his return to Glasgow, Prince Charles was delighted to find that the French had sent him reinforcements. These were not the professional troops that his army commander Lord Murray wanted, but half a dozen heavy cannon. These guns were at once sent into the siege lines around Stirling Castle,which was still holding out after five months.

The pursuing English armies had meanwhile combined at Newcastle under a new commander, General Henry Hawley and was marching on Edinburgh. Learning of the new threat to Stirling, Hawley decided to march to the relief of the castle. Despite the successes of the clansmen at Prestonpans and Clifton, Hawley had little time for them. He knew all about their aggressive tactics but believed they could be crushed by well-trained men in a strong position under a good commander. He knew his army was composed largely of veterans and had no doubt that he was a superb leader. All he needed was to find the right position.

Unfortunately for Hawley, it was Murray who got into position first. About noon on 17 January, Murray drew his army up on a ridge west of the town of Falkirk where he blocked Hawley's route to Stirling. The Jacobite army was for a time confused when John O'Sullivan, the mercenary who acted as Prince Charles military adviser, disagreed with Murray about the army's positioning. But Murray got his way and the army deployed as ordered.

Hawley, meanwhile, was not only outmanoeuvred but also caught unprepared. When he received news of the Scots army's arrival he was drinking wine over lunch with the famous society beauty, the Countess of Kilmarnock. Racing from his meal, Hawley rode at top speed to where his subordinates were rousing the army from camp and getting them into battle formations. Everything was confusion as men formed, marched and countermarched as orders contradicted each other. And a sudden torrential shower dampened the gunpowder. Cursing loudly, Hawley took command, ordered his regiments into a rough formation and gave the order to march towards the enemy.

Callendar House, where the English General Hawley left his hat in his haste to reach the battlefield when the Jacobites unexpectedly arrived on the scene.

Only then did Hawley realize he had left his hat behind with the Countess.

The Opposing Armies

The two armies which met at Falkirk were not too dissimilar in size, though Hawley with 9,000 men had a slightly larger force than the Jacobites. The main differences between the armies were in the equipment and training of the men.

The bulk of Hawley's army, some 6,500 men were regular redcoat infantry from the British army. He had with him the 1st, 3rd, 4th, 13th, 14th, 27th, 34th, 36th, 37th, 59th and 62nd Regiments of Foot. Most of these were English regiments, though the 27th was Irish and the 1st had been raised in Lowland Scotland.

All these units were equipped and trained in orthodox European fashion. They were equipped with muskets and bayonets. They were trained to form up in lines three men deep and fire volleys of musketry, reloading and firing every thirty seconds or so. It was expected that they would stand in line, exchanging fire with the enemy until one side retreated, when the victors would follow up with an advance with bayonets. It was on these men that Hawley relied to win the battle.

Hawley was a professional soldier and no fool. He had studied accounts of the earlier Jacobite victories and learned that their successes had been based on the Highland charge. The answer to these ferocious tactics, Hawley believed, was simple. He ordered his officers to make their men fix bayonets and load their muskets before going into action. When the Highlanders advanced, the men were not to return their fire at sixty yards. Instead they were to keep their muskets loaded until the clansmen were storming forward and just ten yards, or even less, away. The redcoats should then deliver a crushing volley at pointblank range, and immediately charge forward with the bayonet.

It was a novel and logical answer to the famous Highland tactics. Hawley was relying on his men standing immobile while being shot at, then remaining calm in the face of a charge by thousands of screaming Highlanders, urged on by bagpipes. It was a lot to ask of men, but the regiments were veterans of battles in Europe. Hawley was confident.

Hawley's army also included 700 dragoons; horsemen who were equipped with short muskets and bayonets as well as with swords. Their traditional role was to ride to where they were needed, then dismount and form lines to fight as infantry. Thus they combined firepower with speed. There was an increasing tendency, however, for the dragoons to act as cavalry and charge the enemy using their swords as weapons. It was in this latter role that Hawley intended to use them.

In addition, Hawley had the Glasgow Militia. These men had marched out of their city as the Jacobites marched in. Although equipped and trained as regular infantry, they had seen no active service and Hawley doubted their ability to carry out his new tactics. He put them on his left rear flank to act as a guard against any attempts to outflank the main army.

Hawley had Highlanders of his own. The mighty Clan Campbell had decided to come out against Bonnie Prince Charles and the Stuart cause. The eldest son of the clan chief had met Hawley's advancing army bringing with him 2,000 clansmen. About half these men were on patrol on the day of battle, but the remainder formed up on on the right rear flank as a guard.

Finally, Hawley had field artillery. These guns could throw balls of about nine pounds in weight over 1,500 yards. In the confusion reigning in the camp when the Jacobites were first seen, however, the guns had got stuck in marshy ground and were not freed in time to take any part in the fighting.

Lord Murray's army was some 8,000 men strong. About half of these men were Highlanders from the Cameron, Fraser, MacPherson, Mackintosh, Mackenzie and MacDonald clans and the Appin Stewarts. The rest were Lowland infantry militia led by the Duke of Atholl and Lords Ogilvy and Gordon. Murray put his clansmen in the front rank with Lowlanders behind. Prince Charles was stationed in the rear of the centre, with a bodyguard of clansmen. The few hundred horsemen were put under Lord Elcho and stationed next to the Prince.

As an experienced commander, Murray had great respect for the English regular infantry. He did not believe that a traditional Highland Charge would be enough to defeat such veterans. Instead, he ordered his clansmen to stand firm and wait for the enemy to attack, firing their muskets at the last possible minute and then charging. Murray intended using the disciplined fire of his Lowland regiments to deal with those enemy regiments which stood firm and brushed off the clansmen. Such tactics would be new to both the clansmen and to the lords commanding the Lowlanders. The men and officers would need close supervision if the tactics were to be followed. Murray put himself in charge of the right wing and his trusted colleague Lord Drummond in charge of the left. At the last moment, the Prince's military adviser – the Irish mercenary named John O'Sullivan – ordered Drummond to take command of the Prince's bodyguard. The left wing was suddenly leaderless.

The Battle

The Battle of Falkirk did not unfold as the commander of either army expected or planned, which lead to much confusion. The weather was windy with a series of heavy rain showers blowing down from the west, hitting the Jacobites in the back and the English in the face.

Hawley was having trouble getting his English infantry into a proper formation for the advance, so he ordered Colonel Ligonier to take the three regiments of dragoons on the left wing against the Jacobite right wing. The cavalry advanced at the trot, intending to increase to the charge at the last moment. But just as Ligonier was about to give this order, Murray fired his pistol and the entire front rank of clans MacDonald and Farquarson erupted in flame as they fired their muskets. Dozens of dragoons were killed and the two right hand regiments, Ligonier's own and Hamilton's, turned and fled. Cobham's regiment, on the left, put

The undulating land across which the English dragoons launched the charge which began the battle. They came up the slope from the right to attack the MacDonalds who, as their proud tradition demanded, held the right flank of the Scottish army.

their spurs to their horses and charged into the clansmen.

The horsemen rode though the MacDonalds and a brutal and confused sword fight broke out, in the course of which the chief of the clan was pinned beneath a wounded horse. The struggle did not last long before Cobham's horsemen were fleeing down hill after their comrades. The MacDonalds poured down the hill in pursuit, drawing their swords and axes ready to take on the English infantry at the foot of the hill. Seeing the MacDonalds surging forward, the Farquarsons and Mackenzies charged forward in their turn.

Murray was aghast. His careful plans were in tatters as he had wanted the clansmen to wait until the English infantry had attacked before charging, not just wait until after the dragoons attacked. But Murray knew, too soon or not, he would now have to use the Lowlanders to support the clansmen, so he ordered Lord Atholl to bring his men forward.

Hawley, meanwhile, was also watching his battle plan collapse. The fleeing dragoons galloped straight through the waiting 8th, 27th, 34th and 37th Infantry, throwing their ranks into complete disorder. Before the infantry could reform the MacDonalds were on them with their cold steel. With no time to deliver Hawley's planned point-blank volley, the English were caught up in a brutal hand-to-hand struggle. When the Farquarson and Mackenzie clans crashed into the fight, the English fled taking the Glaswegians with them.

Murray arrived at the foot of the hill with his Lowlanders to find the enemy gone and the clansmen scattered across the field looting the dead.

On the left flank of the Jacobite army, things were even more confused. Seeing their colleagues to the right surging forward, and with no orders, the clans on the left had moved forward as well. But before reaching the enemy infantry they had come across a steep ravine. Some clansmen clambered down and tried to get up the far side, others veered to the right to get around the obstacle. The different clans got hopelessly muddled up in the process. Only the MacPhersons under their charismatic leader Cluny MacPherson managed to stay together.

At this point the small body of dragoons on the English right wing tried to launch a charge against the disordered clans. Many clansmen fell back, others raced forwards, some tried to find shelter in the ravine. Prince Charles saw the danger and sent the cavalry under Lord Elcho to save the situation, which they did with some skill.

Cluny MacPherson gathered whatever men he could find and led a charge at the enemy to his front. The English were already retreating as they had seen their left flank collapse. Many simply fled before the MacPherson charge, but the 4th, 14th and 59th fell back in disciplined order, firing volleys of musketry into the pursuing clansmen, who soon gave up the chase.

By now it was almost dark. The clansmen on the left had been discouraged by the volleys of musket fire and thought the battle was lost. Murray could not believe the veteran regiments had fled so quickly and thought he was in danger of being lured into a trap. Lord Elcho had returned from his charge to find the Prince had vanished and set off back to camp to try to find him. Prince Charles, meanwhile, had led a mass of 1,500 clansmen in pursuit of the English and had taken up residence in General Hawley's own quarters in Falkirk while his men happily plundered the English camp. Prince Charles even had Hawley's hat.

It was not until well past midnight that the Prince, Murray

and Elcho found each other and managed to restore some sort of order to their army. By that time Hawley had extricated his men and was retreating rapidly towards Edinburgh. There was no chance of turning the English retreat into a rout, so the Jacobites took shelter from what was now driving rain and waited for morning.

Aftermath

After the battle the utterly dispirited Hawley fled to Edinburgh where he gathered his battered army and prepared for the expected Jacobite attack. He had lost over 400 men and his confidence in his troops was shattered. He hanged a few for cowardice.

Prince Charles was intent on capturing Stirling. Murray gathered up the captured weapons, flags and supplies from Falkirk then set off after his master for the siege. And Murray was furious. Although Cluny MacPherson had done his best to sort out the confusion on the Jacobite left, Murray believed that the confusion had been fatal. With proper handling from the beginning the left wing could have turned the English defeat into a sweeping rout. He blamed O'Sullivan for interfering in his plans.

Sensing the disunity in the high command of the army, the clansmen and chiefs began to lose confidence. Many began to slip away for their home glens. Murray conferred with those chiefs who remained. They thought they had been lucky at Falkirk and wanted to fall back into the Highlands where they could ambush any English force which followed them. Those who had gone home had promised to come out again in the spring. Better, the remaining chiefs said, to remuster in the spring rather than sit before Stirling in the bitter winter weather and watch their army melt away through disease and desertion.

Murray and Cluny MacPherson confronted Prince Charles with the views of the clan chiefs. Charles at first refused to have anything to do with the plan, but as the clansmen melted away he finally accepted it. The army crossed the Forth and headed north, while Prince Charles sent out messages for a fresh mustering of Jacobite support in the spring.

Visiting the Battlefield Today

Falkirk does not seem to be very good at battlefields. Like the battlefield of the 1298 conflict, that of the 1745 fight is not

The crumbling monument on the battlefield, erected on the left flank near the ground held by Cluny MacPherson and his clansmen.

signposted, is difficult to find and offers no car parking. There is, however, a monument, though it is crumbling. As with the 1298 battlefield, you really need a map of the city to stand a chance of finding your way around.

Leave Falkirk town centre on the B803, which is not as easy as it sounds given the idiosyncratic road signs in Falkirk. As you start to climb a hill out of the city centre you will come to a mini-roundabout. Take the right hand turn which is Lochgreen Road. After half a mile a narrow road on the right, identified only by signs stating it is closed to vehicles over 7.5 tons in weight, leads to the monument. This stands on the very left wing of the position taken by Bonnie Prince Charlie's army. A footpath leads from the monument eastwards into the ravine which so disrupted the Scottish advance and which is now largely covered by a modern housing estate. You'll need to take care as this area can be slippery when wet.

Return to the B803 and turn right, heading south-west. This takes you across the centre of the battlefield. The English left lay where a modern hospital has been built and the route they took in retreat is now covered by modern housing estates. Fortunately the position taken by the Jacobites at the start of the battle is undeveloped and is largely composed of grazing land. Most of it can be seen from the road, which is just as well because the footpath which allegedly leads from this road across the battlefield to the monument is so overgrown with gorse and nettles, that it is impassable unless you have a machete to hand.

Chapter Twenty-Six

CULLODEN 1746

NOT SCOT V ENG.!

Introduction

More myths, legends and misunderstandings have swirled about the Battle of Culloden than perhaps any other. Prejudices and confusions were rife at the time and the intervening centuries have done little to remove them.

After his victory at Falkirk, Bonnie Prince Charlie reluctantly led his army north to the safety of Inverness to sit out the winter. The clan chiefs had promised to come out again in the spring to support the claim of the Stuart family to the joint thrones of Scotland and England. Charles still hoped for armed support from France, though this had been promised for months and had not arrived. In March the winter weather eased and the clansmen began to gather at Inverness. But there were not as many as Bonnie Prince Charlie had hoped. And the army of his enemies was approaching from Aberdeen.

As the British Government army approached the Jacobite camp around Inverness, it was clear that a battle would have to be fought before all the clans had come out. The formidable Cluny MacPherson and his warriors were on their way, as were many others, but they had not yet arrived. Lord Murray, the experienced commander of the Jacobite army, suggested they should take their stand at Dalcross where the broken ground would favour his clansmen.

Prince Charles, however, preferred the advice of the Irish mercenary, John O'Sullivan. He pointed out that the moor at Culloden was open ground which would favour artillery. Charles was proud of his guns, sent from France or captured from the English at Falkirk, and wanted to give them a good opportunity to prove themselves.

On 15 April the Jacobites drew up for battle at Culloden, but the enemy did not arrive as expected. Unknown to Prince Charles it was the twenty-fifth birthday of the Duke of Cumberland, who commanded the government army, and he

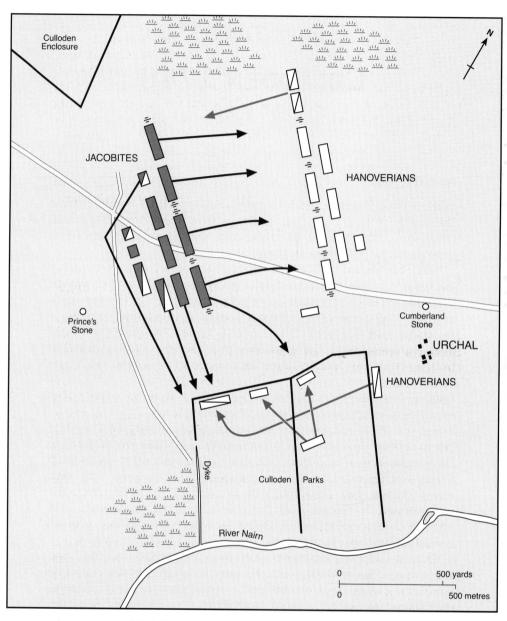

Culloden
Enclosure

JACOBITES

HANOVERIANS

Prince's
Stone

Cumberland
Stone

URCHAL

HANOVERIANS

Dyke

Culloden Parks

River Nairn

0		500 yards
0		500 metres

A frontal assault by the Jacobites was driven back with heavy loss while dragoons on the English left wing pushed forward in a flanking attack.

had given his men the day off from campaigning.

As evening drew on, Murray suggested they should try the trick which had worked so well at the Battle of Prestonpans. Back in September 1745 the Jacobite army had marched at night to get around a marsh so that at dawn they were drawn up on the flank of the enemy and able to deliver a battle-winning charge. Charles agreed and the clansmen set off. The route was over difficult terrain and the army lost its way. At 2 a.m. an alert English scout spotted the advancing Jacobites. With surprise lost, Murray returned to Culloden a little before dawn.

The utterly exhausted clansmen lay down on the heather to sleep. But less than two hours later the Duke of Cumberland came into sight at the head of his army. The clan chiefs had to rouse their exhausted men to face the foe.

The Opposing Armies

The tired and dispirited army which struggled to its feet to fight for Bonnie Prince Charlie at Culloden was barely 5,000 men strong. Of these the majority were Highlanders from the Jacobite clans who had rallied to the Stuart cause. The men of the Appin Stewarts were there, as were the Frasers, Farquarsons, Clan Chattan, Camerons, Chisolms, MacDonalds, Macintoshes, and some Gordons.

These Highlanders were equipped and fought in traditional fashion as they had at Prestonpans. The few who had muskets formed the front rank while those armed only with sword, axe or dirk formed up behind them. The usual tactic was the Highland charge. Such a furious charge had smashed the discipline of militia and veterans alike at Prestonpans and Falkirk. Now the Prince put his faith in its working again, once his prized cannon had softened up the enemy.

The majority of the clansmen were put in the front line, stretching from the walls of Culloden Enclosure on the left to the stone wall around Culloden Parks on the right. Charles put the MacDonalds on the left, which greatly insulted them as for generations they had traditionally held the more prestigious position on the right.

Charles also had a small number of soldiers from the French army under the command of Colonel Stapleton. These were not the thousands of regular troops that Charles had promised the clan chiefs were on their way, but a few companies of Irish exiles in French pay who had been allowed to come to Scotland. These men were equipped with musket and bayonet and trained to march and fire in rigid lines. They were put in the second line, along with the Gordon and Ogilvy men, where they could be used as a reserve.

The Jacobites had some 200 cavalry under Lord Elcho. Equipped with pistols and swords these men could act as a skirmishing line or charge home with cold steel. They were held in the rear, to be directed as needed.

Finally Charles put the heavy guns of which he was so proud in the centre of the front line. From there, he hoped, they could sweep the enemy troops with murderous blasts.

The army of the Duke of Cumberland was almost twice as large as that of Prince Charles. He had most of the regiments which had fought at Falkirk, but with substantial reinforcements in the shape of the 20th, 21st, 24th, 25th and 48th Regiments of Foot, together with some 2,000 fresh dragoons. These new arrivals included many men from the Scottish Lowlands who had opposed the restoration of the Stuart regime. Cumberland also had hundreds of men from Clan Campbell and other Highland clans who likewise opposed Prince Charles. There were almost as many Scots on the government side as were fighting for Charles.

As Cumberland advanced he placed his infantry in two lines, each made up of seven regiments. Each regiment was drawn up three ranks deep. The officers had new orders from Cumberland on how to cope with the Highland charge. The regiments were to fight standing still, bayonets fixed, forcing the Highlanders to attack. The front rank was to kneel with loaded guns while the rear two ranks kept up a rolling fire over their heads at the approaching clansmen. Only at the very last moment, when the attackers were just five yards away, was the front rank to fire, delivering a crushing volley into the clansmen. Then the infantry were to fight with their bayonets. The men were ordered not to fight the Highlander in front of him, for he would be protected by the bayonet-proof leather targe in his left hand, but to stab at the Highlander to their right. The dragoons were stationed on the flanks with orders to charge the enemy when and if the opportunity arose. The guns were stationed at intervals between the front line of infantry.

At the last minute, Cumberland sent the 6th Regiment of Infantry to occupy the walled fields of Culloden Parks from where they could fire into the flank of the enemy. Also pushed fowards into the Culloden Parks were the dragoons, under General Hawley who had lost at Falkirk. They were helped by the Campbell clansmen who tore down the walls of the Parks with their bare hands so that the horsemen could gain access.

As Cumberland made his final dispositions, Lord Elcho rode up to Murray to ask him what he thought of them. 'We are putting an end to a bad affair' replied Murray.

The Battle

The Battle of Culloden began at about 1 p.m. when Lord Bury rode forward from the government line to scout the Jacobite dispositions. A Jacobite gunner tried a shot, but missed, whereupon Prince Charles ordered his artillery to open fire. The gunners aimed at Cumberland and the government banners. One shot killed two men standing just feet from Cumberland, but he was uninjured.

Cumberland now ordered his guns to begin firing. The professional English gunners could aim better and fire faster than the Jacobites. Within a quarter of an hour, Cumberland's guns had disabled all those of Prince Charles. The government guns now began to fire at the clansmen, tearing great holes in their ranks and cutting down hundreds of men. Lochiel, chief of the Cameron clan, had both his legs shattered and was carried from the field.

As the shot and grape tore into the clansmen, Murray sent a messenger to Prince Charles asking permission to attack. No answer came and the cannon continued their killing. The Highlanders did not understand why they stood still to be killed, but wanted to get to grips with the enemy. Finally Charles sent

The red flag bearing a white cockade which marks the position of the centre of the Jacobite front rank as it stood when the battle commenced.

259

Lachlan MacLachlan to order Lord Perth to advance with his men, but the messenger was killed by shot.

Then Clan Macintosh broke ranks and surged forwards screaming their war cries. Clan Chattan went next, disappearing into the billowing smoke drifting forwards from the English guns, and were followed by the Camerons and Murray's own Atholl men. Soon the entire front line of clansmen was racing forward across the moor. Their ranks were cut down by the rolling fire from the redcoat muskets and by the sweeping grapeshot from the cannon.

On the right flank of the charge, the Camerons found themselves taken in the flank by fire from the men behind the stone walls of Culloden Park. On the left the MacDonalds had furthest to go and were taking heavy casualties as they raced over the heather. The central clans reached Cumberland's front line and fell upon the redcoats with fury, driven on by desperation. The infantry met the terrifying sword cuts and axe blows of the clansmen with their ready fixed bayonets. Jabbing to the right as ordered, the infantry began to thin the ranks of the clansmen with ruthless efficiency. Suddenly the clans broke and fled back into the smoke.

On the left the MacDonalds saw the central clans fall back and a force of English dragoons coming up on their left. They too fled, but their clan chief,

The narrow lane where Lord Elcho and the few Jacobite cavalry managed to delay the advance of the English dragoons for vital minutes, allowing many clansmen to escape the slaughter that followed the battle.

Keppoch, refused to retreat and singlehandedly charged the advancing redcoats with sword and pistol, until he was cut down.

Murray had been thrown from his horse as he led the Atholl men forwards. Getting to his feet he saw the ruin of the army and raced to Stapleton, who brought his well trained regulars up to fire volley after volley into the advancing redcoats, gaining precious minutes in which the clansmen could escape.

On the right flank, Elcho and his men were performing a similar duty. The English dragoons were now out of the Parks and were looking to get in among the fleeing enemy with sabre and pistol. But as they emerged from the walled fields they found themselves in a narrow lane faced by Elcho's force. Although heavily outnumbered, Elcho held the dragoons off.

It could not last. In the centre Stapleton saw his men being surrounded and realized there was little more he could achieve. He ordered his men to lay their weapons down in the confident expectation that, as soldiers of an enemy king, they would be spared the summary justice to be given to the clansmen. Pausing only long enough to herd their prisoners to the rear, the government troops now began the pursuit in earnest.

Cumberland had given orders that the clansmen were to be treated as traitors. No trial was necessary, he said, for men found bearing weapons and they could be executed immediately. The dragoons and infantry who followed them obeyed these orders to the letter. Any Highlander caught in the long chase to Inverness was killed on the spot. Those who tried to hide were dragged out and shot. Even some entirely innocent civilians were killed as they were wearing Highland dress.

Toward the end of the day, Cumberland's officers tired of the slaughter of an utterly defeated enemy. When the leader of Clan Fraser was found wounded, Cumberland remarked casually to the Colonel of the 6th Infantry 'Wolfe, shoot me that scoundrel'. Wolfe, later to find fame as the conqueror of Quebec, refused and offered to resign his command. Cumberland relented, but later had the wounded man shot anyway.

It is not known for certain how many clansmen were killed at Culloden and in the brutal chase that followed. Certainly over a thousand lay dead on the battlefield, and hundreds more had been killed by the end of the day. Several hundred wounded died later as Cumberland refused them any medical aid.

Aftermath

While Cumberland and his men were chasing the clansmen towards Inverness, Cluny MacPherson had been marching with his clan's fighting strength to join Prince Charles. He had got as far as Ruthven when he heard the news of Culloden. Pausing at Ruthven, Cluny was met by the tireless Murray, who had rounded up about 1,500 fugitive clansmen. Lord Drummond and Lord Perth, wounded in the shoulder, came in soon after, bringing more men with them.

Although defeated, Murray knew more clansmen were marching to join the Jacobites. He already had 2,000 men and would soon have more. It might yet be possible to cut Cumberland off from his supplies and starve him into retreat. If there was no longer any chance of putting the Stuarts on the throne, at least Murray could put on a show of force and gain good terms of surrender for the clans. The only problem was that the figurehead of the uprising, Prince Charles, was nowhere to be found. Nobody knew if he was alive or dead, or how to find him.

Three days later Murray received a hastily penned note from Prince Charles on a scrap of paper. It said simply that the Prince released the clan chiefs from their oaths of loyalty and that he was going back to France. 'Let every man seek his own safety the best way he can,' concluded the note. It was a great betrayal of the men who had risked life and wealth to follow him. With no

Prince Charlie's Cairn on the shores of Loch Nan Uamh which marks the lonely spot where Bonnie Prince Charlie embarked on a French ship to be carried into exile.

attempt to gain good terms for the men Cumberland had branded traitors, Charles was looking to his own safety. Murray could do nothing except send the clansmen home and advise the clan chiefs to follow him into exile. The chiefs would certainly be executed if they were caught, but there was hope that the humble clansmen might be merely fined or imprisoned for marching to war.

After writing his note, Charles spent months as a hunted fugitive. It was during these weeks that Flora MacDonald helped him escape a party of redcoats by rowing him over the sea to Skye. Eventually, on 20 September, a French ship found Charles and he was carried away into exile. Charles was to live another forty-three years, but he and all Europe knew there was now no chance of a Stuart sitting on the thrones of England and Scotland. Charles's younger brother made a successful career for himself in the Catholic Church, but Charles descended into drunkenness and debauchery.

Back in Scotland the vengeance against the clans who had come out for Charles continued. Their fields were burnt, their castles destroyed and their men summarily killed, beaten or dragged off for trial. In all some 3,500 men, captured in arms against the government, made it to trial in England or the Scottish Lowlands. It is not known how many died before reaching court. Of these the 120 most senior leaders were executed and another 700 or so died in prison from wounds or disease. A few dozen were pardoned, but most were sent to the colonies to work as slave labour for seven years or more. Most never returned to Scotland.

More forceful still were the actions of the government over the following years. There had been a time when it made sense to devolve power over the wild mountain lands to the clan chiefs. But the clans had come out in rebellion in 1689, in 1715, in 1719 and now in 1745. It was decided to break up the entire clan system and with it the Highland way of life. Tartan was banned, playing the bagpipes made illegal, weapons ruthlessly confiscated and the legal powers of the clan chiefs destroyed.

Within forty years the Highlands had been depopulated as sheep replaced clansmen on the hills. The clan system was gone. Highland Scotland was remodelled in the shape of the Lowlands and its culture. Only the shadow of the clans remained in kilts and bagpipes used by men who had never carried a claymore or come out to follow their clan chief in pursuit of blood feud.

Visiting the Battlefield Today

Culloden battlefield is in the care of the National Trust for Scotland. The Visitor Centre located on the B9006, to the west of the junction with the B851, offers ample parking, a gift shop and cafe. The Centre houses an impressive museum of contemporary weapons and displays which explain the lead up to the battle and the events of the day. The battlefield itself, adjacent to the Visitor Centre, is well tended and crossed by gravel paths. The location of each regiment and clan at the opening of the battle is indicated by markers and it is easy to trace what happened on the ground. The famous Cairn and clan monuments lie along a path just off the battlefield.

Only two important features lie off the National Trust land and both are best visited on foot, leaving your car in the Centre car park. Turn right out of the car park and walk across a crossroads to reach the Cumberland Stone. Local tradition has it that the Duke of Cumberland stood on top of this huge boulder to survey the battlefield before the action began. Metal hoops hammered into the boulder enable you to climb to the top of the stone with rather more ease than the corpulent Cumberland. To find the lane where Lord Elcho and his cavalry heroically held off the English dragoons, turn left on leaving the car park and walk along the B9006 to the lane which turns left off the road at the far edge of the National Trust land. Follow this lane for 200 yards or so until it plunges into woodland, which is where the cavalry fighting took place.

The heather-covered moorland of Culloden battlefield. This view is from behind the English lines looking towards the Jacobite position. The modern Visitor Centre and the clan graves are in the grove of trees to the left of the picture.

Index

Page numbers in *italic* indicate pictures.
Page numbers in **bold** indicate a main entry.